D1229564

GRUMBLE

YOU'RE THE
DOG NOW,
MAN!

ALBATROSS FUNNYBOOKS PRESENTS

GRUMBLE

VOLUME I
YOU'RE THE DOG NOW, MAN!

HAVERHILL
PUBLIC LIBRARY

This item was purchased with
funds from private donors to
maintain the collection of the
Haverhill Public Library.

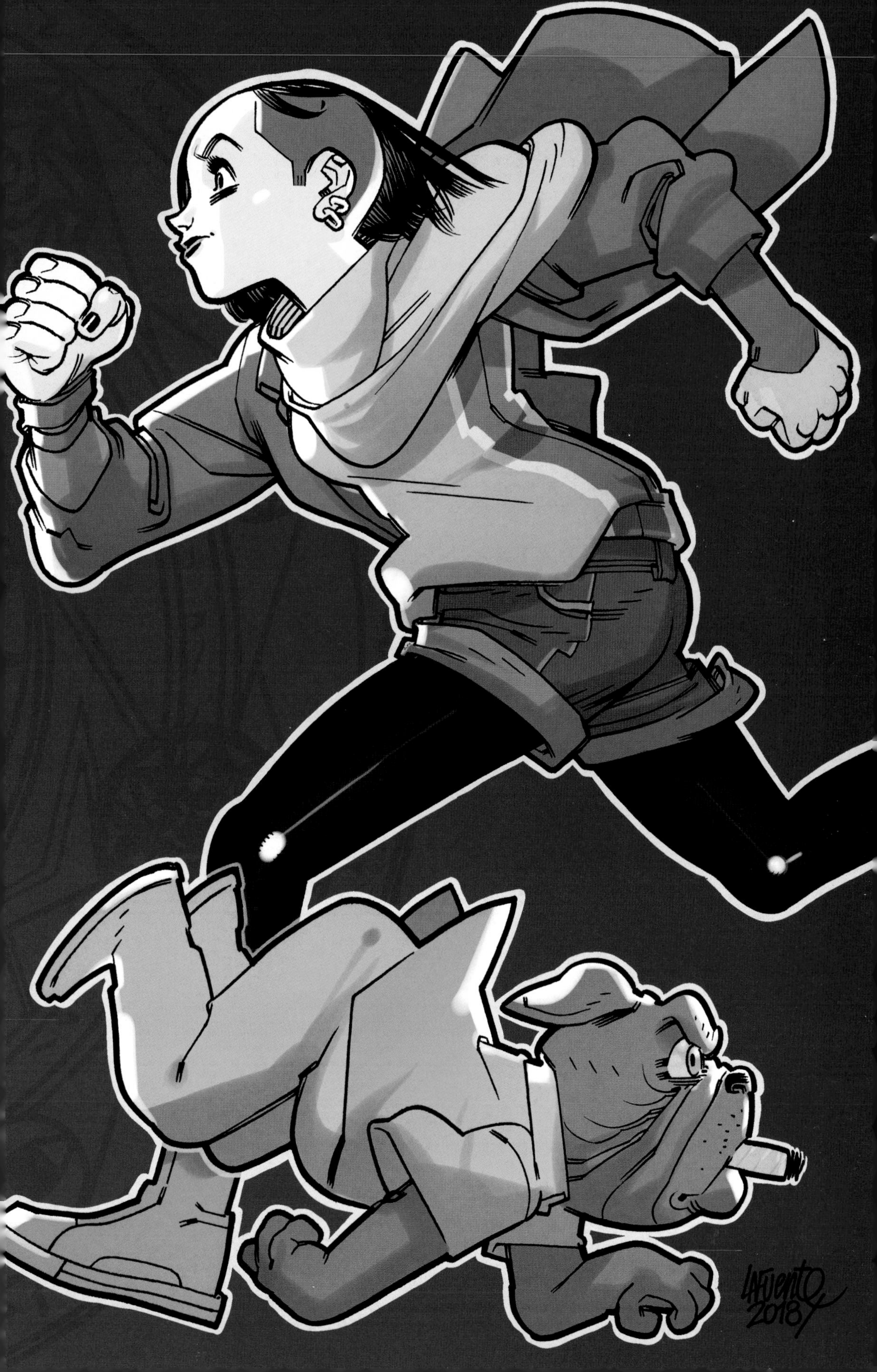
LAFUENTE
2018

CREATED BY

RAFER ROBERTS - WRITER   **MIKE NORTON** - ARTIST

MARISSA LOUISE - COLOR ARTIST

CRANK! - LETTERER

ALEJANDRO ARBONA w/**DANNY KHAZEM** - EDITOR

COVERS BY
MIKE NORTON & MARISSA LOUISE, DAVID LAFUENTE,
JENNY FRISON, FAREL DALRYMPLE, JIM MAHFOOD,
EVAN DORKIN & ADDISON DUKE

GRUMBLE: YOU'RE THE DOG NOW, MAN Published by ALbatross Funnybooks, PO Box 60627, Nashville TN 37206. Grumble™&© 2019 Mike Norton and Rafer Roberts. All contents and related characters™&© Mike Norton and Rafer Roberts. All rights reserved. No portion of this product may be reproduced or transmitted, by any form or by any means, without express written permission of Mike Norton and Rafer Roberts. Albatross Funnybooks and the Albatross Funnybooks logo are registered trademarks of Eric Powell. Names, characters, places, and incidents featured in this publication are fictional. Any similarity to persons living or dead, places and incidents is unintended or for satirical purposes.   Printed in Canada.

BOOK ONE

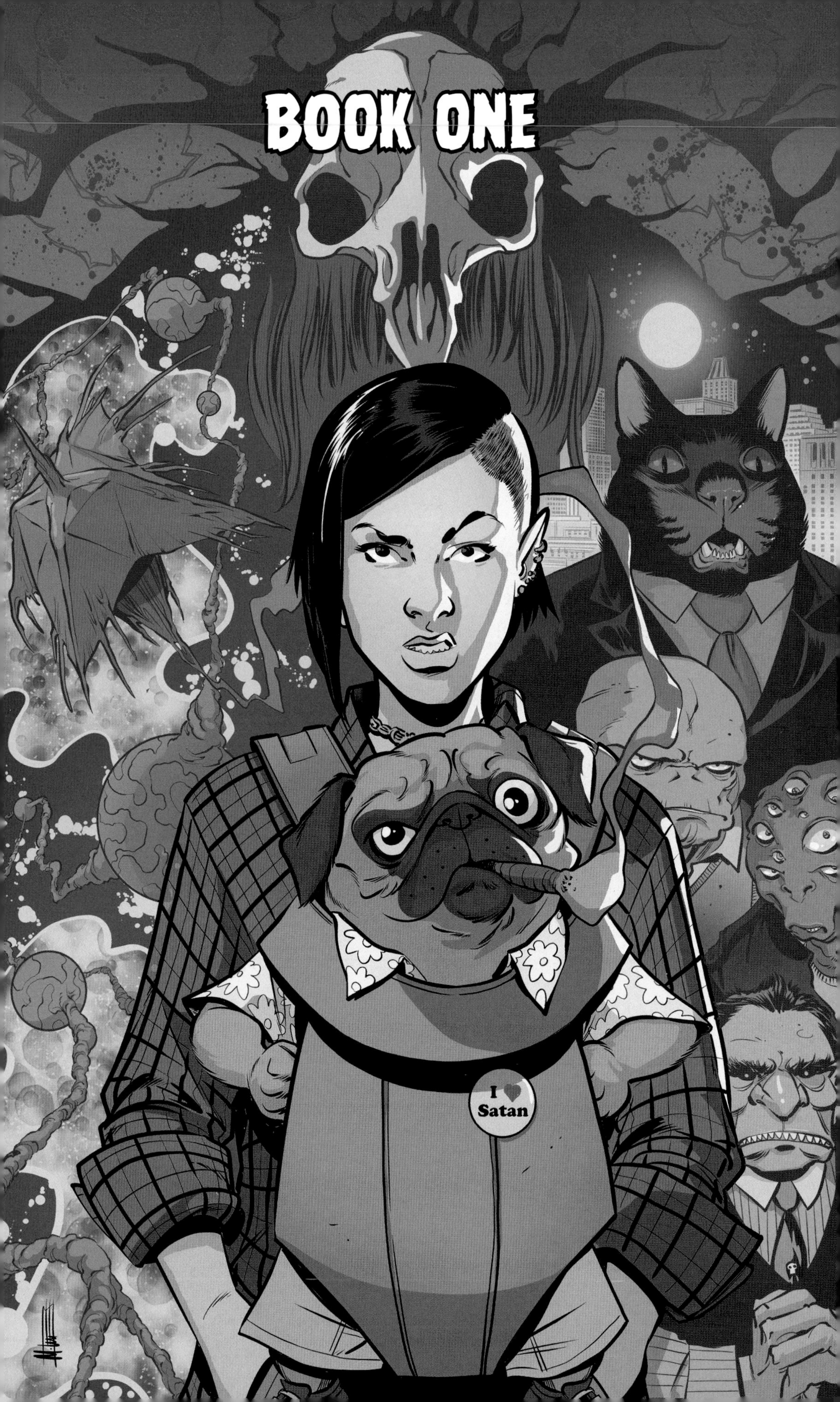
I ♥ Satan

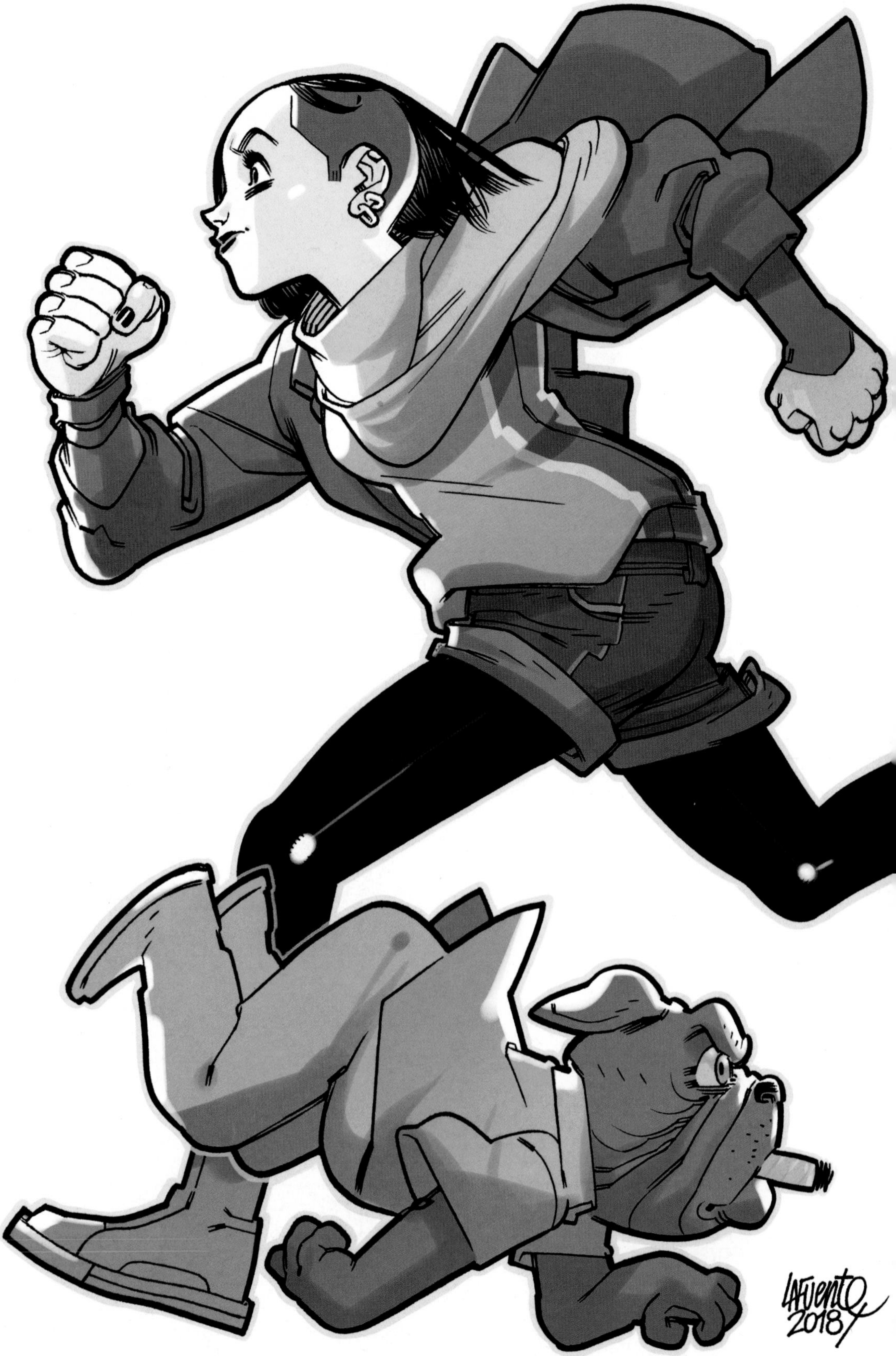
LAFUENTE 2018

SPECIAL EDITION COVER ART BY DAVID LAFUENTE.

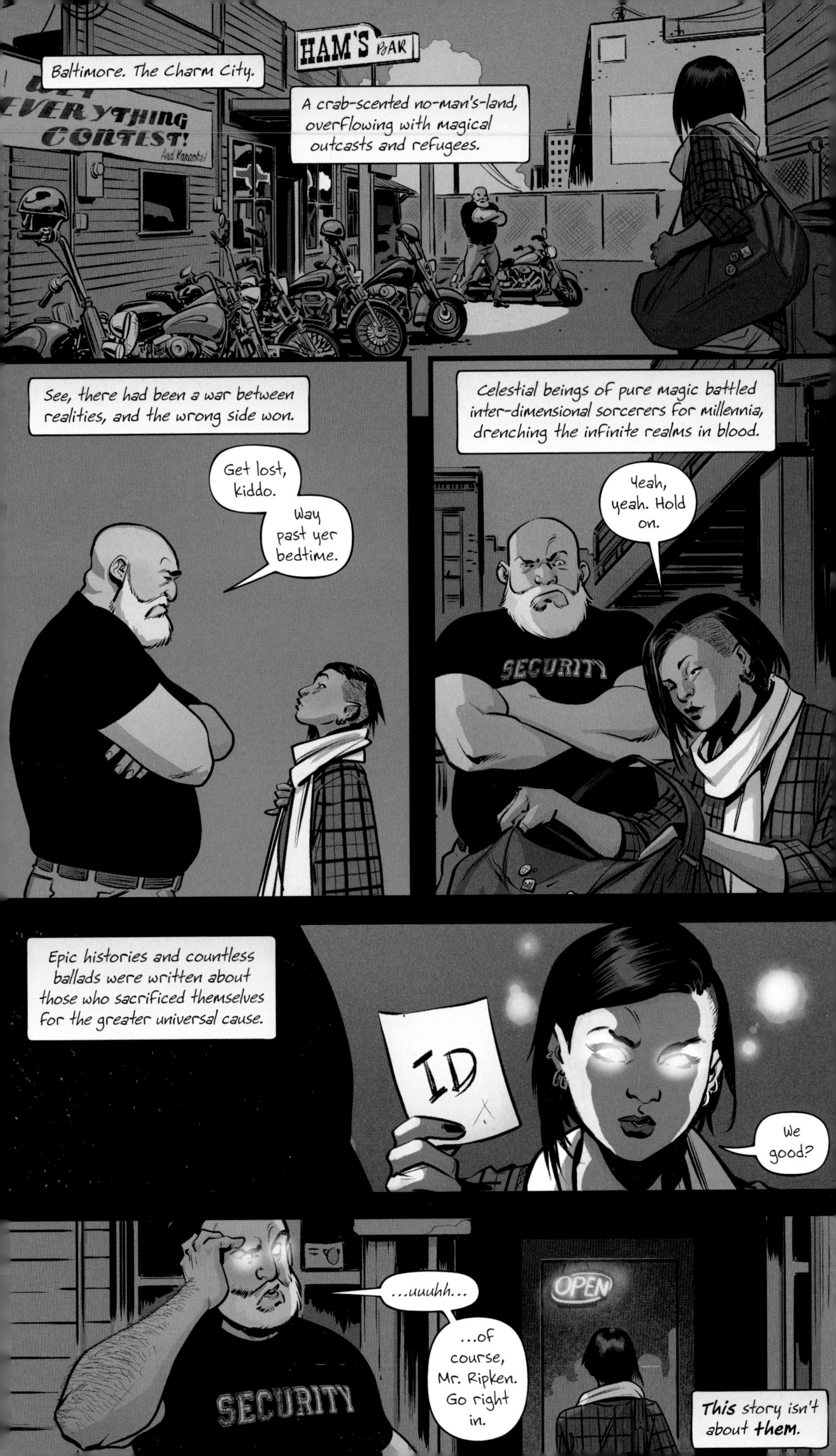
Baltimore. The Charm City.
HAM'S BAR
EVERYTHING CONTEST!
And Karaoke!
A crab-scented no-man's-land, overflowing with magical outcasts and refugees.
See, there had been a war between realities, and the wrong side won.
Get lost, kiddo.
Way past yer bedtime.
Celestial beings of pure magic battled inter-dimensional sorcerers for millennia, drenching the infinite realms in blood.
Yeah, yeah. Hold on.
SECURITY
Epic histories and countless ballads were written about those who sacrificed themselves for the greater universal cause.
ID
We good?
...uuuhh...
...of course, Mr. Ripken. Go right in.
OPEN
SECURITY
This story isn't about **them**.

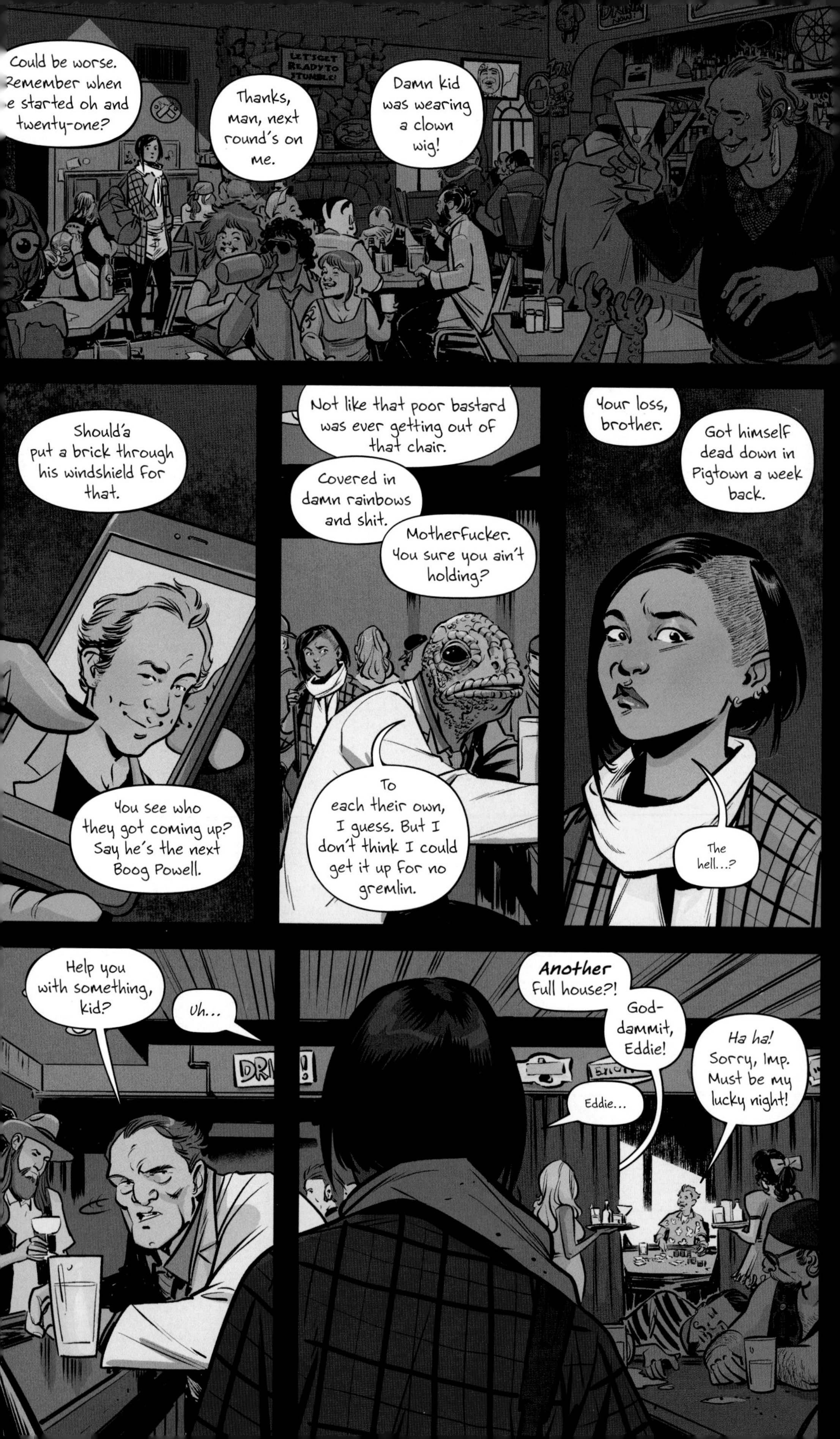
Could be worse. Remember when e started oh and twenty-one?
LET'S GET READY TO STUMBLE!
Thanks, man, next round's on me.
Damn kid was wearing a clown wig!
Should'a put a brick through his windshield for that.
You see who they got coming up? Say he's the next Boog Powell.
Not like that poor bastard was ever getting out of that chair.
Covered in damn rainbows and shit.
Motherfucker. You sure you ain't holding?
To each their own, I guess. But I don't think I could get it up for no gremlin.
Your loss, brother.
Got himself dead down in Pigtown a week back.
The hell...?
Help you with something, kid?
Uh...
Another full house?!
God-dammit, Eddie!
Eddie...
Ha ha! Sorry, Imp. Must be my lucky night!

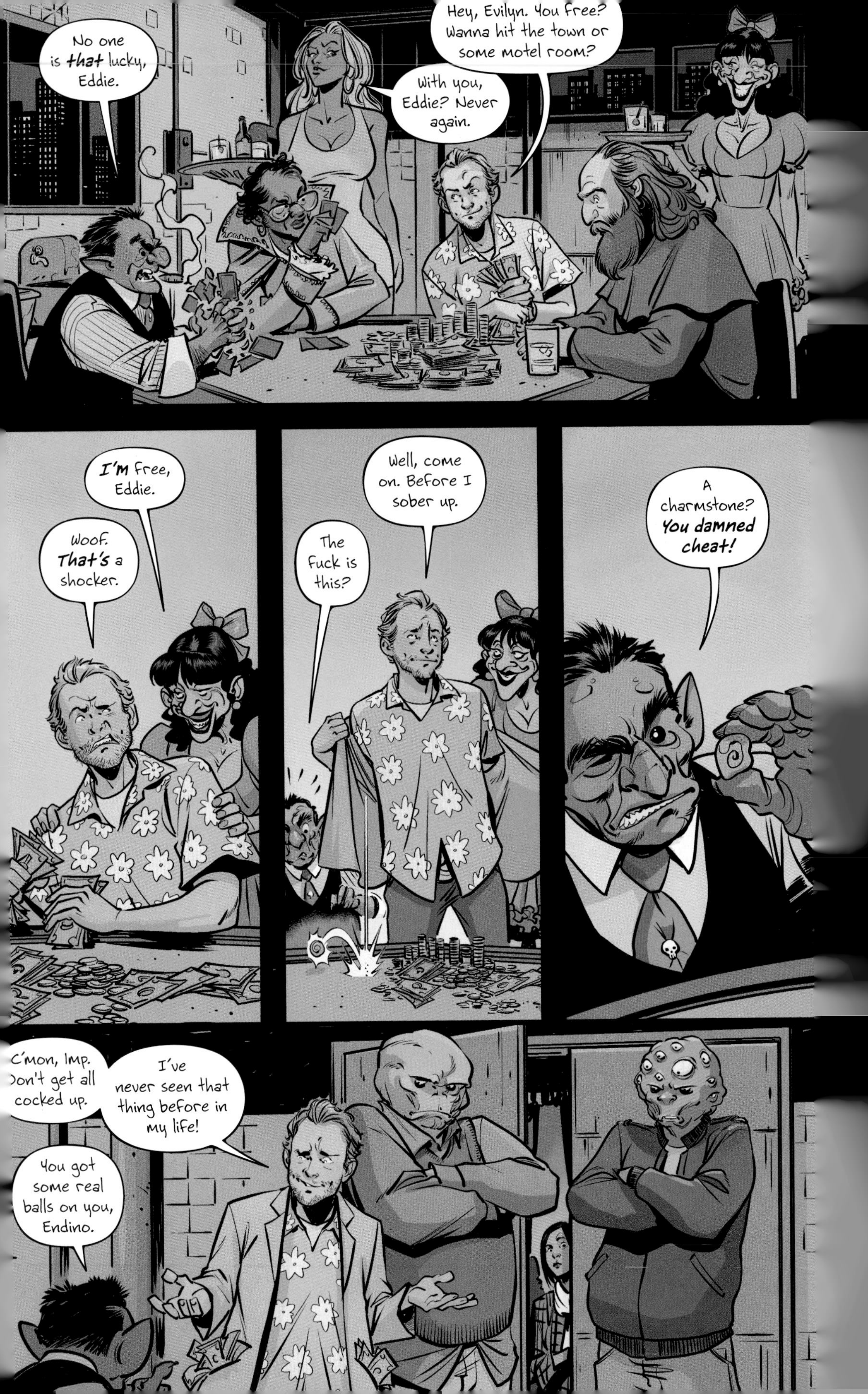
No one is that lucky, Eddie.
Hey, Evilyn. You free? Wanna hit the town or some motel room?
With you, Eddie? Never again.
I'M free, Eddie.
Woof. That's a shocker.
Well, come on. Before I sober up.
The fuck is this?
A charmstone? You damned cheat!
C'mon, Imp. Don't get all cocked up.
I've never seen that thing before in my life!
You got some real balls on you, Endino.

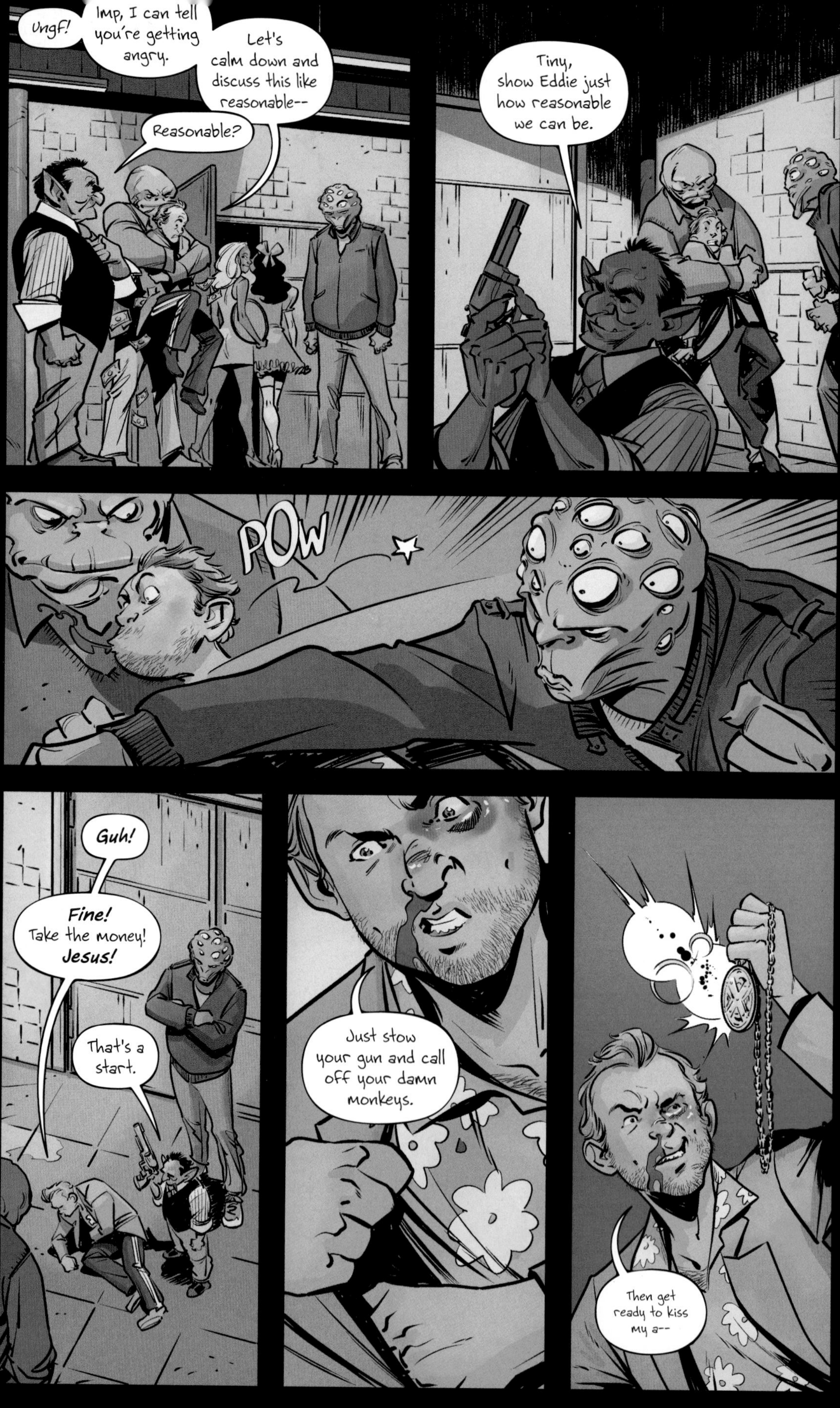
Ungf!
Imp, I can tell you're getting angry.
Let's calm down and discuss this like reasonable--
Reasonable?
Tiny, show Eddie just how reasonable we can be.
POW
Guh!
Fine! Take the money! Jesus!
That's a start.
Just stow your gun and call off your damn monkeys.
Then get ready to kiss my a--

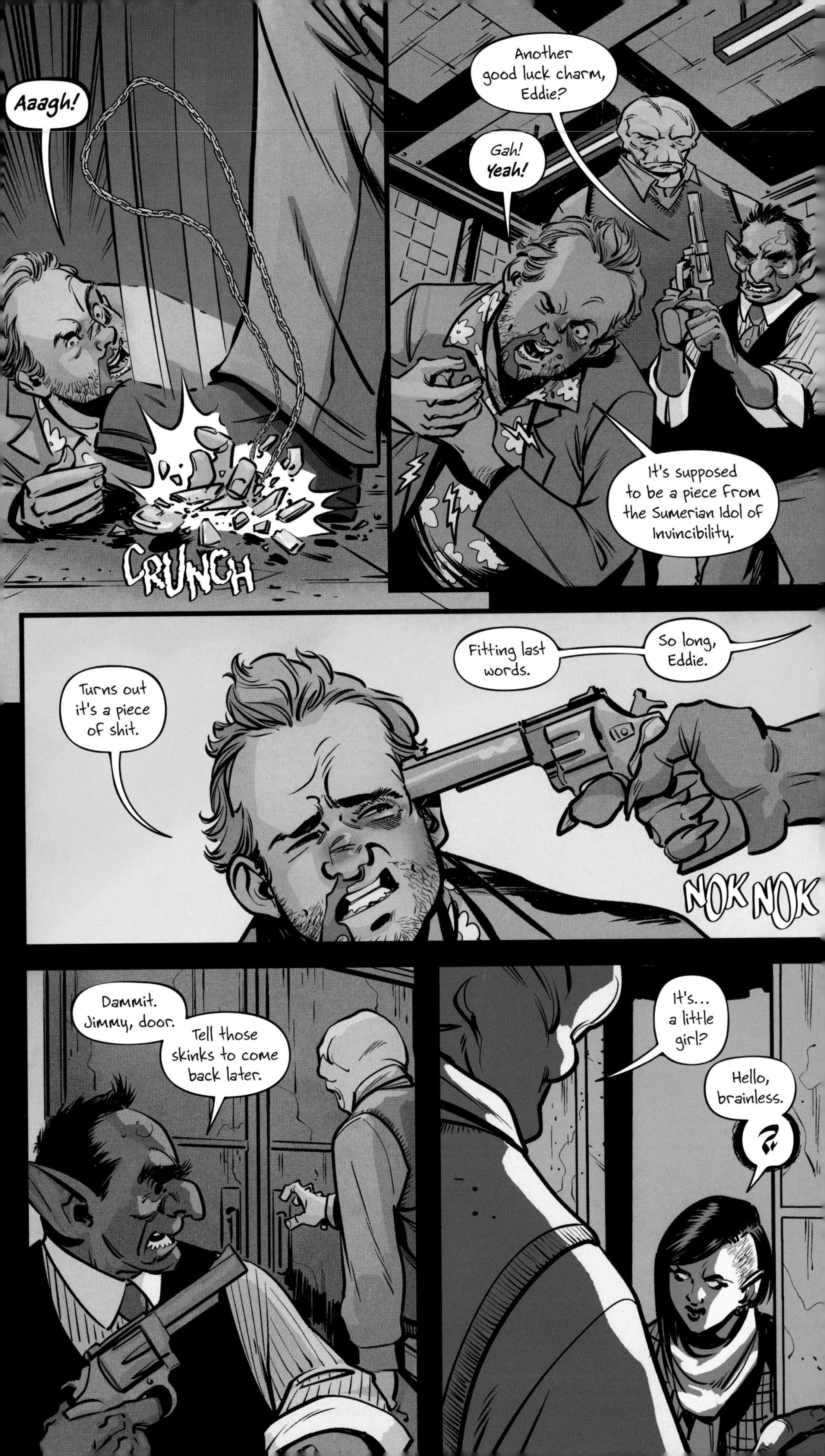
Aaagh!
CRUNCH
Another good luck charm, Eddie?
Gah! Yeah!
It's supposed to be a piece from the Sumerian Idol of Invincibility.
Turns out it's a piece of shit.
Fitting last words.
So long, Eddie.
NOK NOK
Dammit. Jimmy, door.
Tell those skinks to come back later.
It's... a little girl?
Hello, brainless.

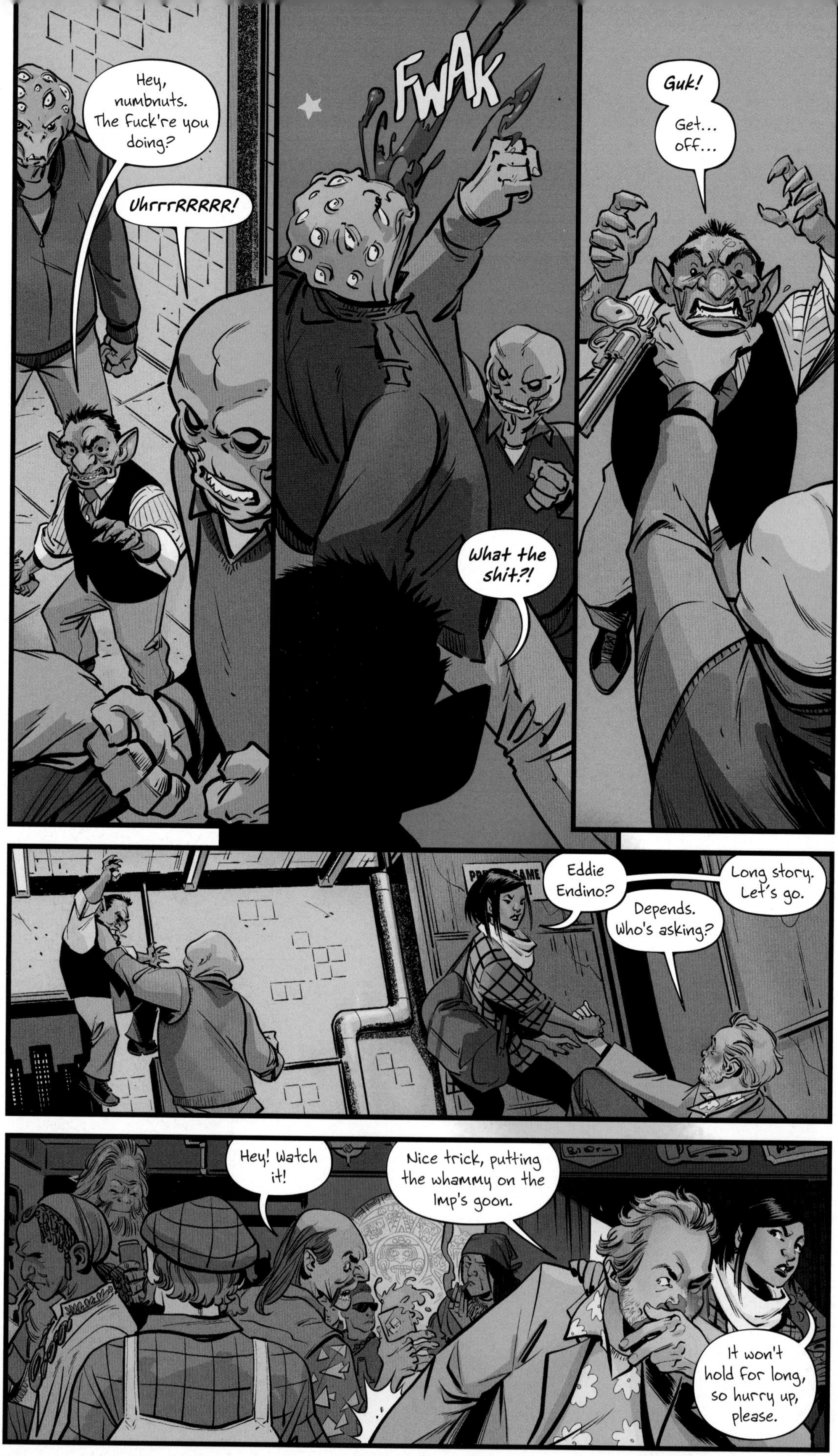
Hey, numbnuts. The fuck're you doing?
UhrrrRRRRR!
FWAK
What the shit?!
Guk!
Get... off...
Eddie Endino?
Depends. Who's asking?
Long story. Let's go.
Hey! Watch it!
Nice trick, putting the whammy on the Imp's goon.
It won't hold for long, so hurry up, please.

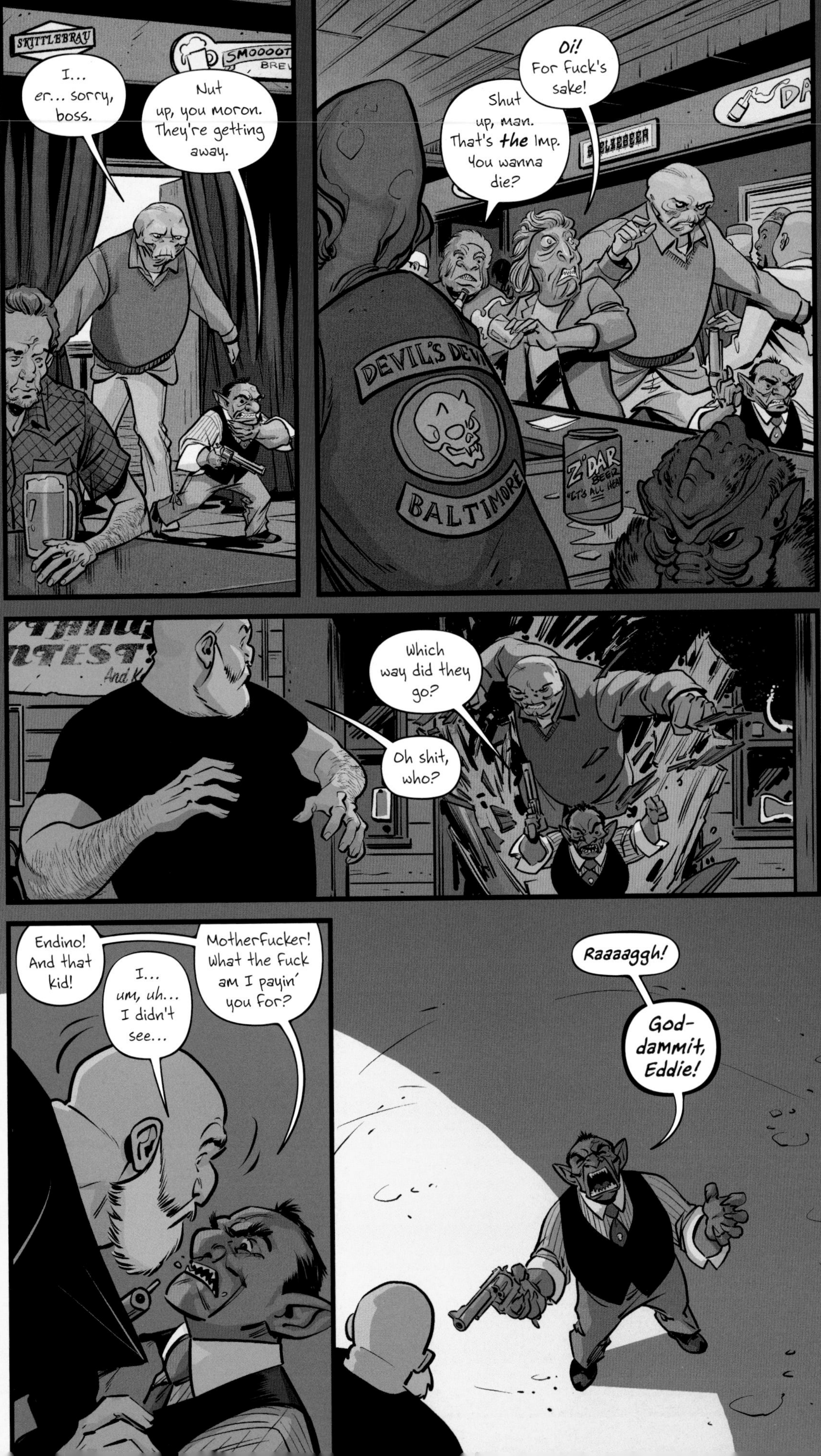
SKITTLEBRAU
SMOOOOT BREW
I... er... sorry, boss.
Nut up, you moron. They're getting away.
Oi! For fuck's sake!
Shut up, man. That's *the* Imp. You wanna die?
DEVIL'S DEV
BALTIMORE
Z'DAR BEER
Which way did they go?
Oh shit, who?
Endino! And that kid!
I... um, uh... I didn't see...
Motherfucker! What the fuck am I payin' you for?
Raaaaggh!
God-dammit, Eddie!

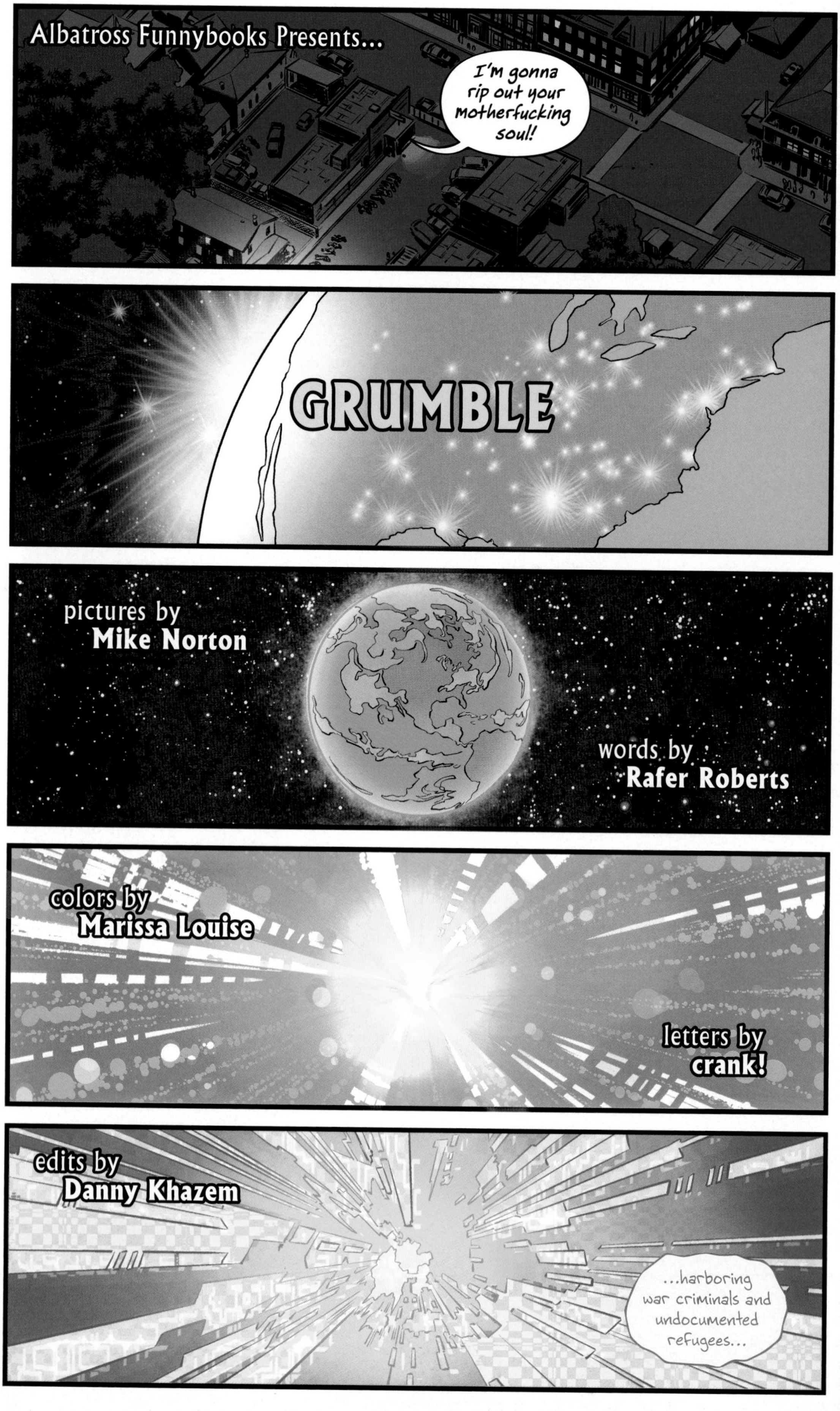
Albatross Funnybooks Presents...
I'm gonna rip out your motherfucking soul!
GRUMBLE
pictures by Mike Norton
words by Rafer Roberts
colors by Marissa Louise
letters by crank!
edits by Danny Khazem
...harboring war criminals and undocumented refugees...

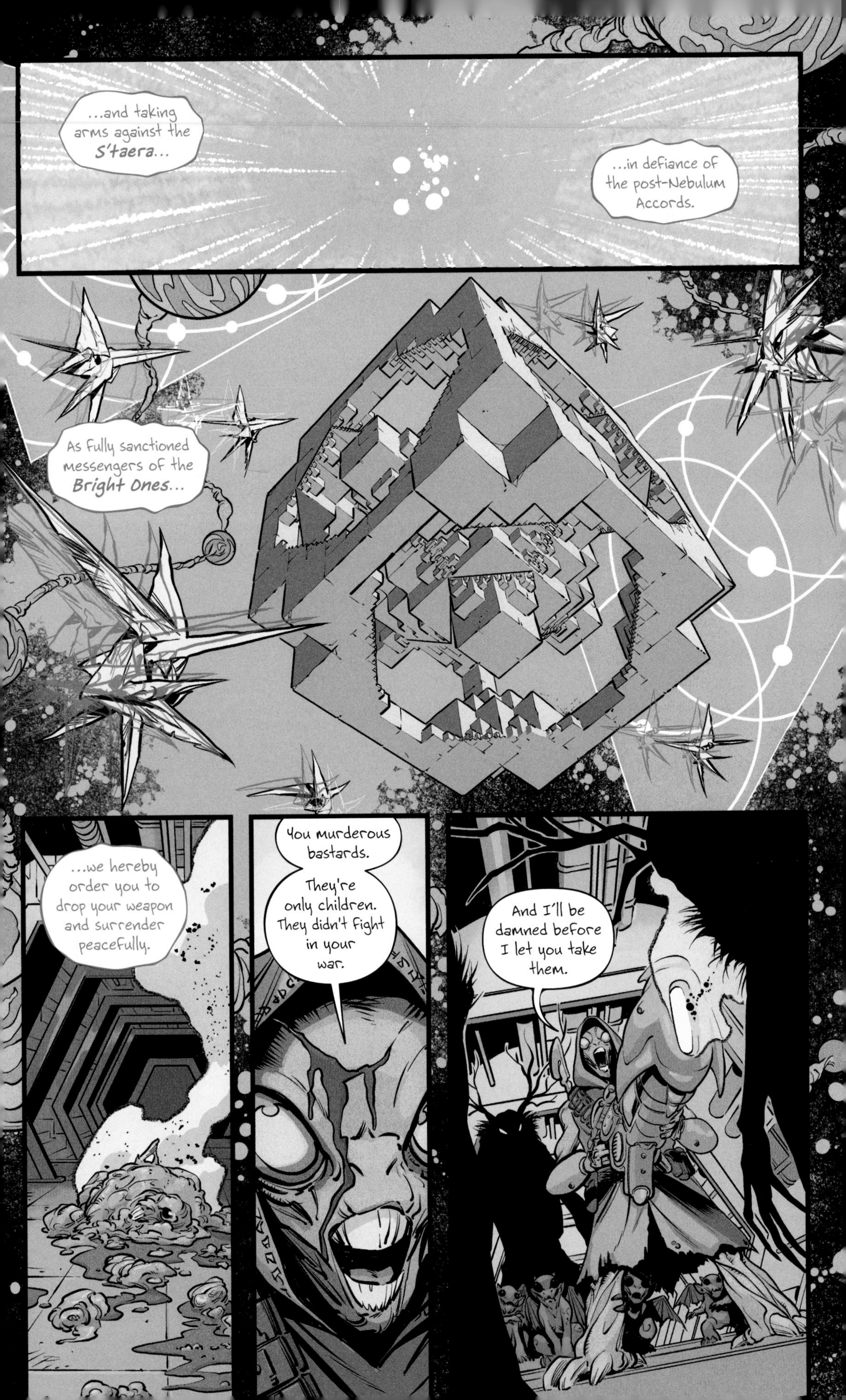
...and taking arms against the S'taera...
...in defiance of the post-Nebulum Accords.
As fully sanctioned messengers of the Bright Ones...
...we hereby order you to drop your weapon and surrender peacefully.
You murderous bastards.
They're only children. They didn't fight in your war.
And I'll be damned before I let you take them.

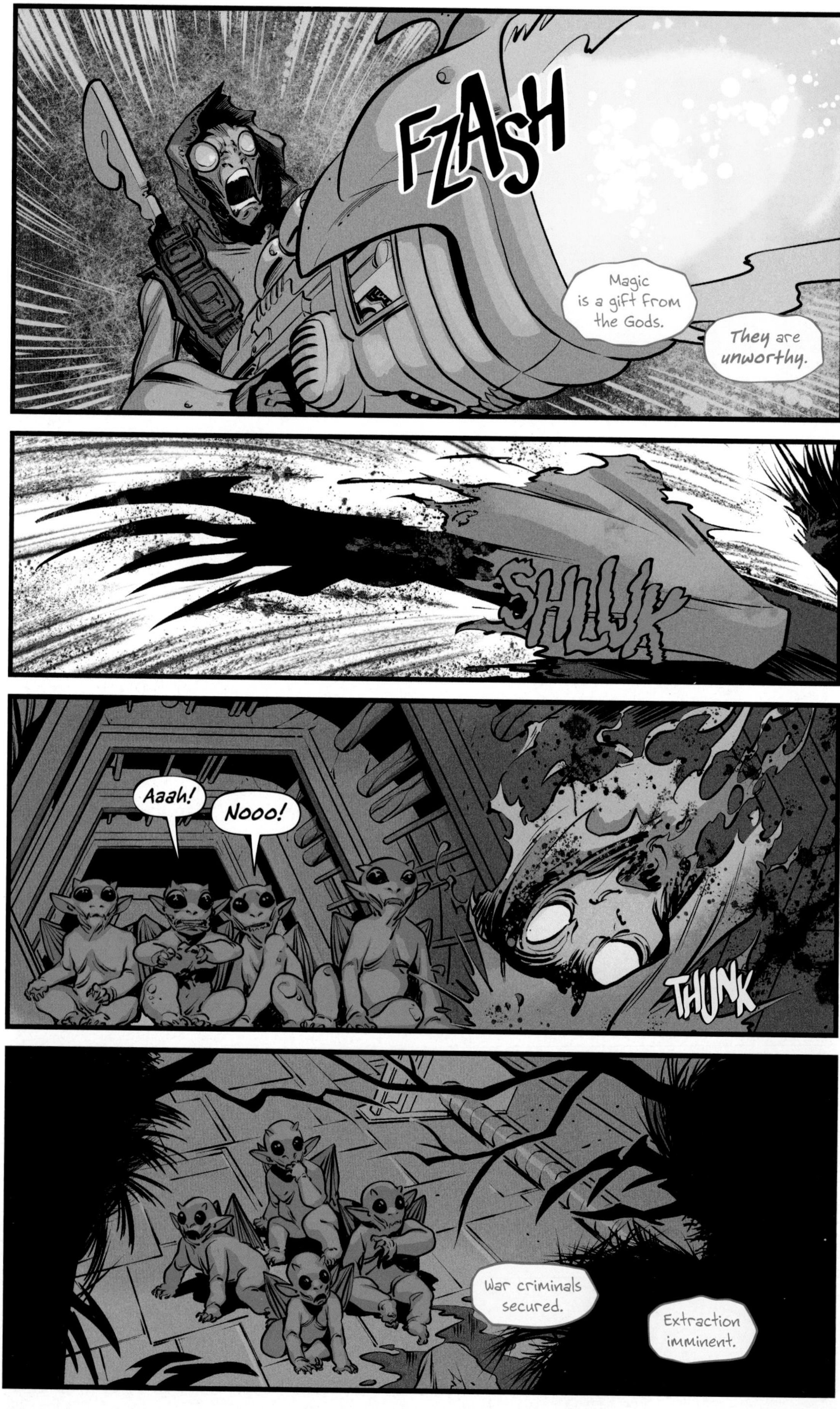
FZASH
Magic is a gift from the Gods.
They are unworthy.
SHLUK
Aaah!
Nooo!
THUNK
War criminals secured.
Extraction imminent.

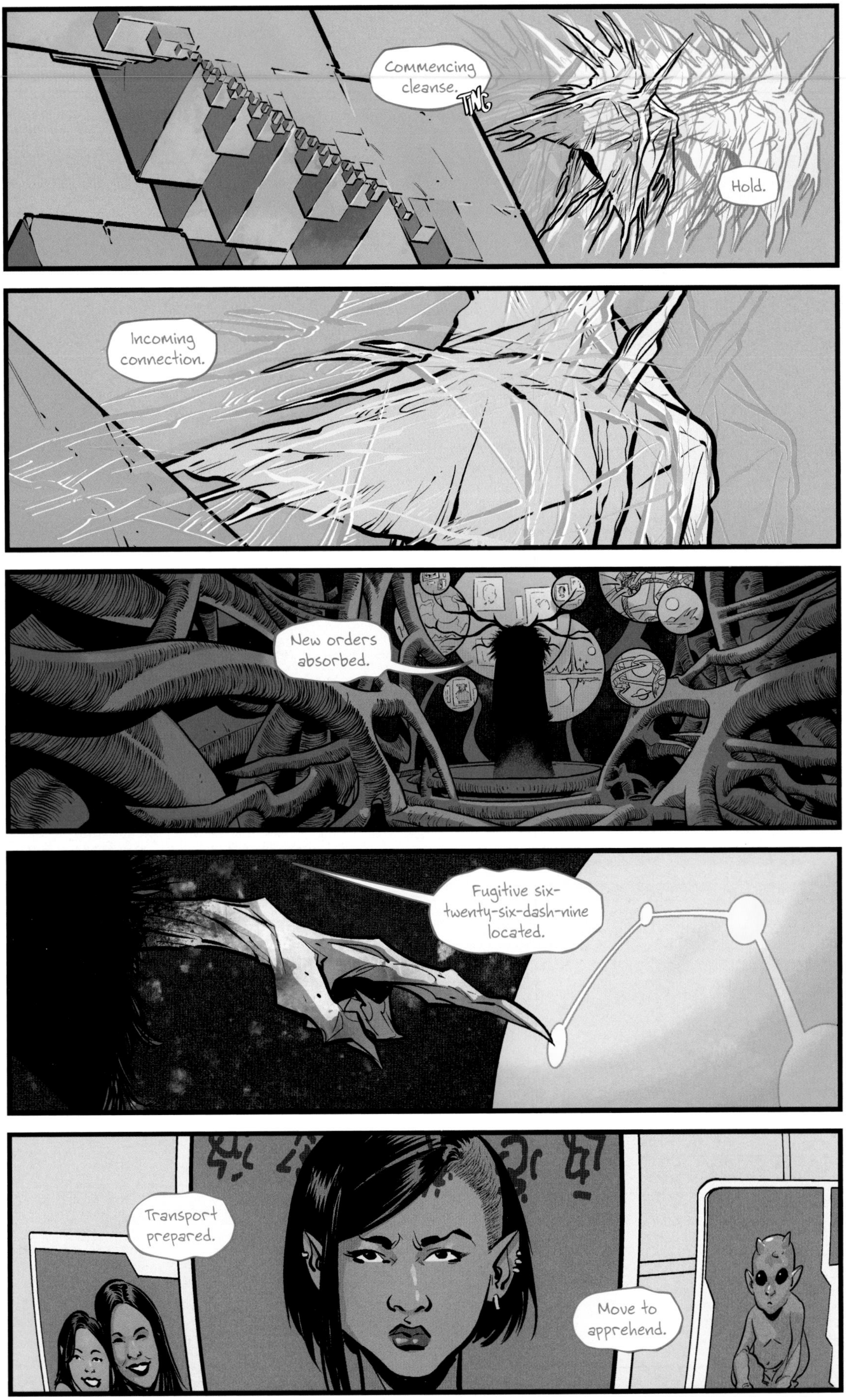
Commencing cleanse.
TNG
Hold.
Incoming connection.
New orders absorbed.
Fugitive six-twenty-six-dash-nine located.
Transport prepared.
Move to apprehend.

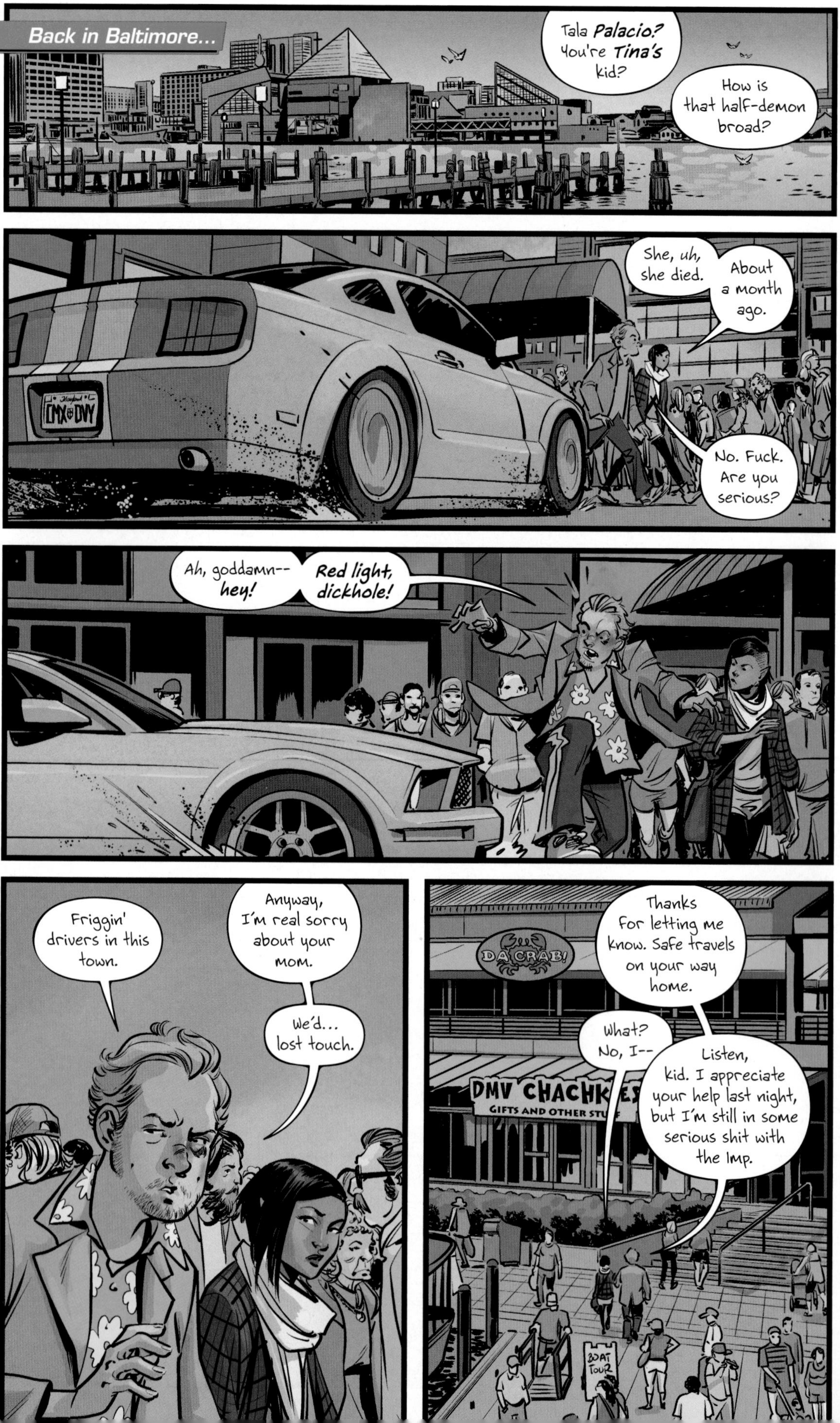
Back in Baltimore...
Tala *Palacio?* You're *Tina's* kid?
How is that half-demon broad?
She, uh, she died.
About a month ago.
No. Fuck. Are you serious?
CMX DVY
Ah, goddamn-- **hey!**
Red light, dickhole!
Friggin' drivers in this town.
Anyway, I'm real sorry about your mom.
We'd... lost touch.
Thanks for letting me know. Safe travels on your way home.
What? No, I--
Listen, kid. I appreciate your help last night, but I'm still in some serious shit with the Imp.
DA CRAB!
GIFTS AND OTHER STUFF
BOAT TOUR

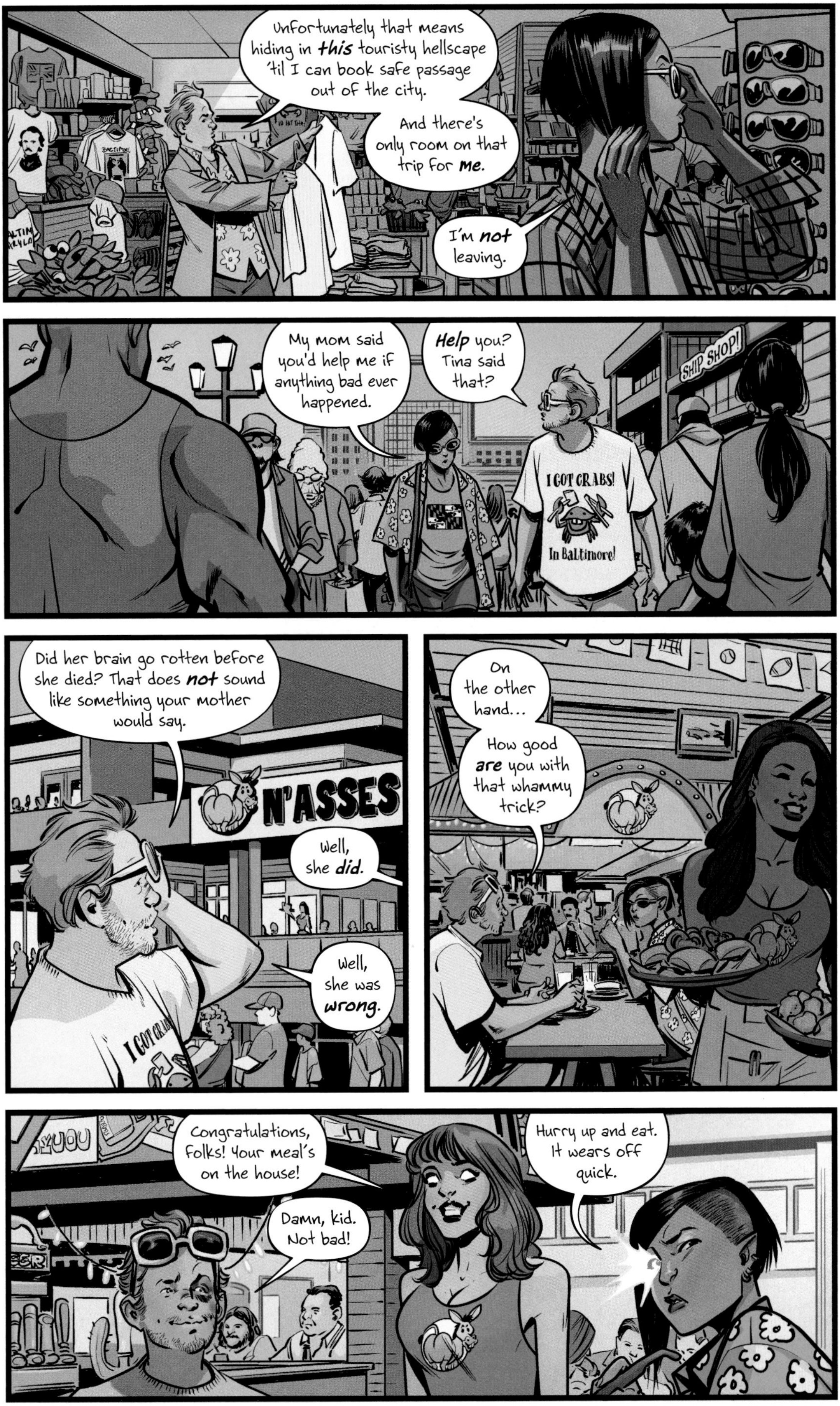
Unfortunately that means hiding in ***this*** touristy hellscape 'til I can book safe passage out of the city.
And there's only room on that trip for ***me.***
I'm ***not*** leaving.
SHIP SHOP!
My mom said you'd help me if anything bad ever happened.
Help you? Tina said that?
I GOT CRABS! In Baltimore!
Did her brain go rotten before she died? That does ***not*** sound like something your mother would say.
N'ASSES
Well, she ***did.***
Well, she was ***wrong.***
On the other hand...
How good ***are*** you with that whammy trick?
Congratulations, Folks! Your meal's on the house!
Damn, kid. Not bad!
Hurry up and eat. It wears off quick.

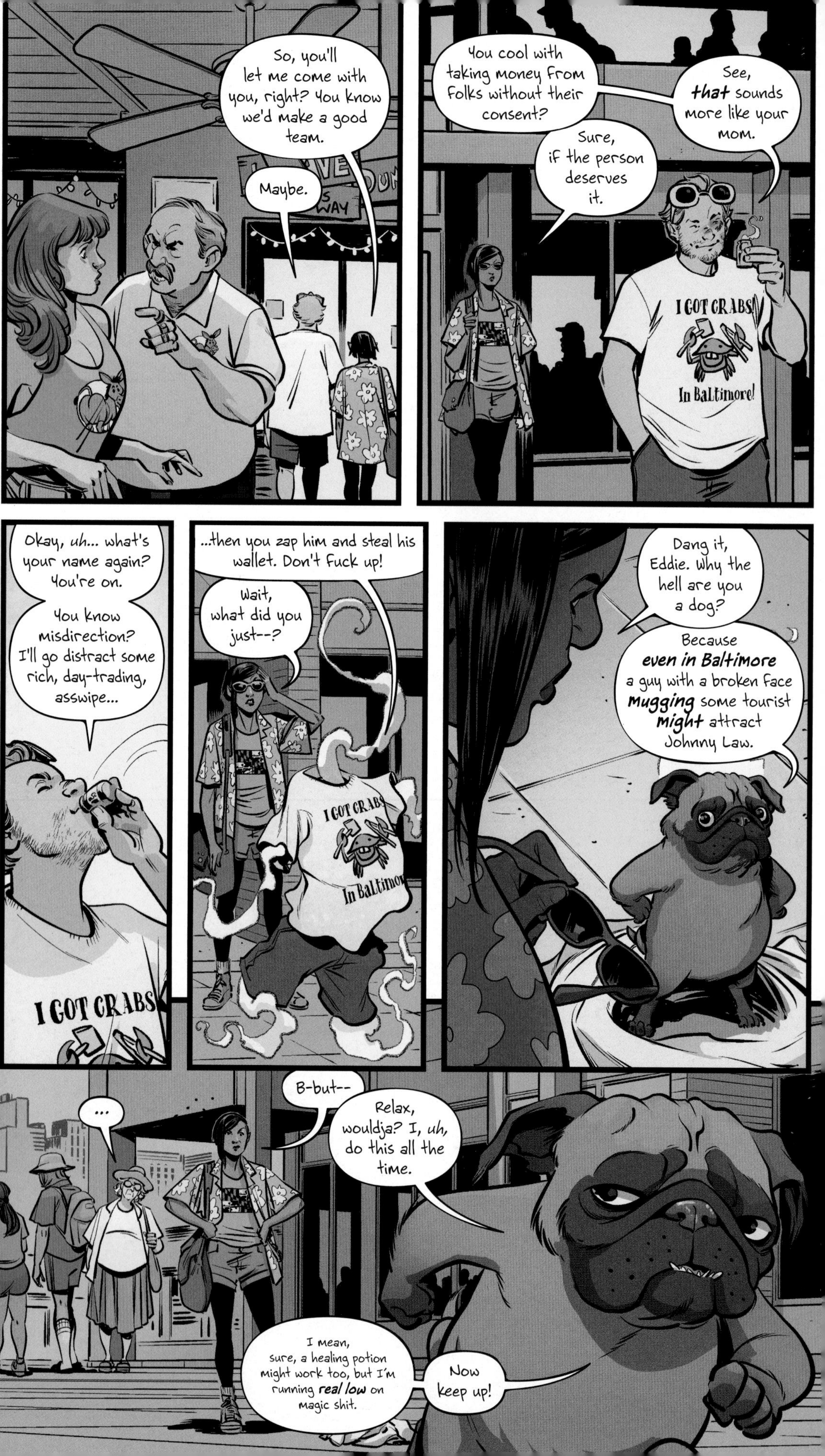
So, you'll let me come with you, right? You know we'd make a good team.
Maybe.
You cool with taking money from folks without their consent?
Sure, if the person deserves it.
See, **that** sounds more like your mom.
I GOT CRABS In Baltimore!
Okay, *uh*... what's your name again? You're on.
You know misdirection? I'll go distract some rich, day-trading, asswipe...
I GOT CRABS
...then you zap him and steal his wallet. Don't fuck up!
Wait, what did you just--?
I GOT CRABS In Baltimo
Dang it, Eddie. Why the hell are you a dog?
Because **even in Baltimore** a guy with a broken face **mugging** some tourist **might** attract Johnny Law.
...
B-but--
Relax, wouldja? I, uh, do this all the time.
I mean, sure, a healing potion might work too, but I'm running **real low** on magic shit.
Now keep up!

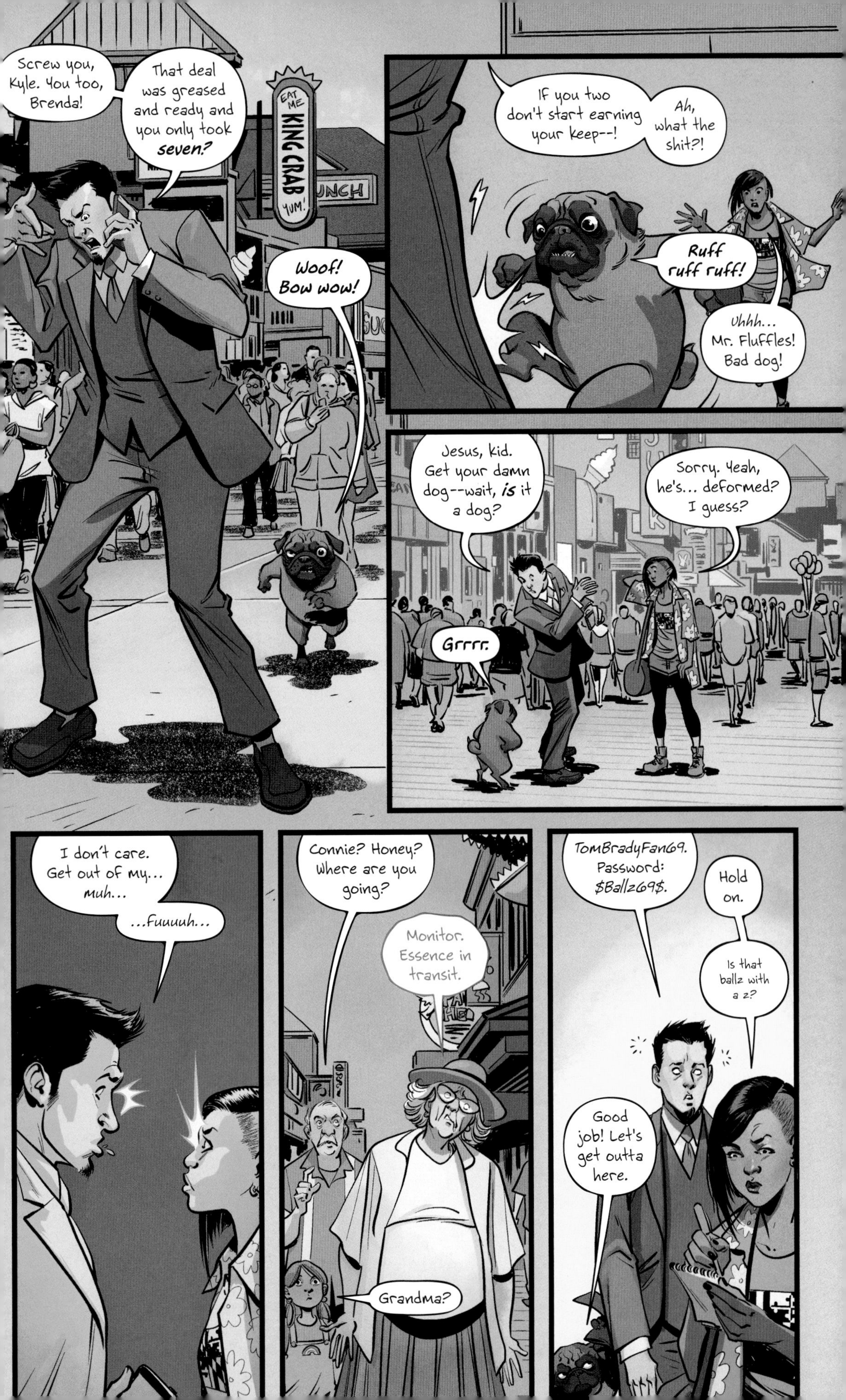
Screw you, Kyle. You too, Brenda!
That deal was greased and ready and you only took seven?
EAT ME
KING CRAB
YUM!
LUNCH
Woof! Bow wow!
If you two don't start earning your keep--!
Ah, what the shit?!
Ruff ruff ruff!
Uhhh... Mr. Fluffles! Bad dog!
Jesus, kid. Get your damn dog--wait, is it a dog?
Sorry. Yeah, he's... deformed? I guess?
Grrrr.
I don't care. Get out of my... muh...
...fuuuuh...
Connie? Honey? Where are you going?
Monitor. Essence in transit.
Grandma?
TomBradyFan69. Password: $Ballz69$.
Hold on.
Is that ballz with a z?
Good job! Let's get outta here.

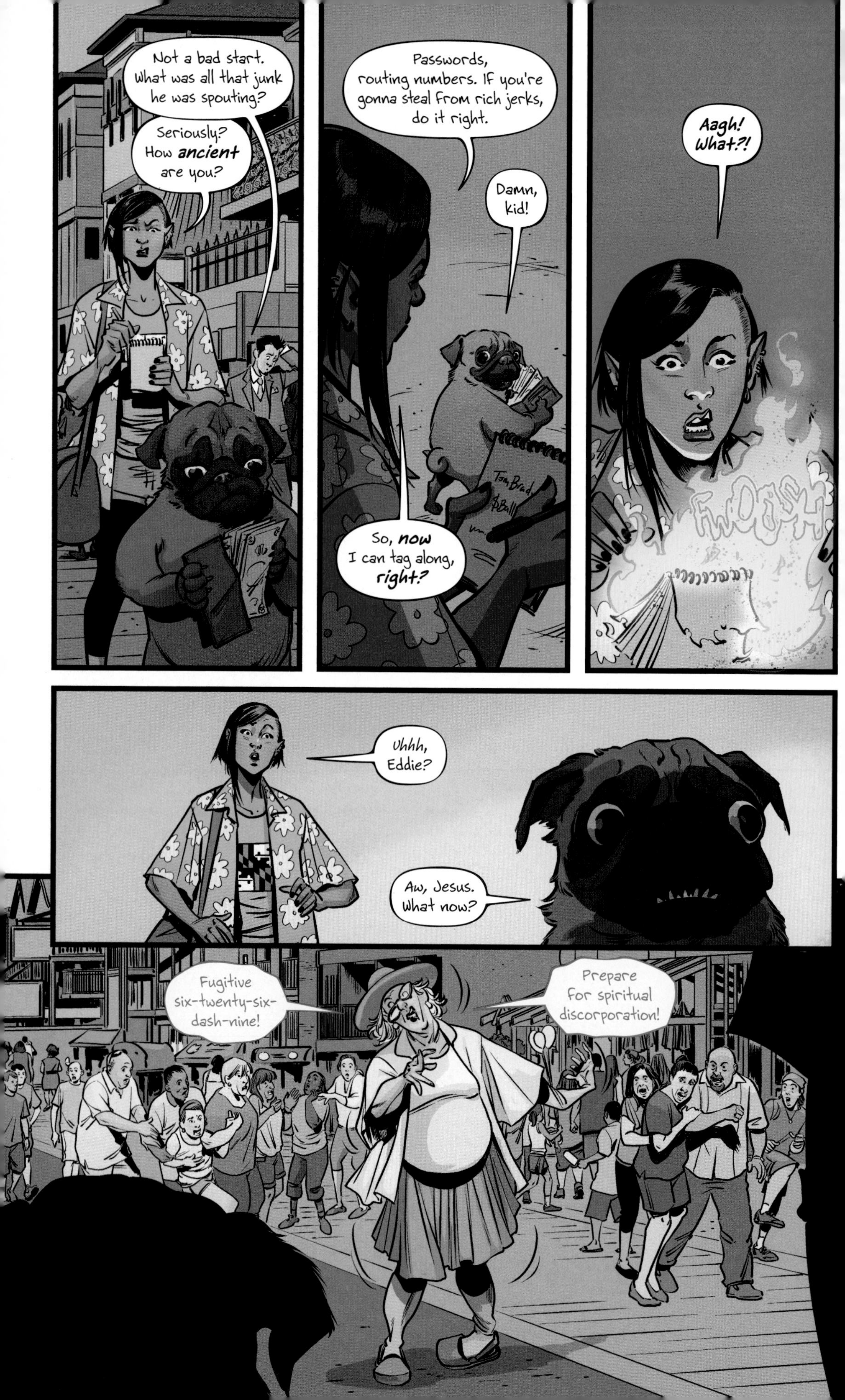
Not a bad start. What was all that junk he was spouting?
Seriously? How **ancient** are you?
Passwords, routing numbers. If you're gonna steal from rich jerks, do it right.
Damn, kid!
So, **now** I can tag along, **right?**
Aagh! What?!
FWOOSH
Uhhh, Eddie?
Aw, Jesus. What now?
Fugitive six-twenty-six-dash-nine!
Prepare for spiritual discorporation!

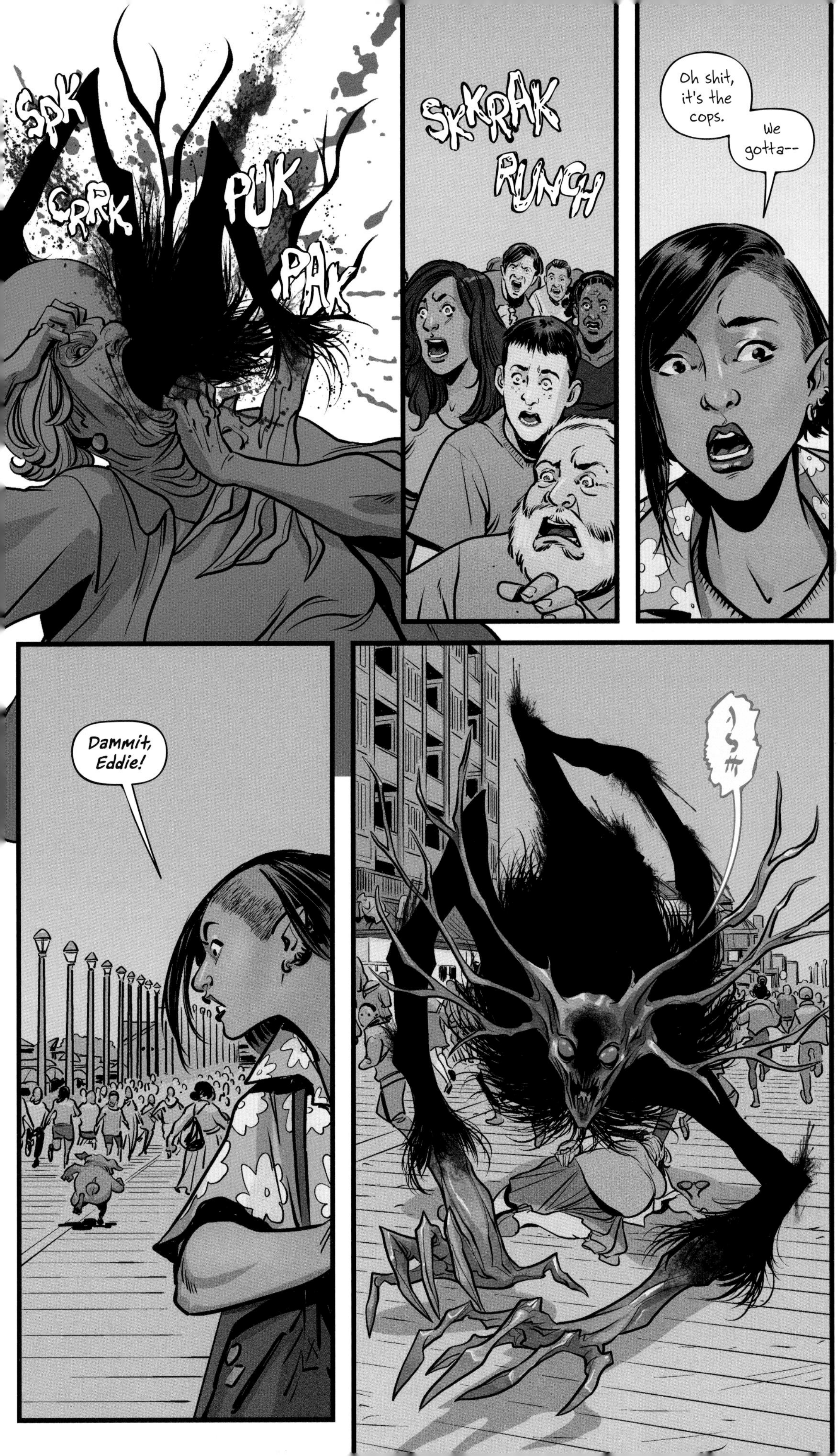
SPK
CRRK
PUK
PAK
SKKRAK
RUNCH
Oh shit, it's the cops.
We gotta--
Dammit, Eddie!

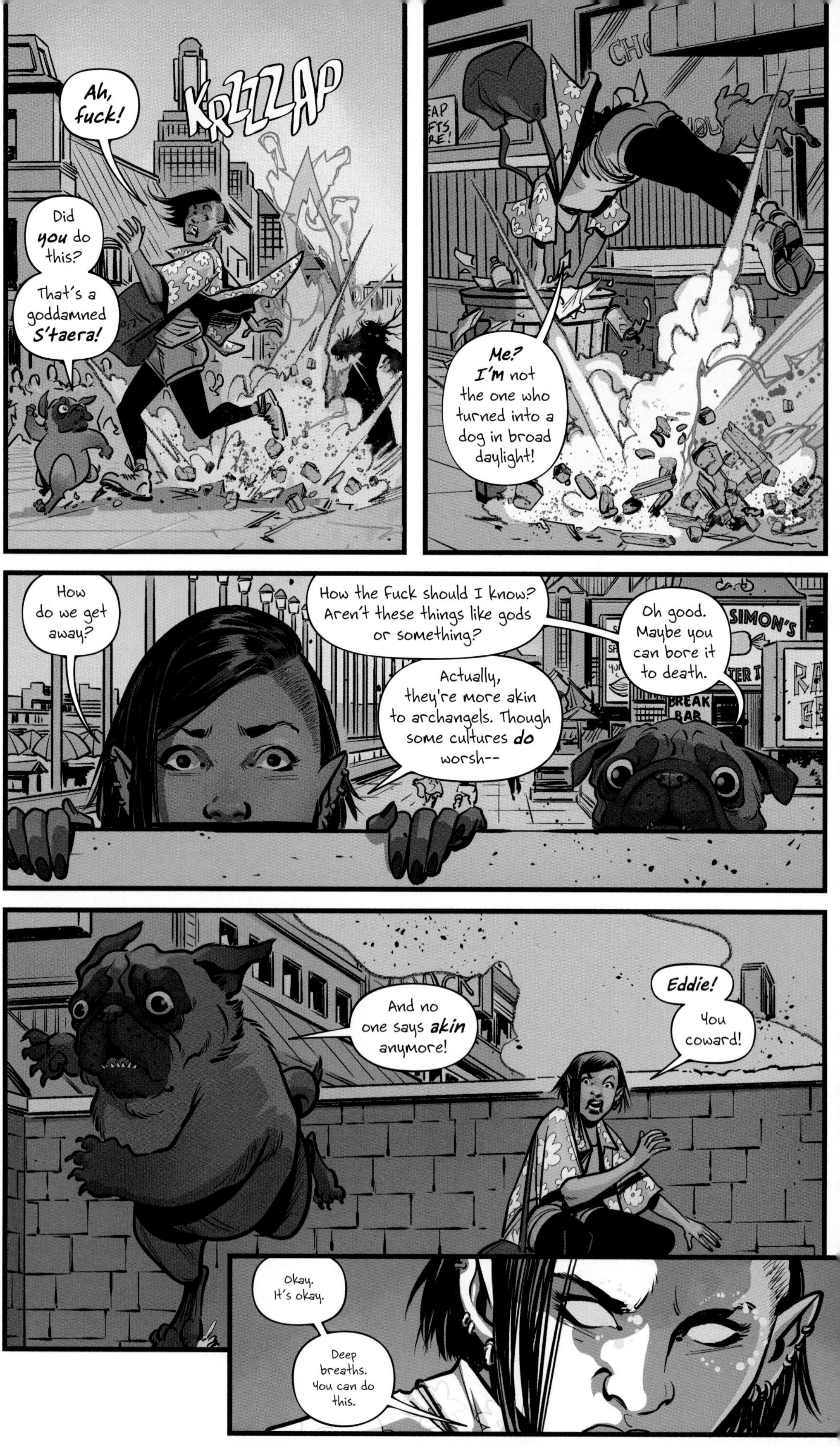
Ah, fuck!
KRZZZAP
Did you do this?
That's a goddamned S'taera!
Me? I'M not the one who turned into a dog in broad daylight!
How do we get away?
How the fuck should I know? Aren't these things like gods or something?
Actually, they're more akin to archangels. Though some cultures do worsh--
Oh good. Maybe you can bore it to death.
SIMON'S
BREAK BAR
And no one says akin anymore!
Eddie!
You coward!
Okay. It's okay.
Deep breaths. You can do this.

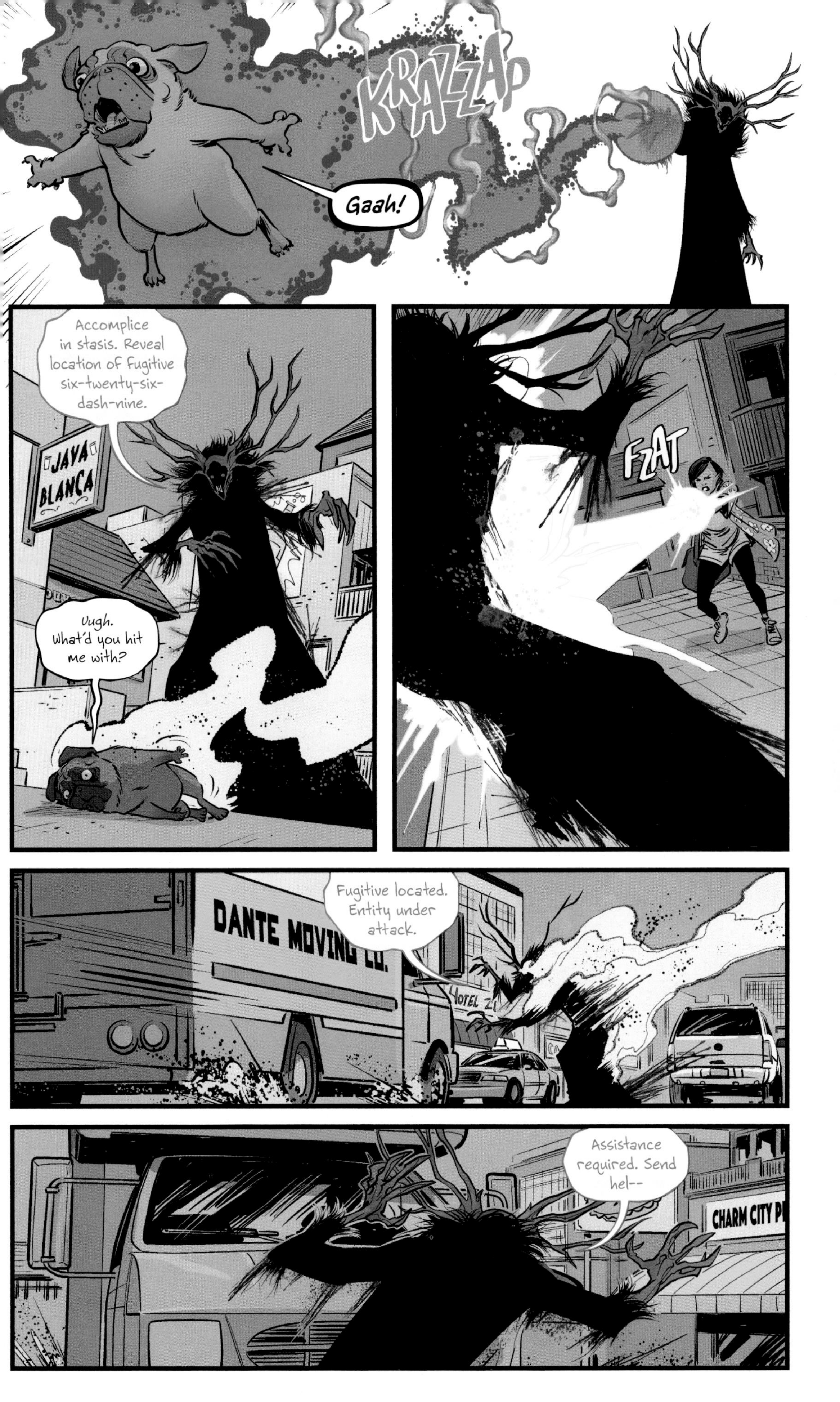
KRAZZZAP
Gaah!
Accomplice in stasis. Reveal location of fugitive six-twenty-six-dash-nine.
JAVA BLANCA
Ugh. What'd you hit me with?
FZAT
DANTE MOVING CO.
Fugitive located. Entity under attack.
HOTEL Z
Assistance required. Send hel--
CHARM CITY P

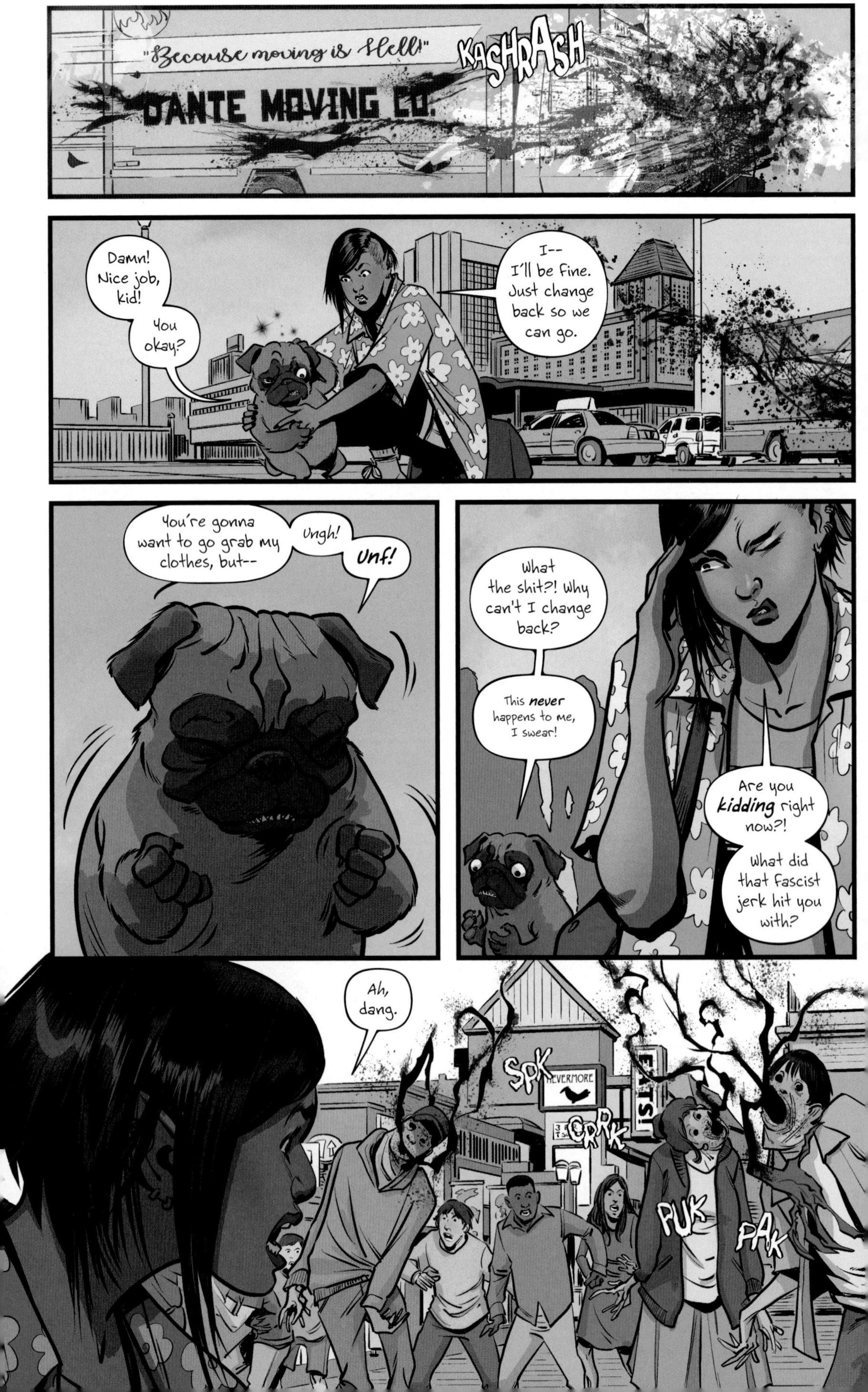
"Because moving is Hell!"
DANTE MOVING CO.
KASHRASH
Damn! Nice job, kid!
You okay?
I-- I'll be fine. Just change back so we can go.
You're gonna want to go grab my clothes, but--
Ungh!
Unf!
What the shit?! Why can't I change back?
This never happens to me, I swear!
Are you kidding right now?!
What did that fascist jerk hit you with?
Ah, dang.
SPK
NEVERMORE
EATS!
CRRK
PUK
PAK

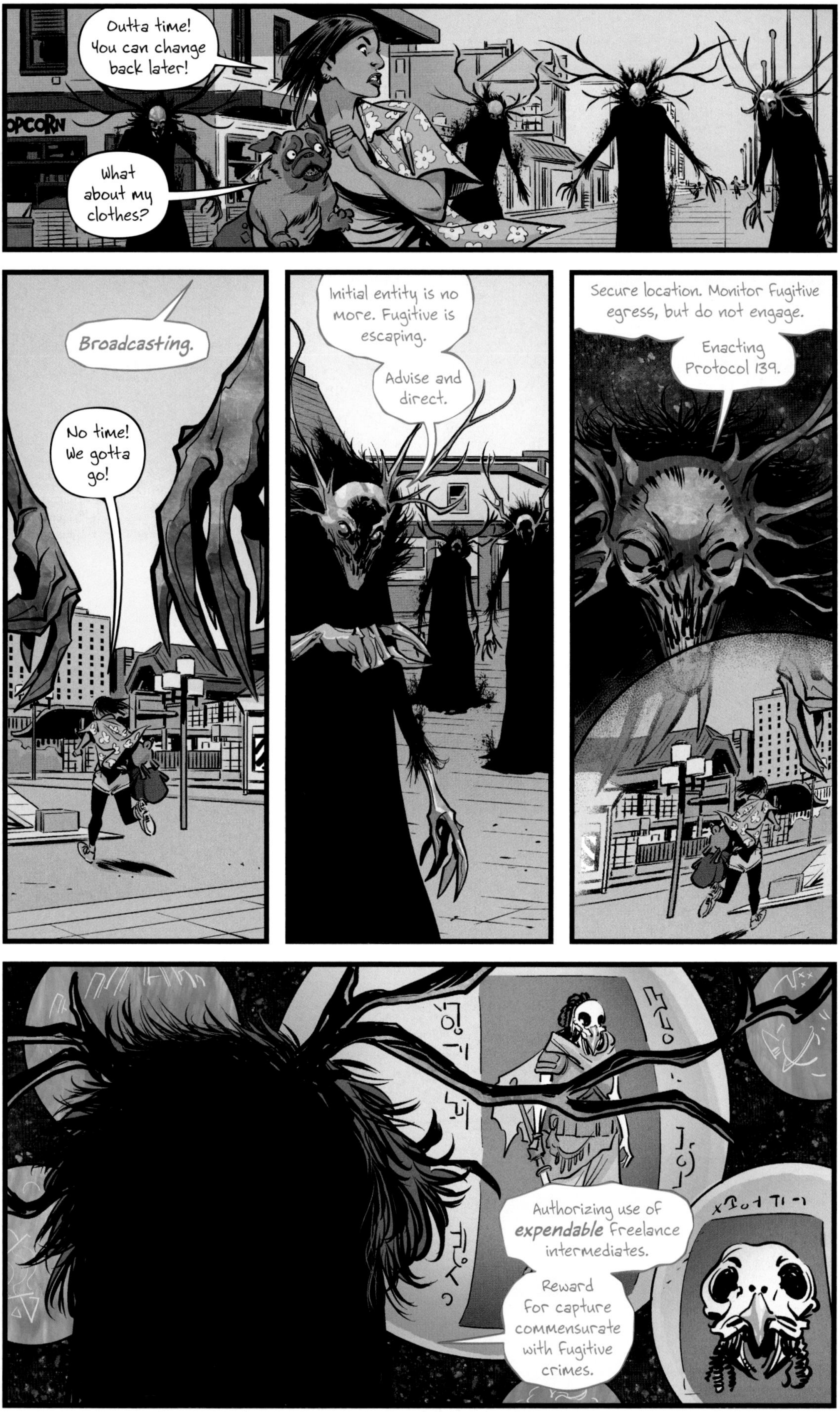

Outta time! You can change back later!
What about my clothes?
POPCORN
Broadcasting.
No time! We gotta go!
Initial entity is no more. Fugitive is escaping.
Advise and direct.
Secure location. Monitor Fugitive egress, but do not engage.
Enacting Protocol 139.
Authorizing use of ***expendable*** freelance intermediates.
Reward for capture commensurate with Fugitive crimes.

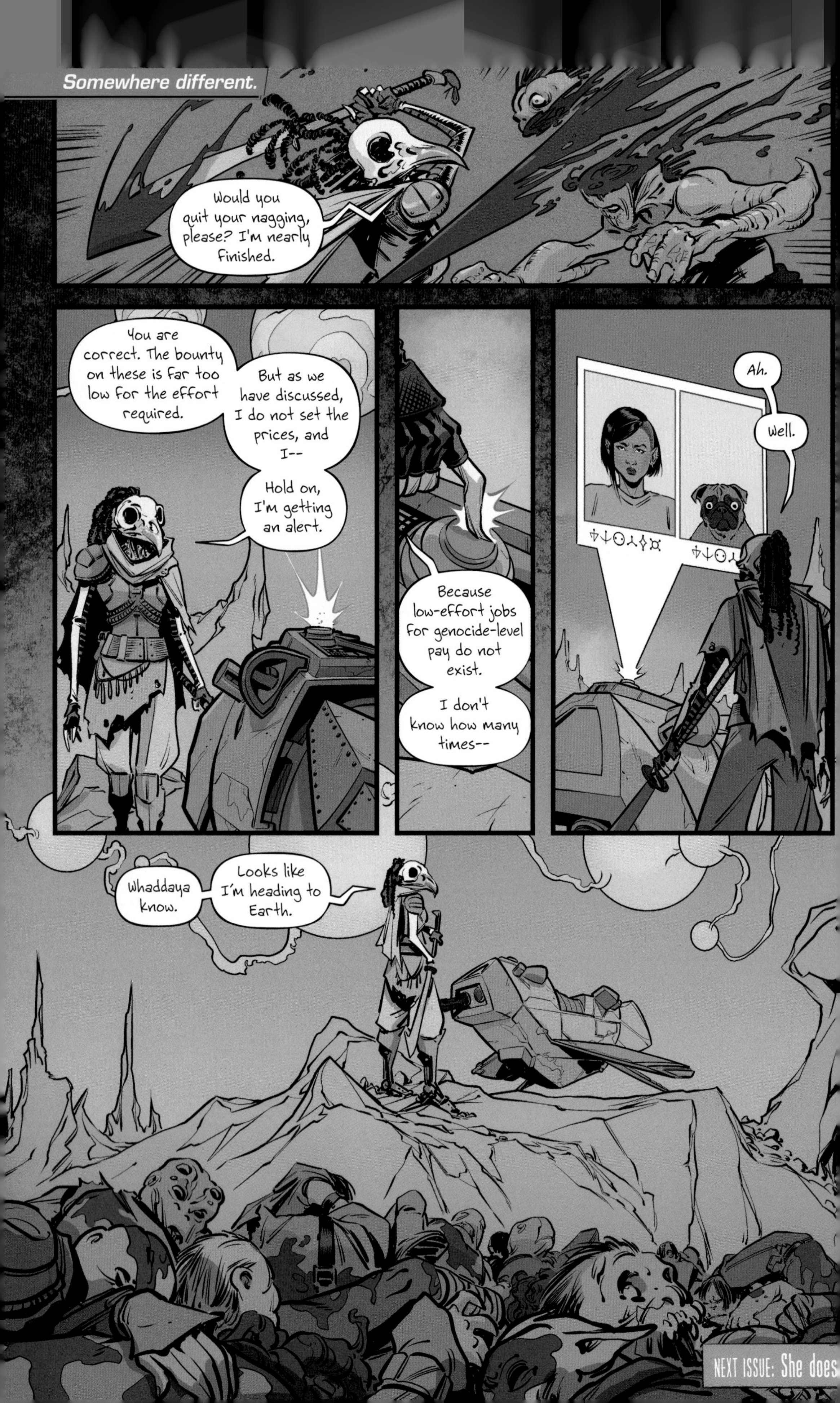

Somewhere different.
Would you quit your nagging, please? I'm nearly finished.
You are correct. The bounty on these is far too low for the effort required.
But as we have discussed, I do not set the prices, and I--
Hold on, I'm getting an alert.
Because low-effort jobs for genocide-level pay do not exist.
I don't know how many times--
Ah.
Well.
Whaddaya know.
Looks like I'm heading to Earth.
NEXT ISSUE: She does

BOOK TWO

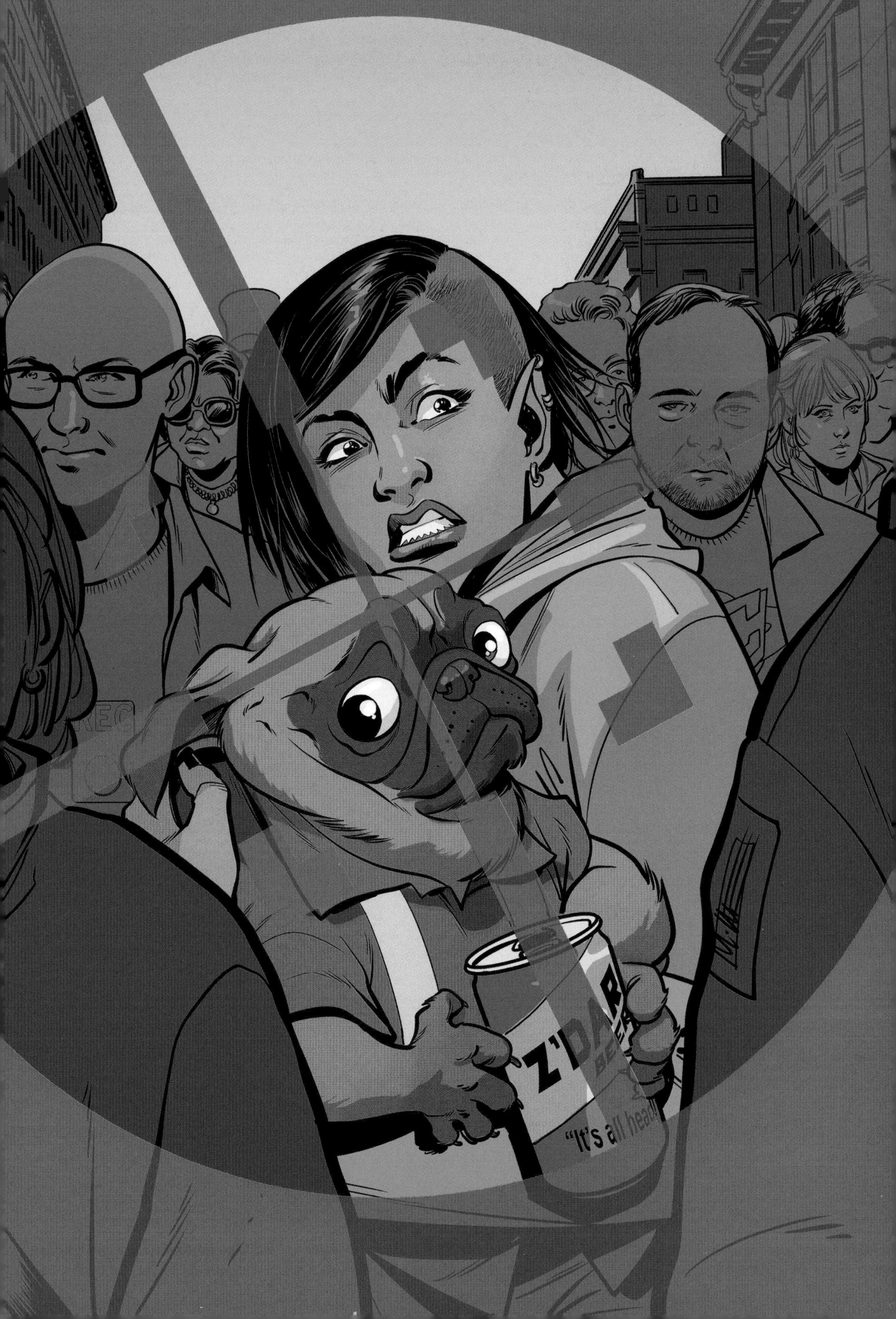
Z'DAR
“It's all

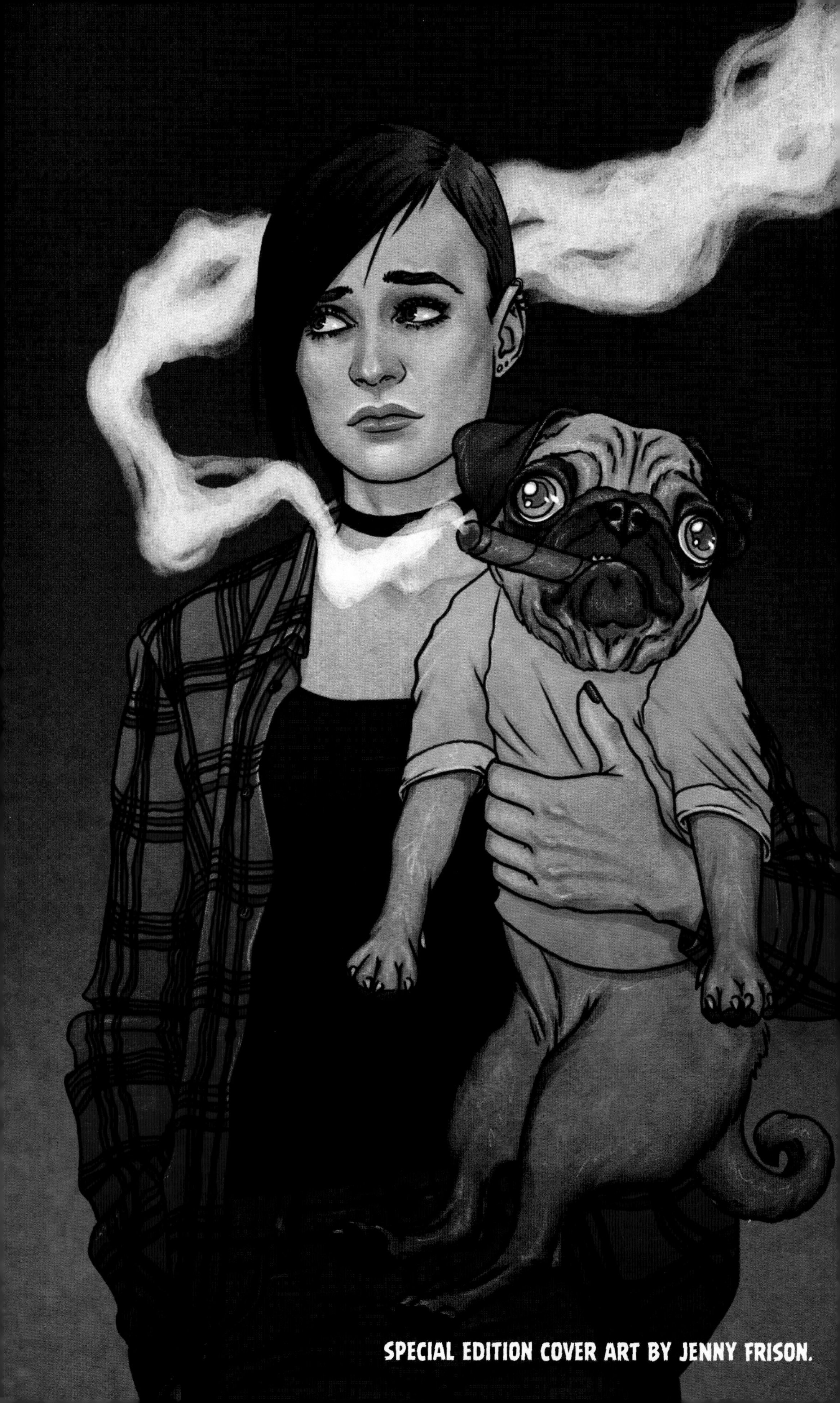

SPECIAL EDITION COVER ART BY JENNY FRISON.

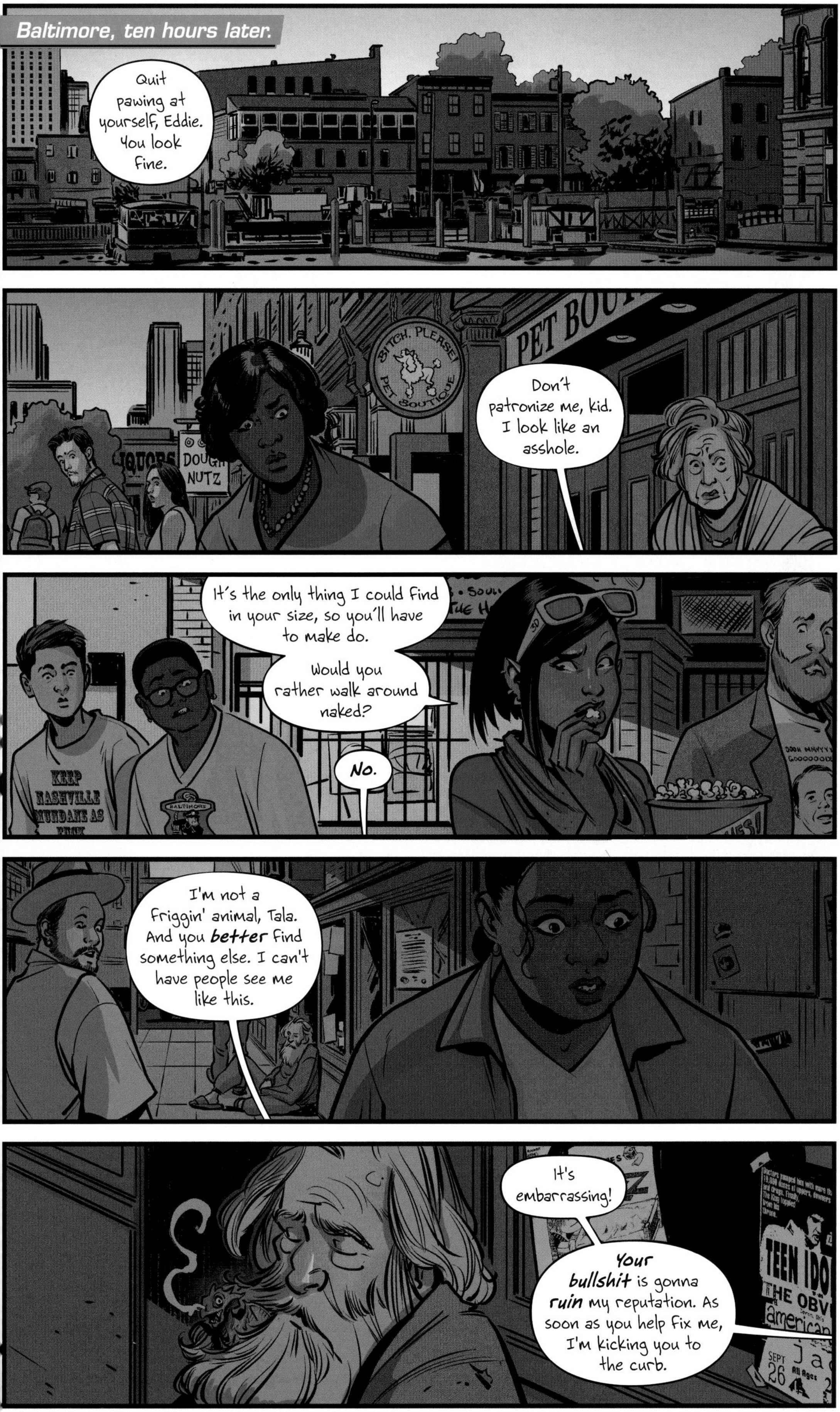
Baltimore, ten hours later.
Quit pawing at yourself, Eddie. You look fine.
BITCH, PLEASE! PET BOUTIQUE
LIQUORS
DOUGH NUTZ
Don't patronize me, kid. I look like an asshole.
It's the only thing I could find in your size, so you'll have to make do.
Would you rather walk around naked?
No.
KEEP NASHVILLE MUNDANE AS
BALTIMORE
I'm not a friggin' animal, Tala. And you **better** find something else. I can't have people see me like this.
It's embarrassing!
Your bullshit is gonna ***ruin*** my reputation. As soon as you help fix me, I'm kicking you to the curb.
SEPT 26
All Ages

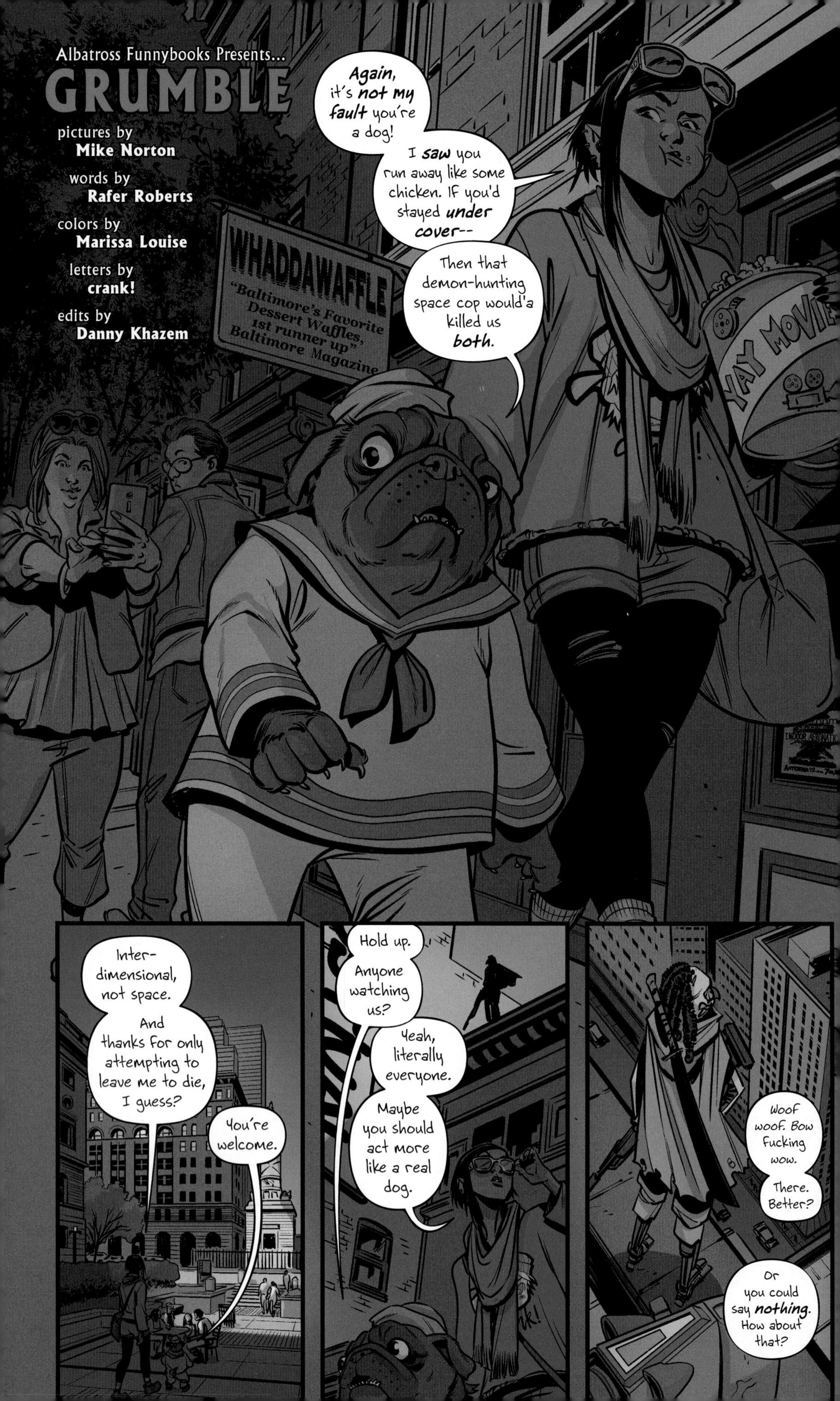
Albatross Funnybooks Presents...
GRUMBLE
pictures by Mike Norton
words by Rafer Roberts
colors by Marissa Louise
letters by crank!
edits by Danny Khazem
WHADDAWAFFLE
"Baltimore's Favorite Dessert Waffles, 1st runner up" Baltimore Magazine
Again, it's not my fault you're a dog!
I saw you run away like some chicken. If you'd stayed under cover--
Then that demon-hunting space cop would'a killed us both.
YAY MOVIE
Inter-dimensional, not space.
And thanks for only attempting to leave me to die, I guess?
You're welcome.
Hold up.
Anyone watching us?
Yeah, literally everyone.
Maybe you should act more like a real dog.
Woof woof. Bow Fucking wow.
There. Better?
Or you could say nothing. How about that?

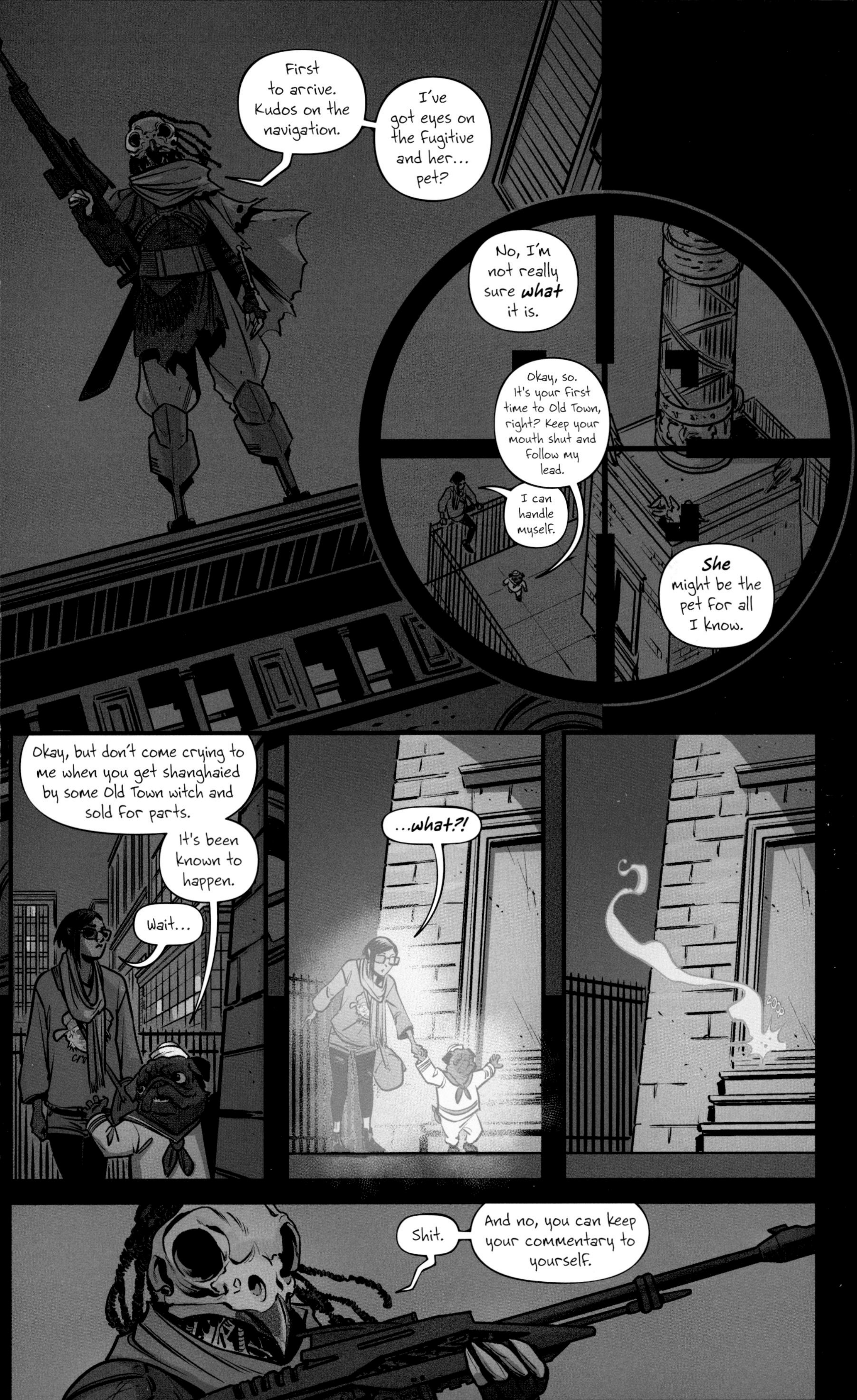
First to arrive. Kudos on the navigation.
I've got eyes on the Fugitive and her... pet?
No, I'm not really sure **what** it is.
Okay, so. It's your first time to Old Town, right? Keep your mouth shut and follow my lead.
I can handle myself.
She might be the pet for all I know.
Okay, but don't come crying to me when you get shanghaied by some Old Town witch and sold for parts.
It's been known to happen.
Wait...
...**what?!**
Shit.
And no, you can keep your commentary to yourself.

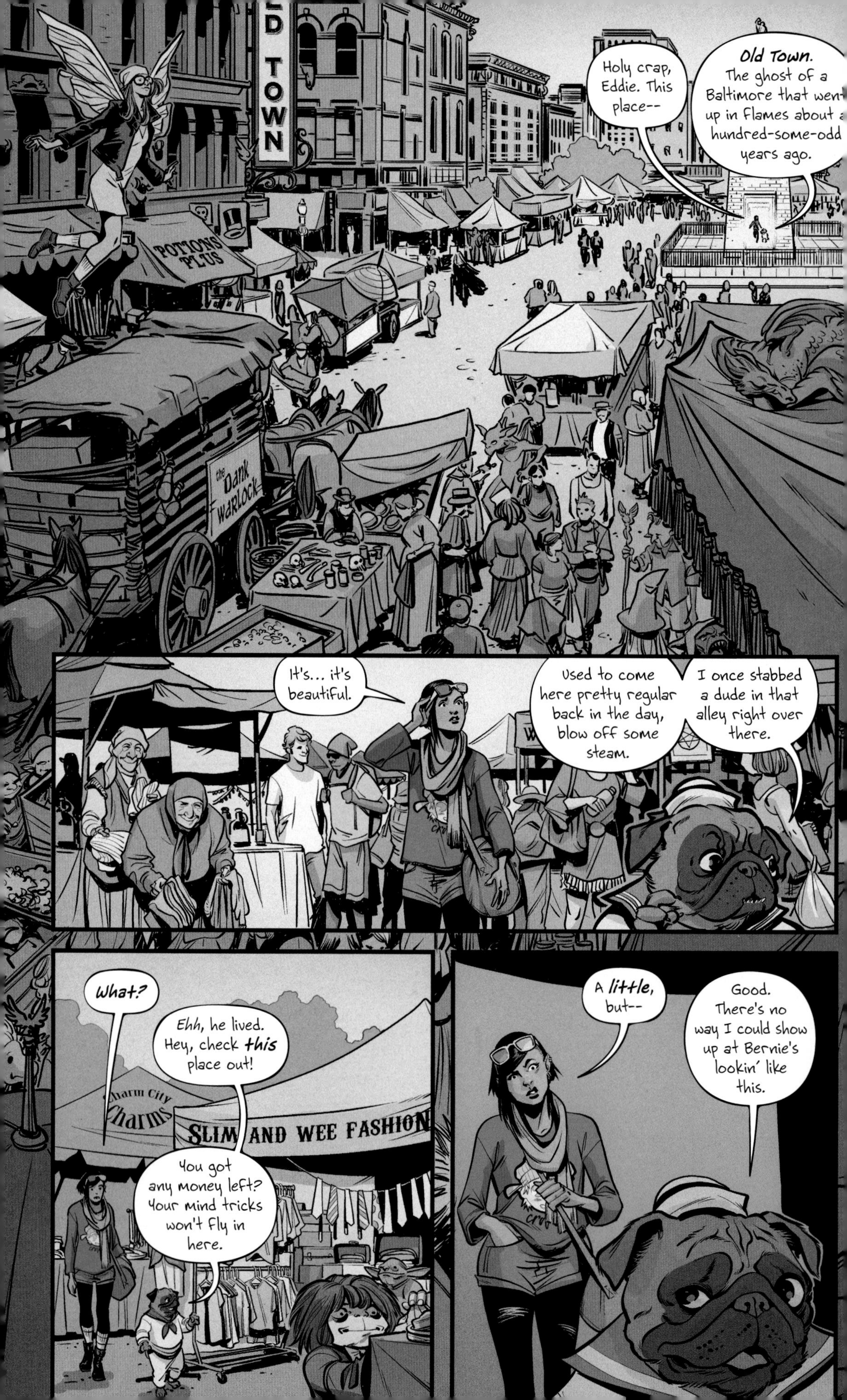

D TOWN
POTIONS PLUS
the Dank Warlock
Holy crap, Eddie. This place--
Old Town. The ghost of a Baltimore that went up in flames about a hundred-some-odd years ago.
It's... it's beautiful.
Used to come here pretty regular back in the day, blow off some steam.
I once stabbed a dude in that alley right over there.
What?
Ehh, he lived. Hey, check this place out!
Charm City Charms
SLIM AND WEE FASHION
You got any money left? Your mind tricks won't fly in here.
A little, but--
Good. There's no way I could show up at Bernie's lookin' like this.

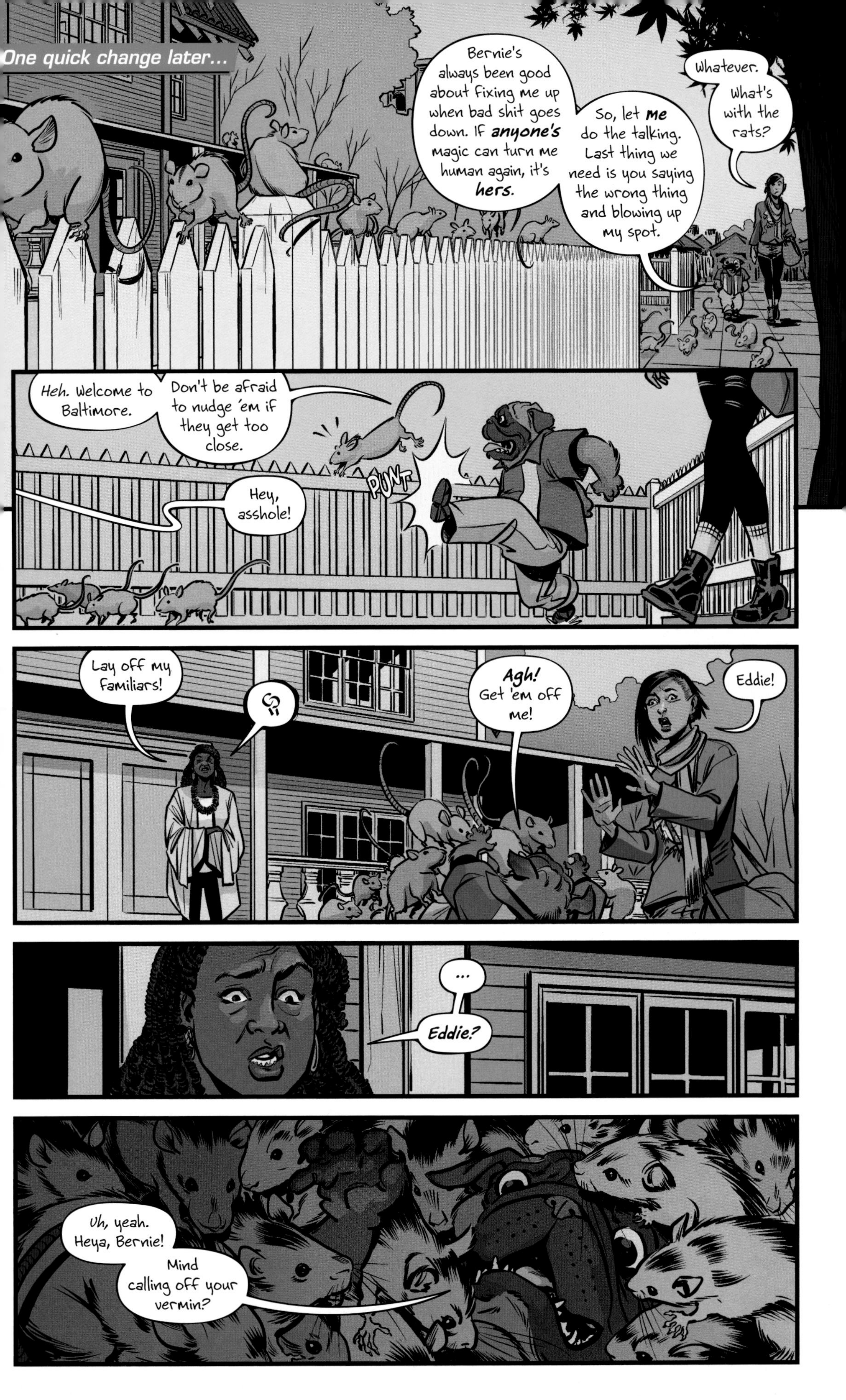

One quick change later...
Bernie's always been good about fixing me up when bad shit goes down. If anyone's magic can turn me human again, it's hers.
So, let me do the talking. Last thing we need is you saying the wrong thing and blowing up my spot.
Whatever.
What's with the rats?
Heh. Welcome to Baltimore.
Don't be afraid to nudge 'em if they get too close.
PUNT
Hey, asshole!
Lay off my familiars!
Agh! Get 'em off me!
Eddie!
...
Eddie?
Uh, yeah. Heya, Bernie!
Mind calling off your vermin?

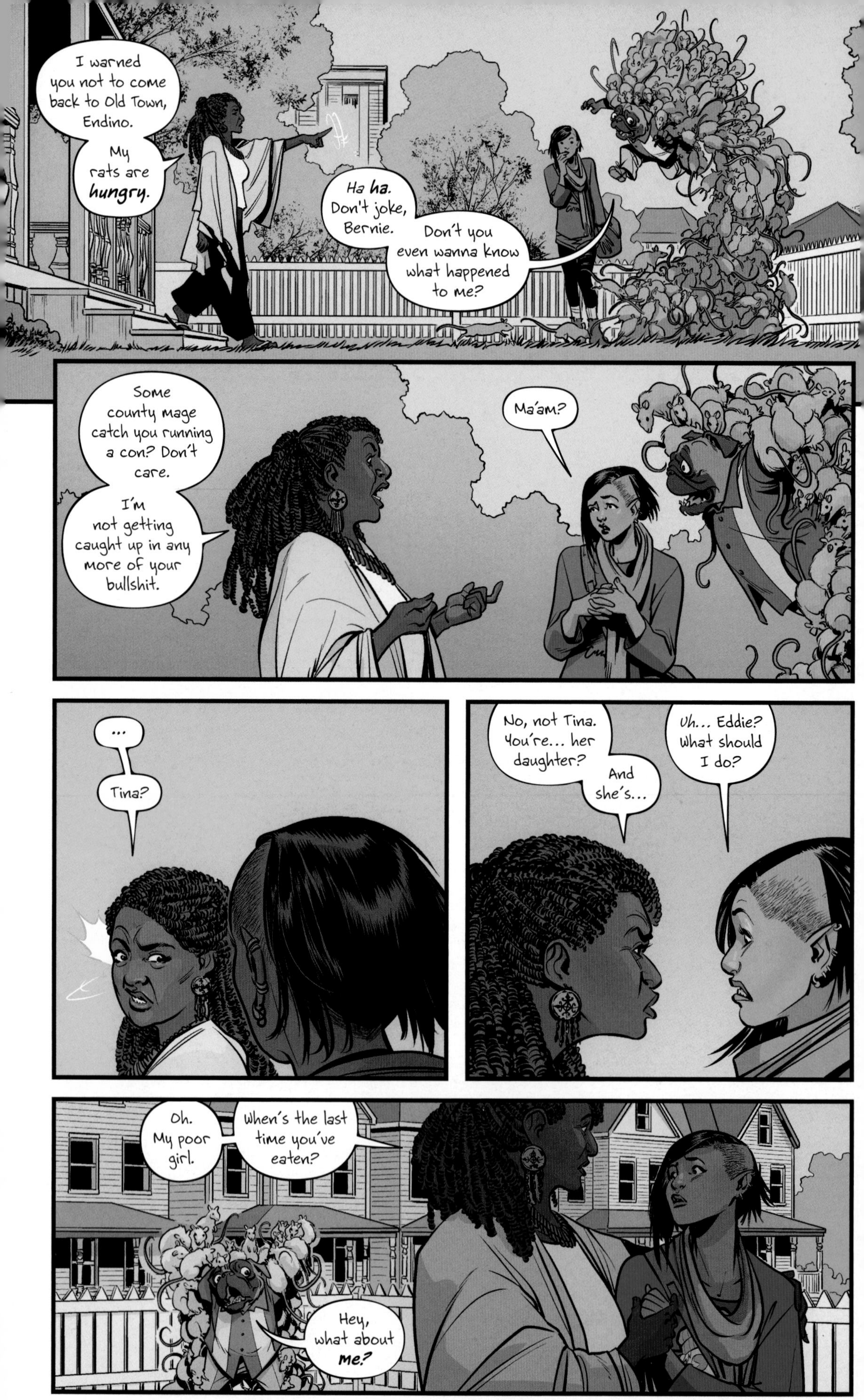
I warned you not to come back to Old Town, Endino.
My rats are **hungry**.
Ha **ha**. Don't joke, Bernie.
Don't you even wanna know what happened to me?
Some county mage catch you running a con? Don't care.
I'm not getting caught up in any more of your bullshit.
Ma'am?
...
Tina?
No, not Tina. You're... her daughter?
And she's...
Uh... Eddie? What should I do?
Oh. My poor girl.
When's the last time you've eaten?
Hey, what about **me?**

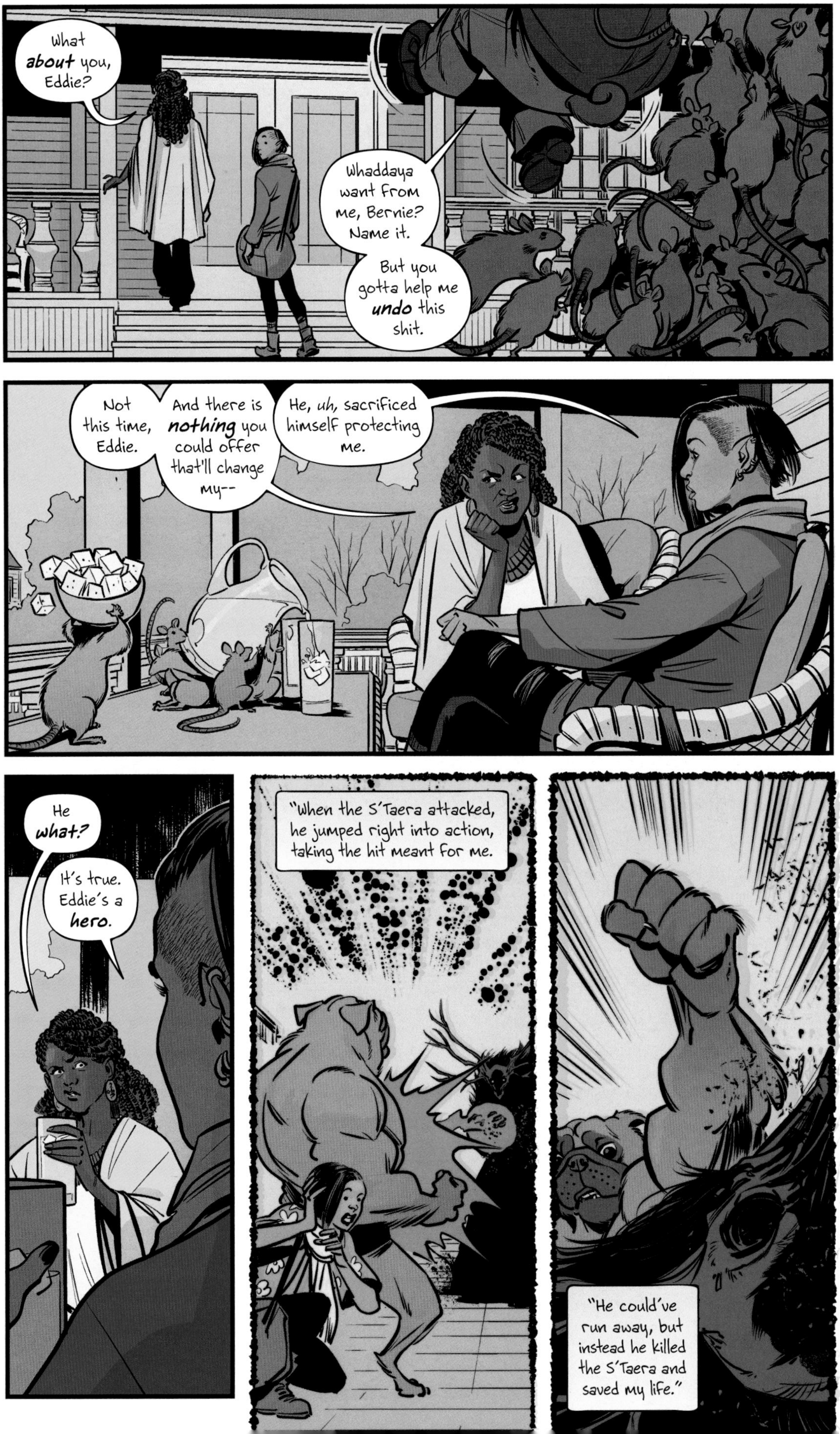
What about you, Eddie?
Whaddaya want from me, Bernie? Name it.
But you gotta help me undo this shit.
Not this time, Eddie.
And there is nothing you could offer that'll change my--
He, uh, sacrificed himself protecting me.
He what?
It's true. Eddie's a hero.
"When the S'Taera attacked, he jumped right into action, taking the hit meant for me.
"He could've run away, but instead he killed the S'Taera and saved my life."

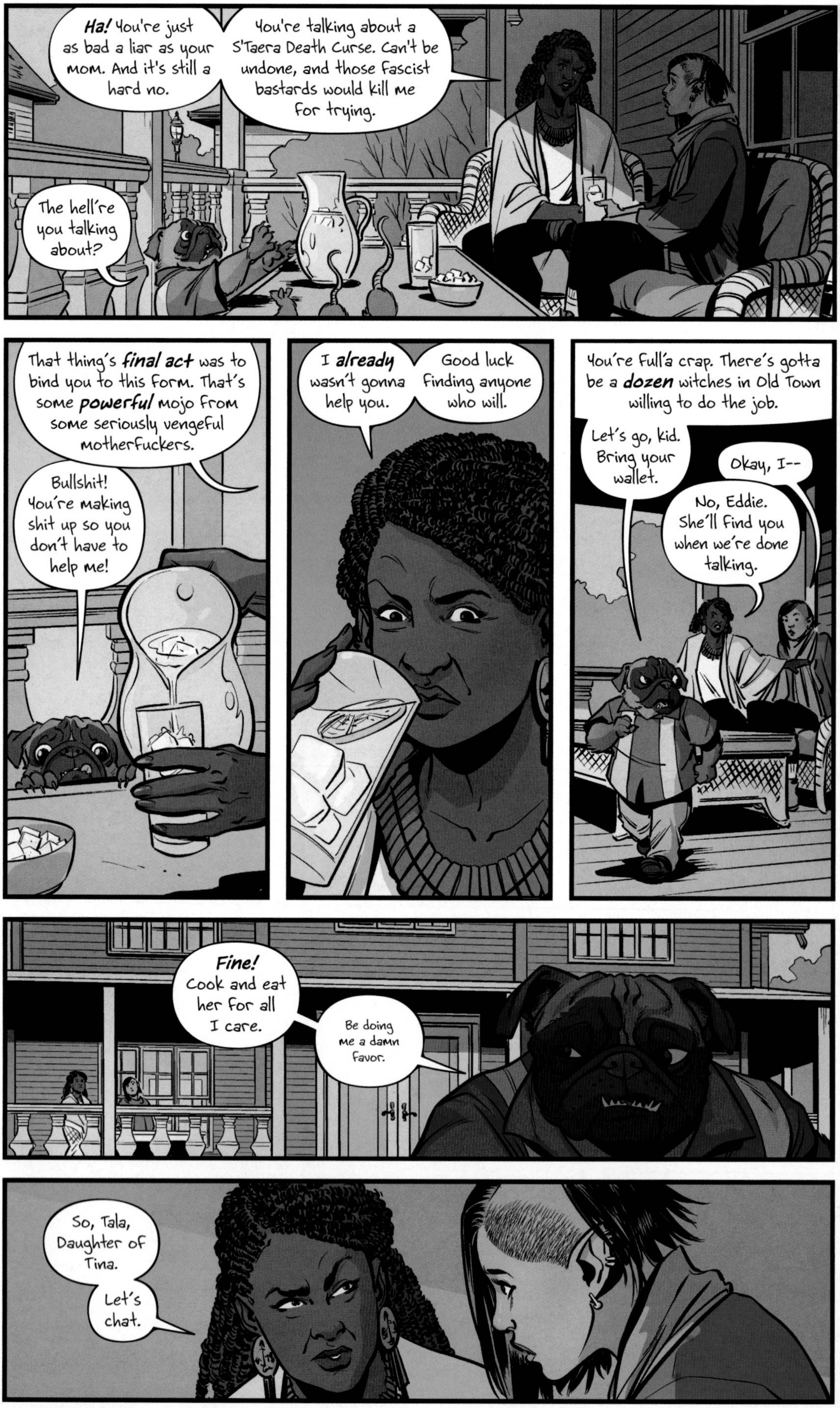
Ha! You're just as bad a liar as your mom. And it's still a hard no.
You're talking about a S'Taera Death Curse. Can't be undone, and those fascist bastards would kill me for trying.
The hell're you talking about?
That thing's final act was to bind you to this form. That's some powerful mojo from some seriously vengeful motherfuckers.
Bullshit! You're making shit up so you don't have to help me!
I already wasn't gonna help you.
Good luck finding anyone who will.
You're full'a crap. There's gotta be a dozen witches in Old Town willing to do the job.
Let's go, kid. Bring your wallet.
Okay, I--
No, Eddie. She'll find you when we're done talking.
Fine! Cook and eat her for all I care.
Be doing me a damn favor.
So, Tala, Daughter of Tina.
Let's chat.

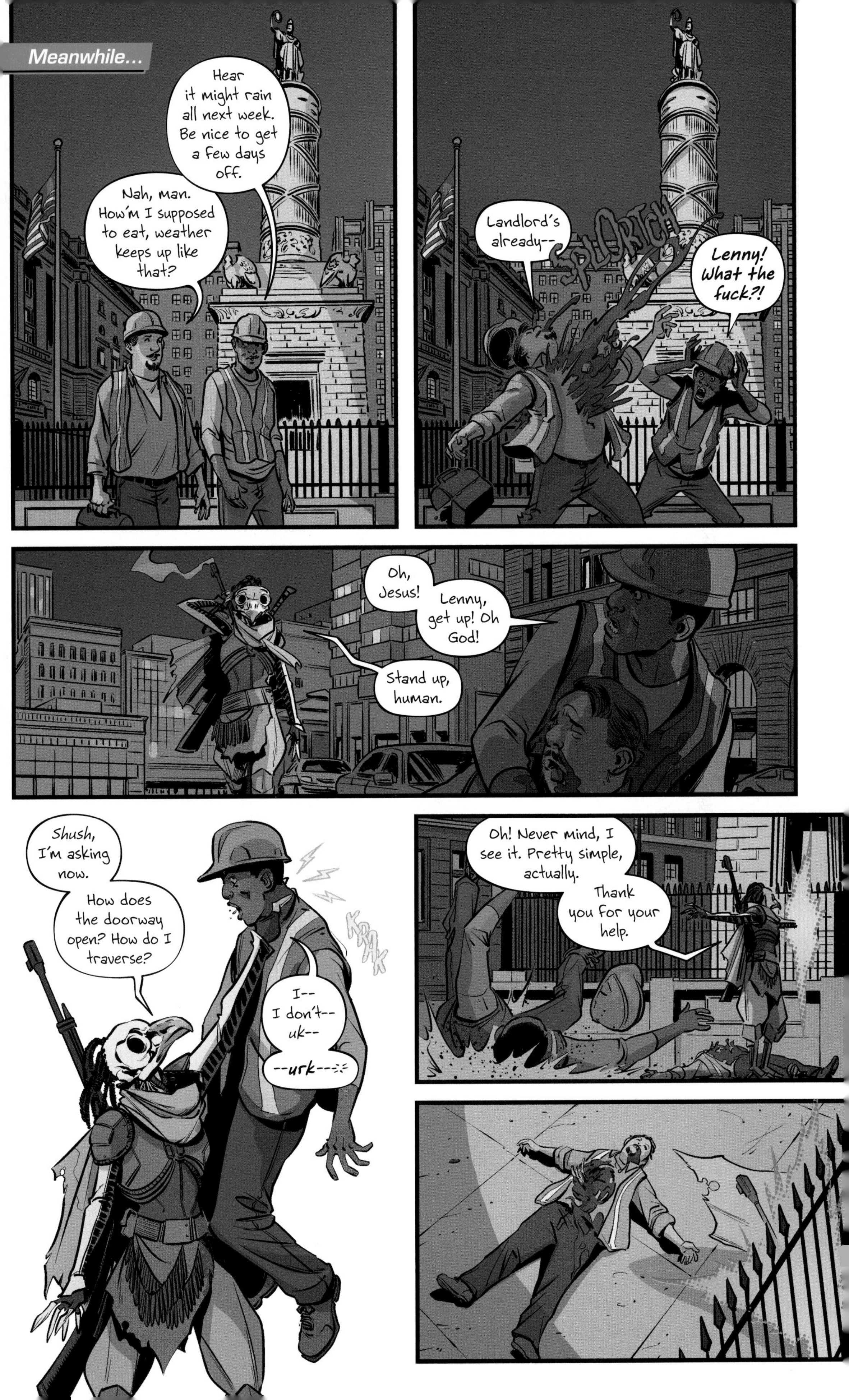
Meanwhile...
Hear it might rain all next week. Be nice to get a few days off.
Nah, man. How'm I supposed to eat, weather keeps up like that?
Landlord's already--
SPLORTCH
Lenny! What the fuck?!
Oh, Jesus!
Lenny, get up! Oh God!
Stand up, human.
Shush, I'm asking now.
How does the doorway open? How do I traverse?
KRAK
I-- I don't-- uk--
--urk--
Oh! Never mind, I see it. Pretty simple, actually.
Thank you for your help.

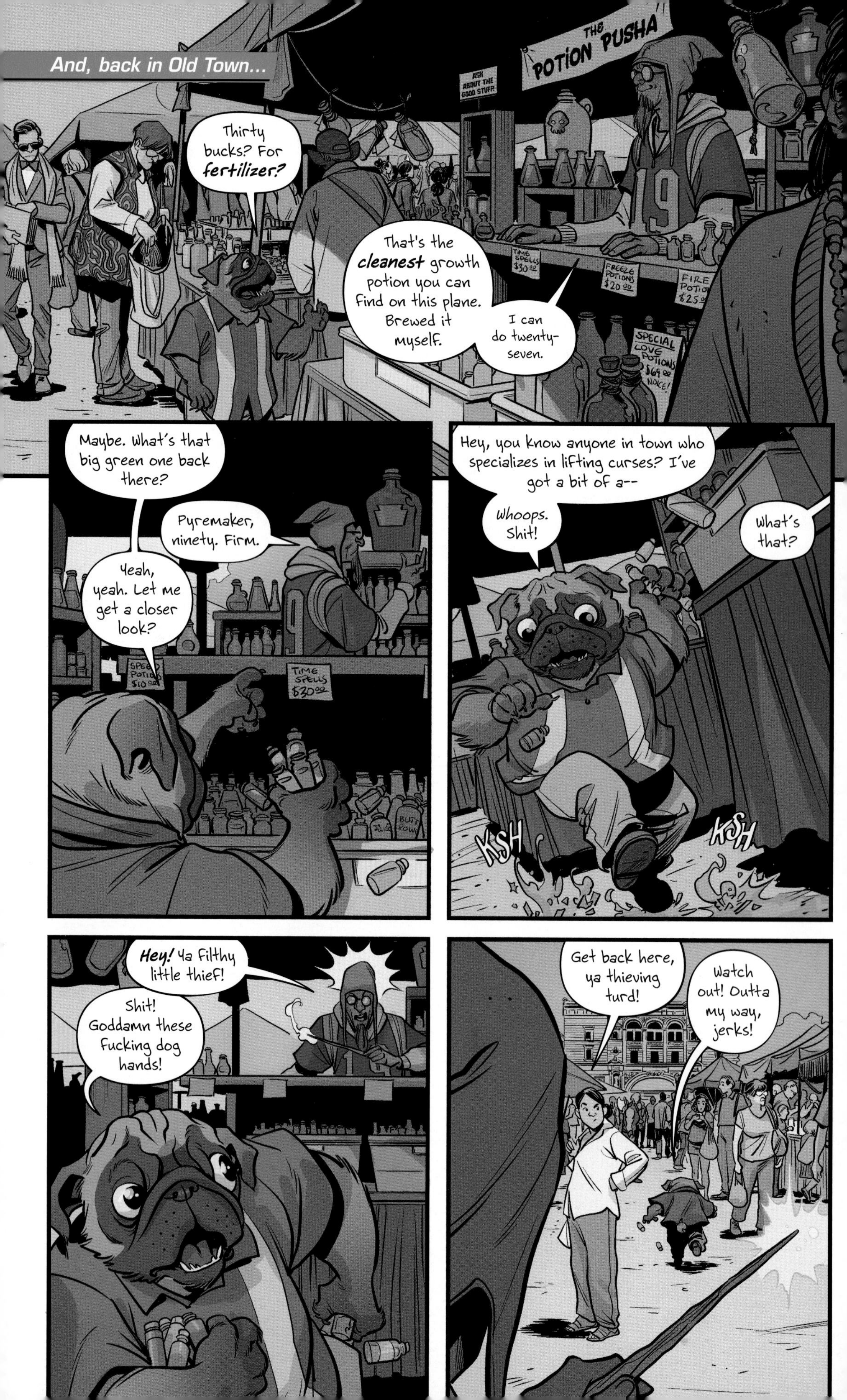
And, back in Old Town...
THE POTION PUSHA
ASK ABOUT THE GOOD STUFF
Thirty bucks? For fertilizer?
That's the cleanest growth potion you can find on this plane. Brewed it myself.
I can do twenty-seven.
TIME SPELLS $30.00
FREEZE POTIONS $20.00
FIRE POTIONS $25.00
SPECIAL LOVE POTIONS $69.00 NOICE!
Maybe. What's that big green one back there?
Pyremaker, ninety. Firm.
Yeah, yeah. Let me get a closer look?
TIME SPELLS $30.00
Hey, you know anyone in town who specializes in lifting curses? I've got a bit of a--
Whoops. Shit!
What's that?
KSH
KSH
Hey! Ya filthy little thief!
Shit! Goddamn these fucking dog hands!
Get back here, ya thieving turd!
Watch out! Outta my way, jerks!

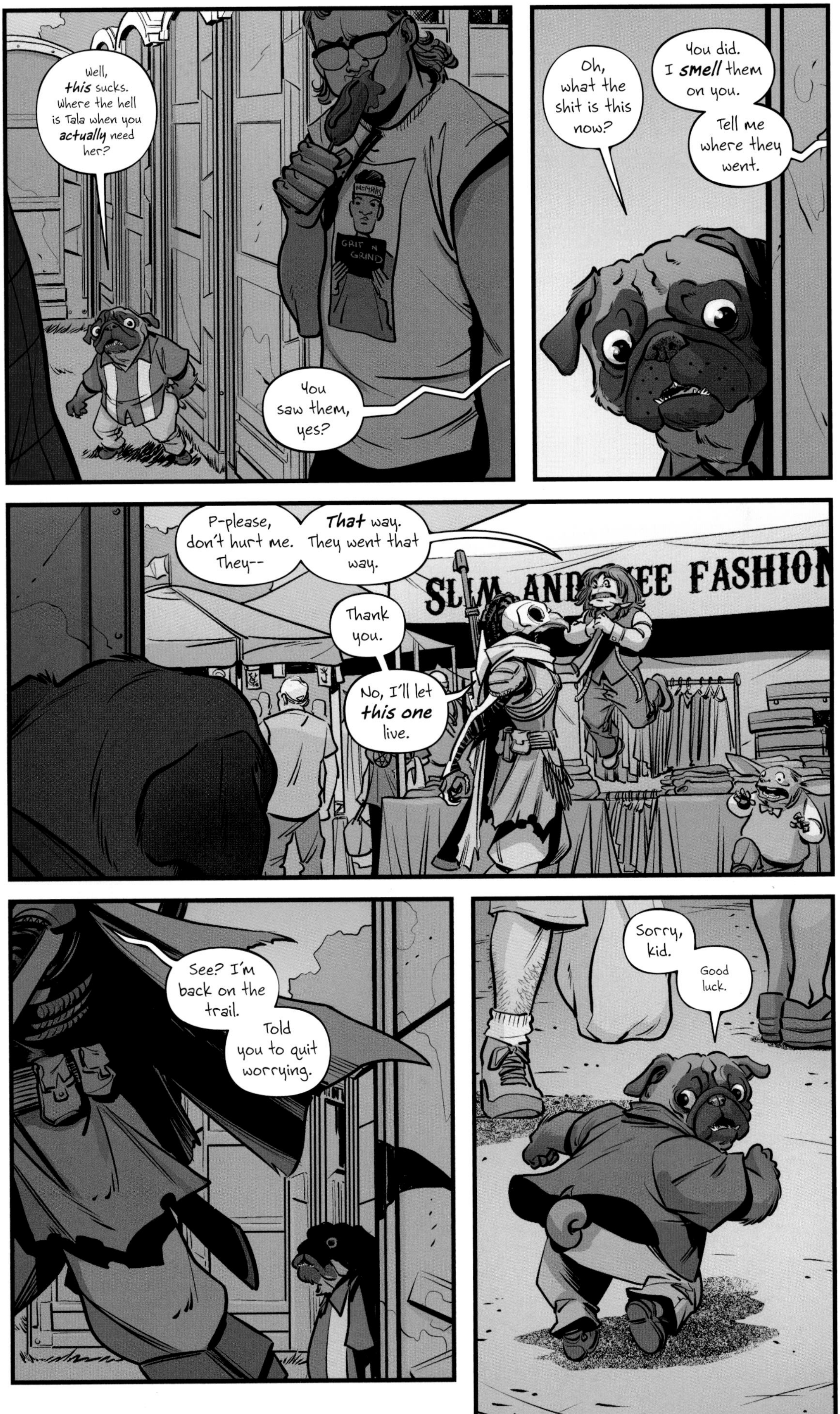
Well, this sucks. Where the hell is Tala when you actually need her?
MEMPHIS
GRIT N GRIND
You saw them, yes?
Oh, what the shit is this now?
You did. I smell them on you.
Tell me where they went.
P-please, don't hurt me. They--
That way. They went that way.
SLIM AND
EE FASHION
Thank you.
No, I'll let this one live.
See? I'm back on the trail.
Told you to quit worrying.
Sorry, kid.
Good luck.

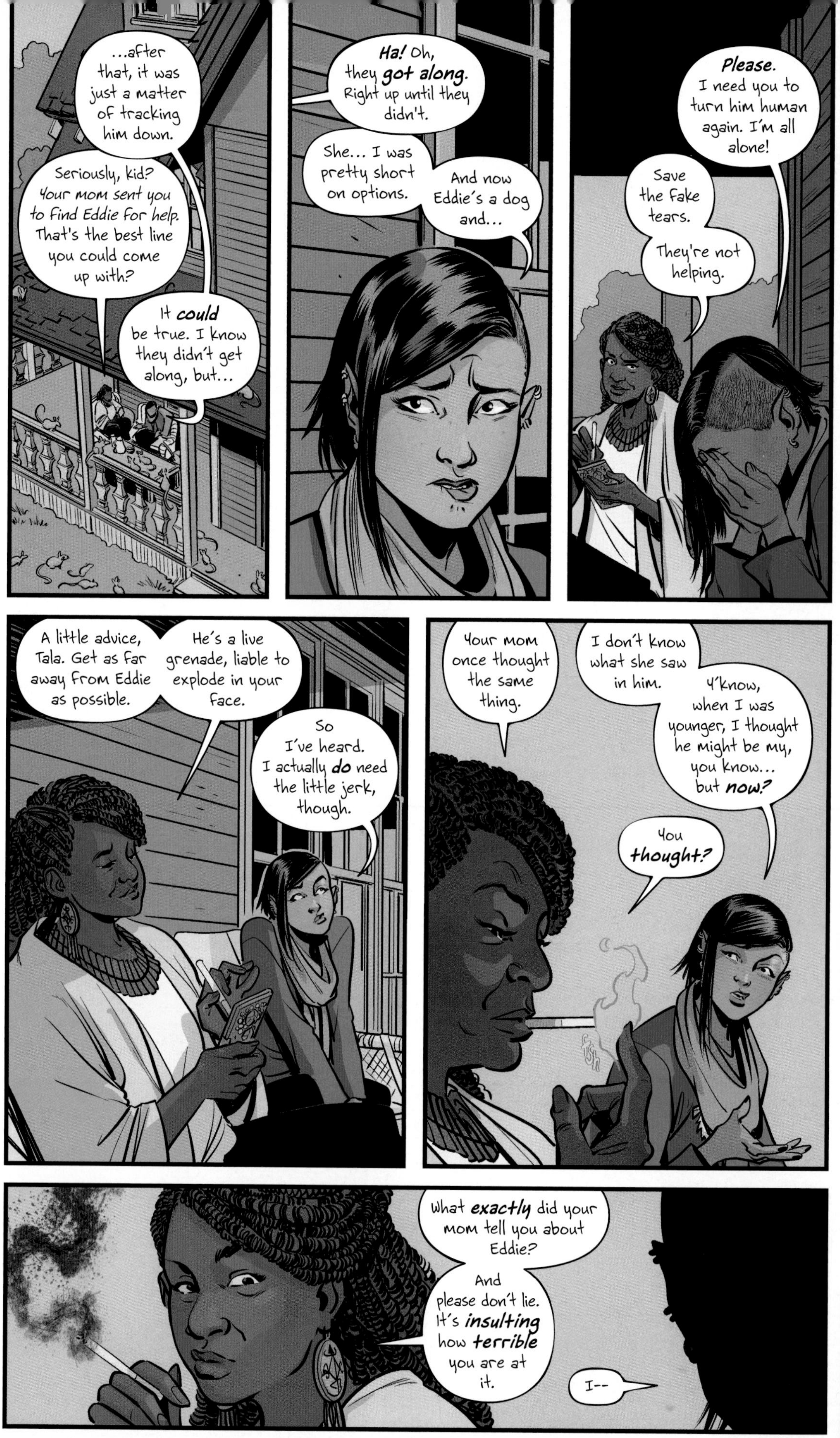
...after that, it was just a matter of tracking him down.
Seriously, kid? Your mom sent you to find Eddie for help. That's the best line you could come up with?
It **could** be true. I know they didn't get along, but...
Ha! Oh, they **got along.** Right up until they didn't.
She... I was pretty short on options.
And now Eddie's a dog and...
Please. I need you to turn him human again. I'm all alone!
Save the fake tears.
They're not helping.
A little advice, Tala. Get as far away from Eddie as possible.
He's a live grenade, liable to explode in your face.
So I've heard. I actually **do** need the little jerk, though.
Your mom once thought the same thing.
I don't know what she saw in him.
Y'know, when I was younger, I thought he might be my, you know... but **now?**
You **thought?**
FISH
What **exactly** did your mom tell you about Eddie?
And please don't lie. It's **insulting** how **terrible** you are at it.
I--

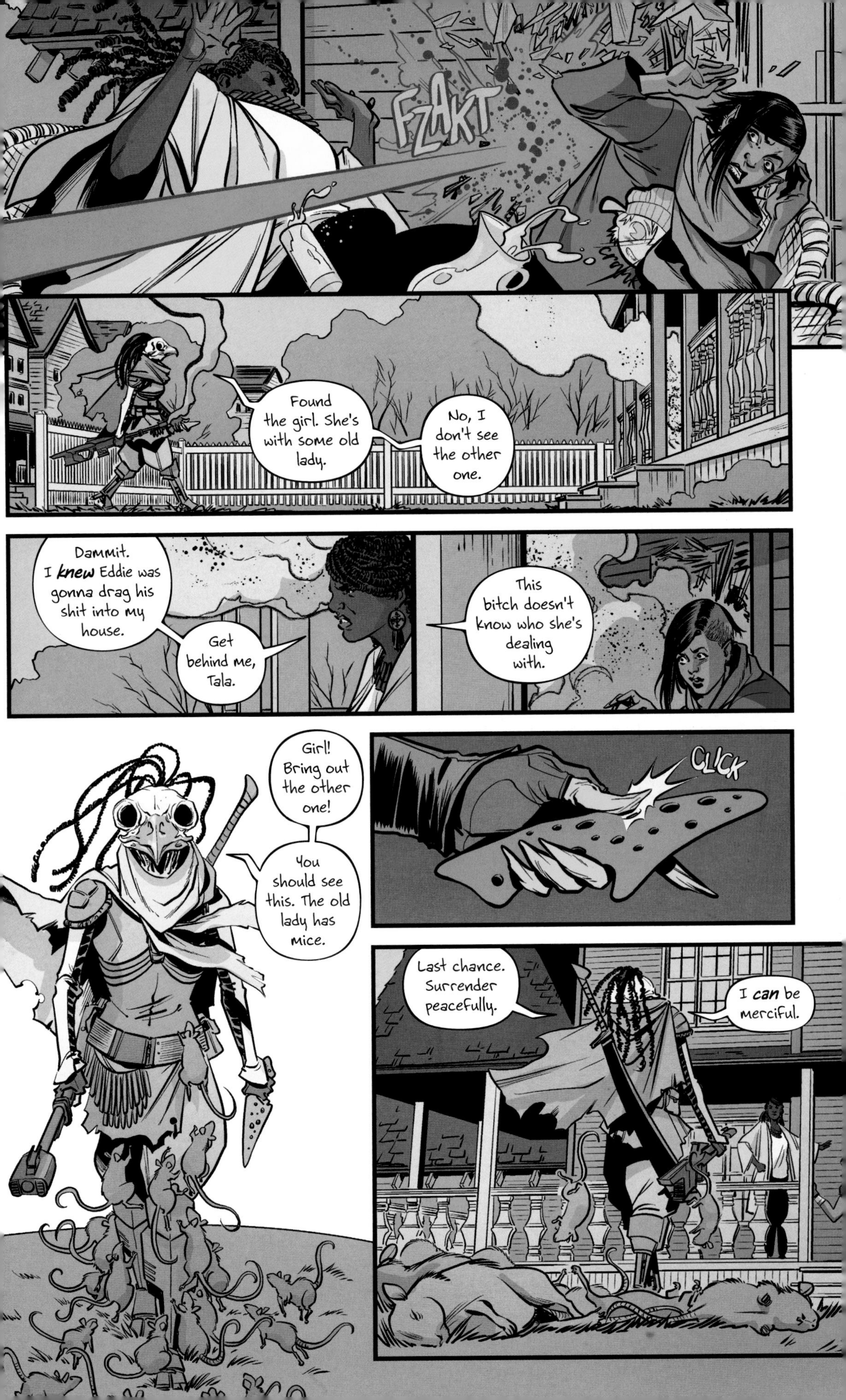
FZAKT
crunk
Found the girl. She's with some old lady.
No, I don't see the other one.
Dammit. I *knew* Eddie was gonna drag his shit into my house.
Get behind me, Tala.
This bitch doesn't know who she's dealing with.
Girl! Bring out the other one!
You should see this. The old lady has mice.
CLICK
Last chance. Surrender peacefully.
I *can* be merciful.

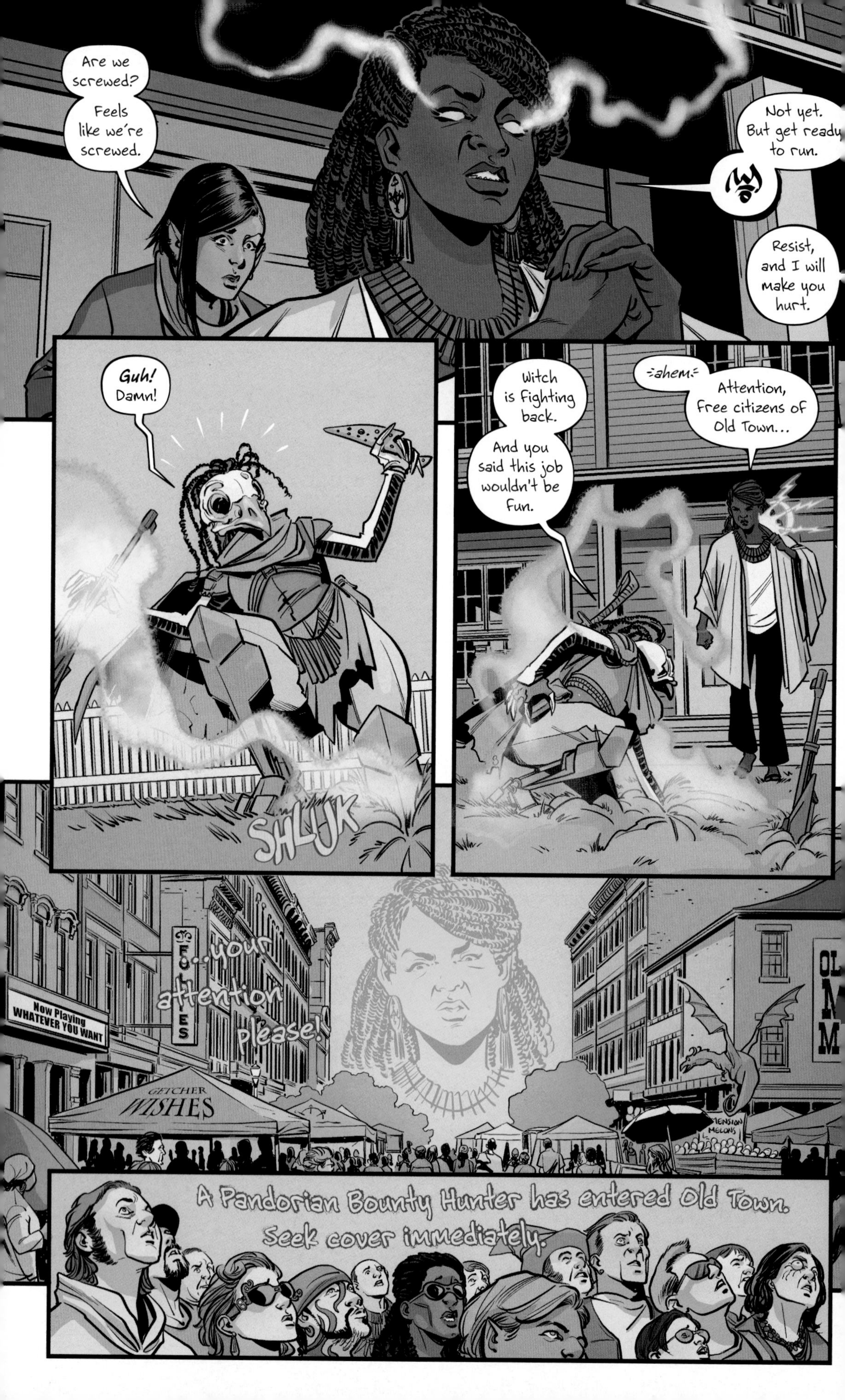
Are we screwed?
Feels like we're screwed.
Not yet. But get ready to run.
Resist, and I will make you hurt.
Guh! Damn!
SHLUK
Witch is fighting back.
And you said this job wouldn't be fun.
ahem
Attention, free citizens of Old Town...
Now Playing WHATEVER YOU WANT
GETCHER WISHES
...your attention please!
A Pandorian Bounty Hunter has entered Old Town.
Seek cover immediately.

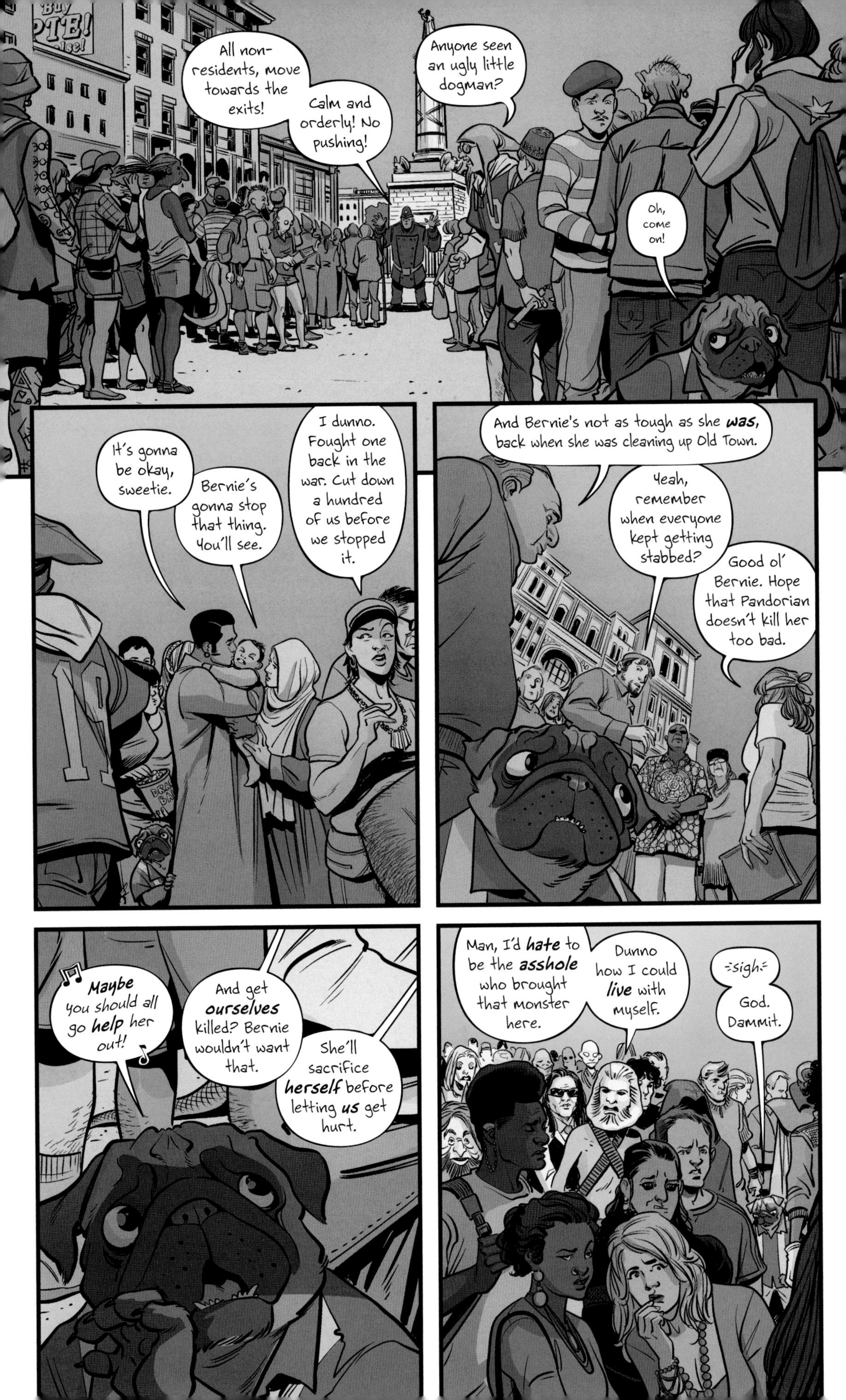
All non-residents, move towards the exits!
Calm and orderly! No pushing!
Anyone seen an ugly little dogman?
Oh, come on!
It's gonna be okay, sweetie.
Bernie's gonna stop that thing. You'll see.
I dunno. Fought one back in the war. Cut down a hundred of us before we stopped it.
And Bernie's not as tough as she **was**, back when she was cleaning up Old Town.
Yeah, remember when everyone kept getting stabbed?
Good ol' Bernie. Hope that Pandorian doesn't kill her too bad.
Maybe you should all go **help** her out!
And get **ourselves** killed? Bernie wouldn't want that.
She'll sacrifice **herself** before letting **us** get hurt.
Man, I'd **hate** to be the **asshole** who brought that monster here.
Dunno how I could **live** with myself.
sigh
God. Dammit.

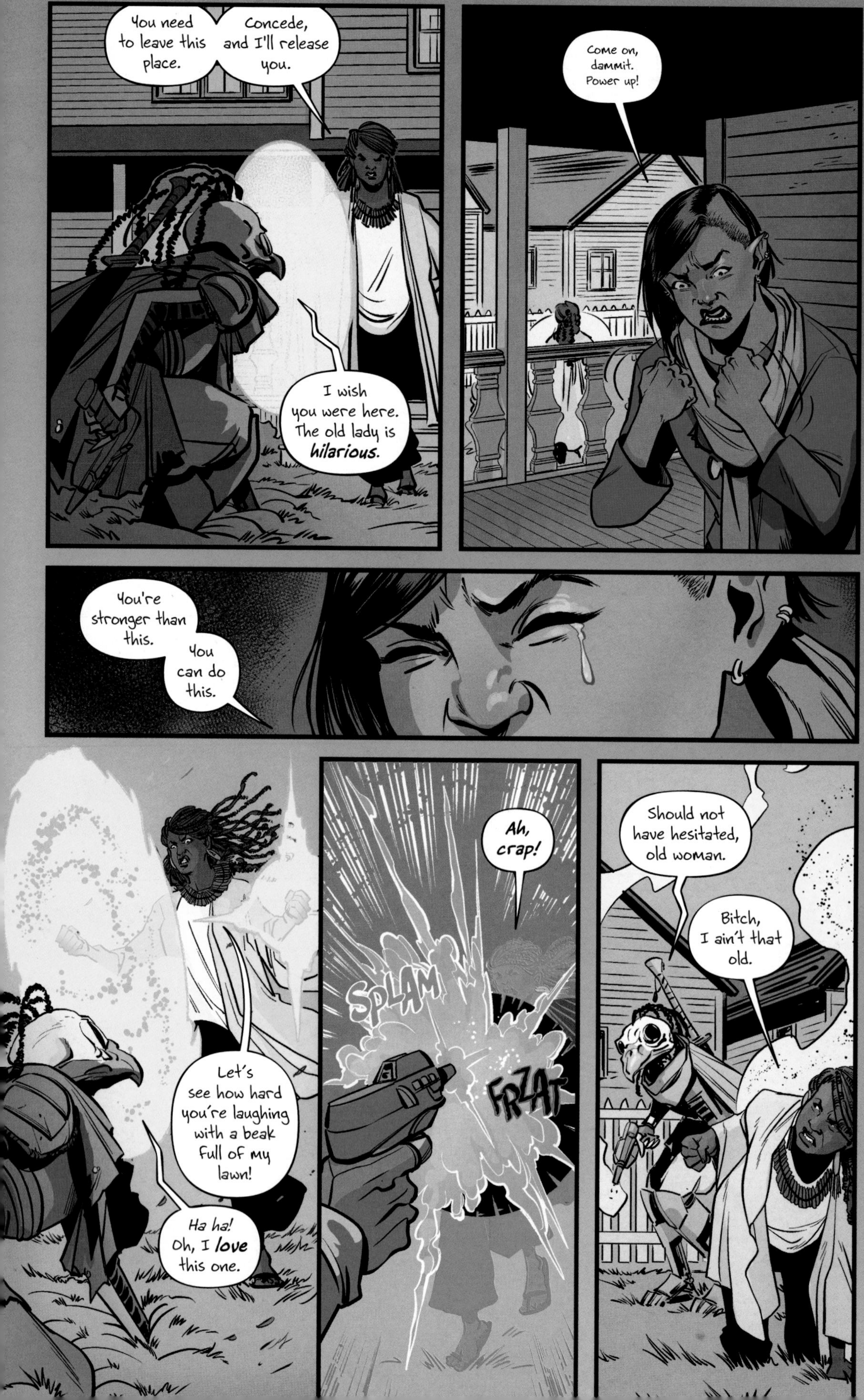
You need to leave this place.
Concede, and I'll release you.
I wish you were here. The old lady is hilarious.
Come on, dammit. Power up!
You're stronger than this.
You can do this.
Let's see how hard you're laughing with a beak full of my lawn!
Ha ha! Oh, I love this one.
Ah, crap!
SPLAM
FRZAT
Should not have hesitated, old woman.
Bitch, I ain't that old.

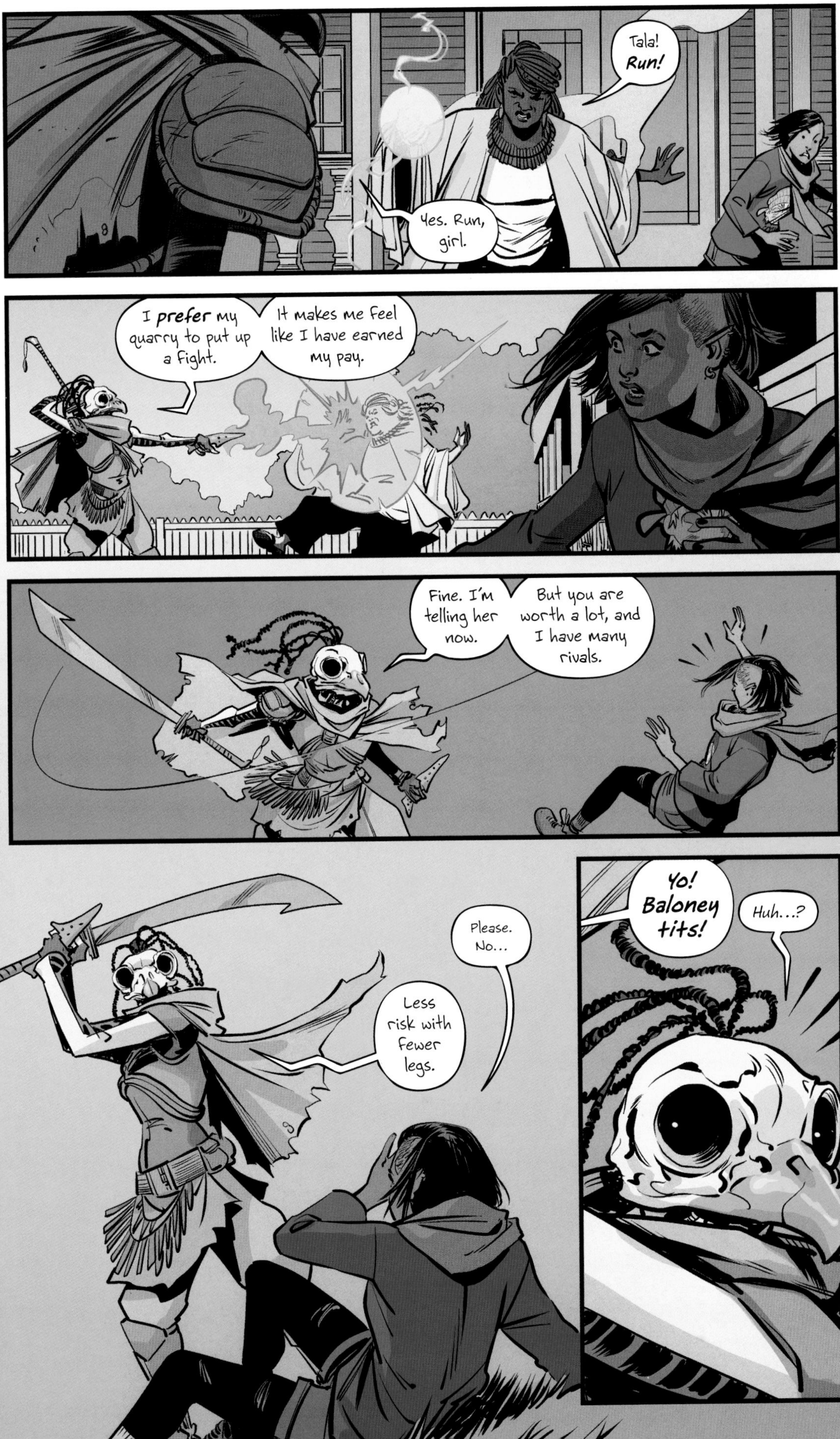
Tala!
Run!
Yes. Run, girl.
I prefer my quarry to put up a fight.
It makes me feel like I have earned my pay.
Fine. I'm telling her now.
But you are worth a lot, and I have many rivals.
Please. No...
Less risk with fewer legs.
Yo! Baloney tits!
Huh...?

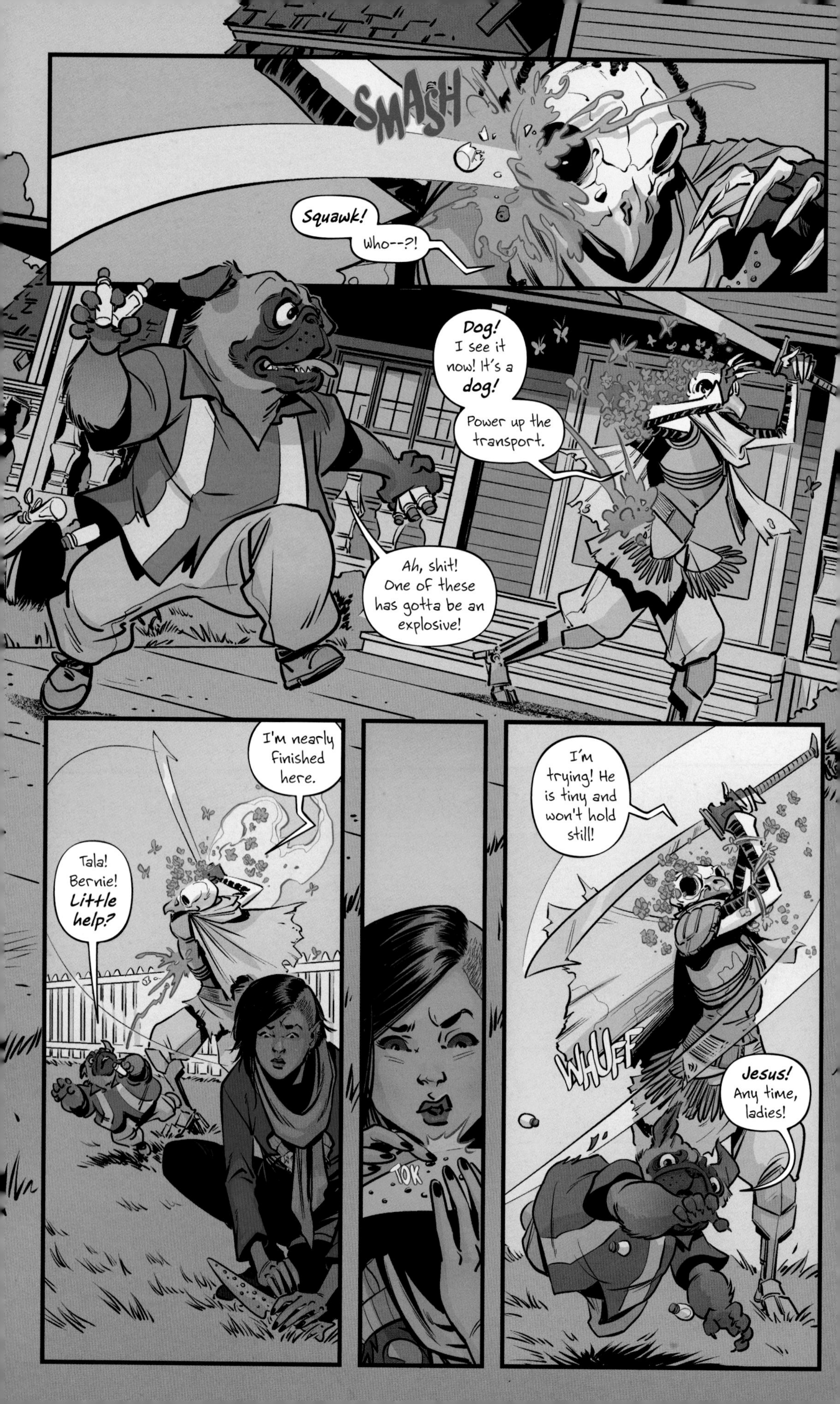
SMASH
Squawk!
Who--?!
Dog! I see it now! It's a dog!
Power up the transport.
Ah, shit! One of these has gotta be an explosive!
I'm nearly finished here.
Tala! Bernie! Little help?
TOK
I'm trying! He is tiny and won't hold still!
WHUFF
Jesus! Any time, ladies!

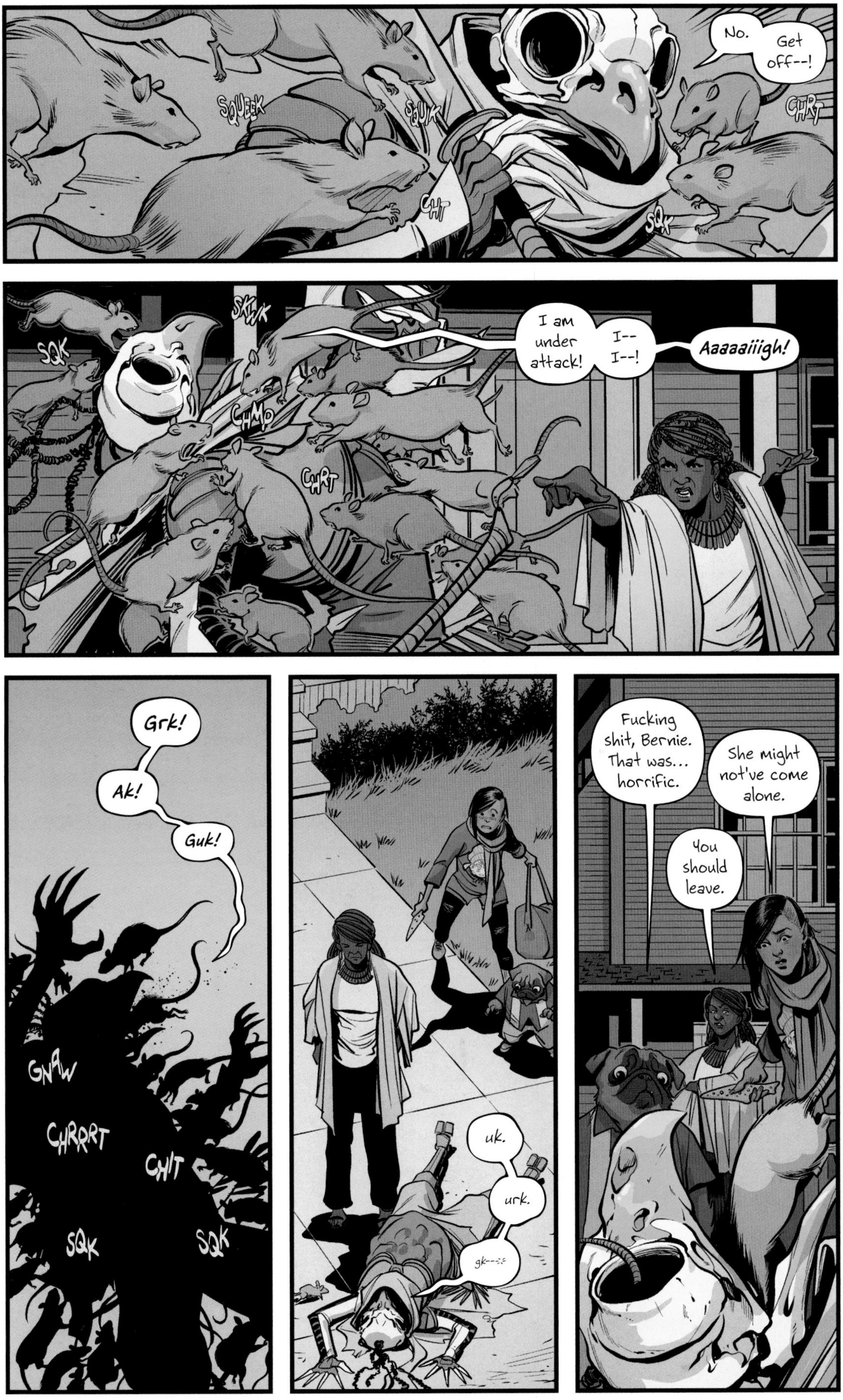

SQUEEK
SQUIK
No.
Get off--!
CHRT
CHIT
SQK
SKWK
SQK
I am under attack!
I-- I--!
Aaaaaiiigh!
CHMP
CHRT
Grk!
Ak!
Guk!
GNAW
CHRRRT
CHIT
SQK
SQK
uk.
urk.
Fucking shit, Bernie. That was... horrific.
She might not've come alone.
You should leave.

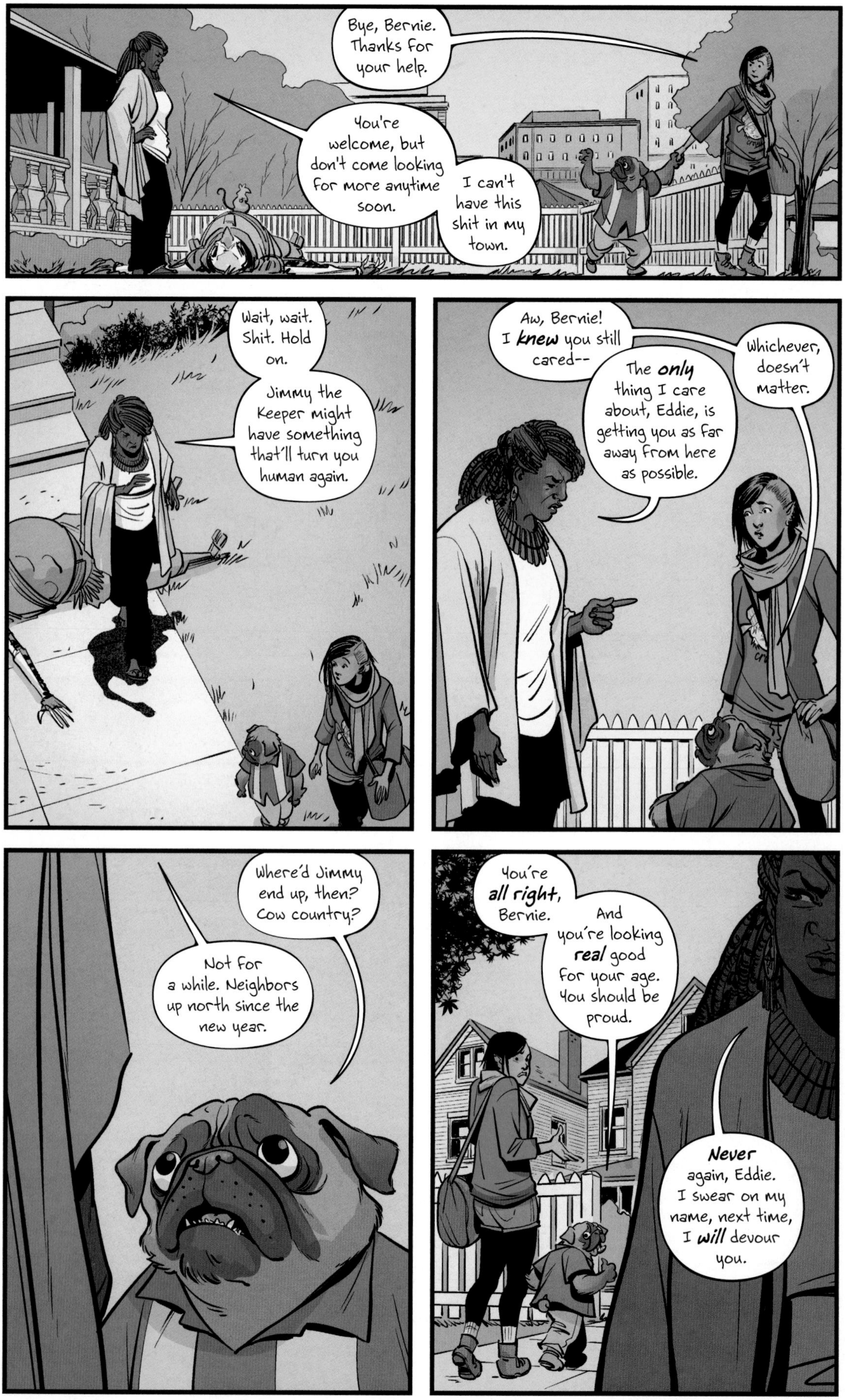

Bye, Bernie. Thanks for your help.
You're welcome, but don't come looking for more anytime soon.
I can't have this shit in my town.
Wait, wait. Shit. Hold on.
Jimmy the Keeper might have something that'll turn you human again.
Aw, Bernie! I **knew** you still cared--
The **only** thing I care about, Eddie, is getting you as far away from here as possible.
Whichever, doesn't matter.
Where'd Jimmy end up, then? Cow country?
Not for a while. Neighbors up north since the new year.
You're **all right,** Bernie.
And you're looking **real** good for your age. You should be proud.
Never again, Eddie. I swear on my name, next time, I **will** devour you.

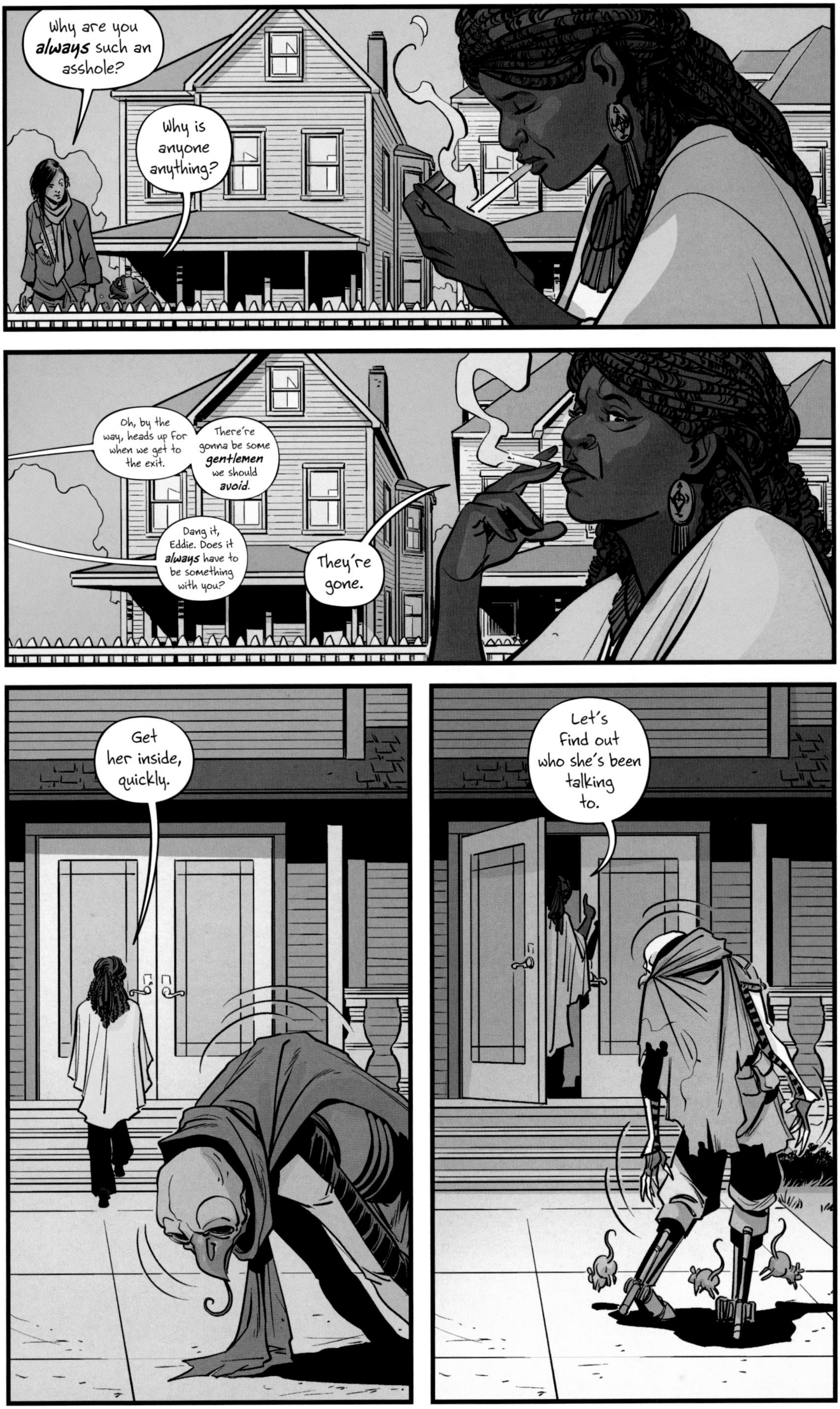

Why are you always such an asshole?
Why is anyone anything?
Oh, by the way, heads up for when we get to the exit.
There're gonna be some gentlemen we should avoid.
Dang it, Eddie. Does it always have to be something with you?
They're gone.
Get her inside, quickly.
Let's find out who she's been talking to.

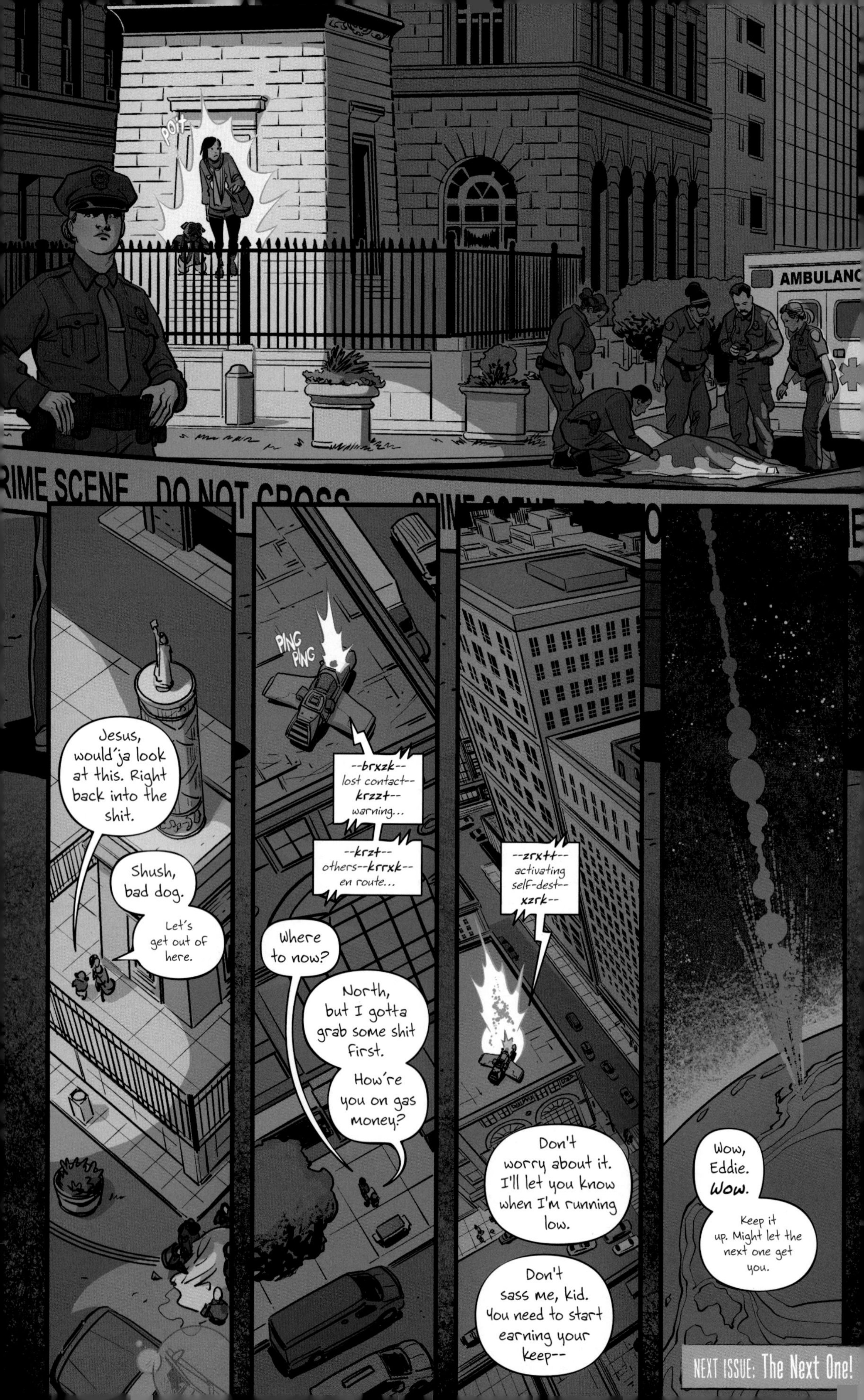

POIT
AMBULANCE
CRIME SCENE DO NOT CROSS
Jesus, would'ja look at this. Right back into the shit.
Shush, bad dog.
Let's get out of here.
PING PING
--brxzk-- lost contact-- krzzt-- warning...
--krzt-- others--krrxk-- en route...
Where to now?
North, but I gotta grab some shit first.
How're you on gas money?
--zrxtt-- activating self-dest-- xzrk--
Don't worry about it. I'll let you know when I'm running low.
Don't sass me, kid. You need to start earning your keep--
Wow, Eddie. Wow.
Keep it up. Might let the next one get you.
NEXT ISSUE: The Next One!

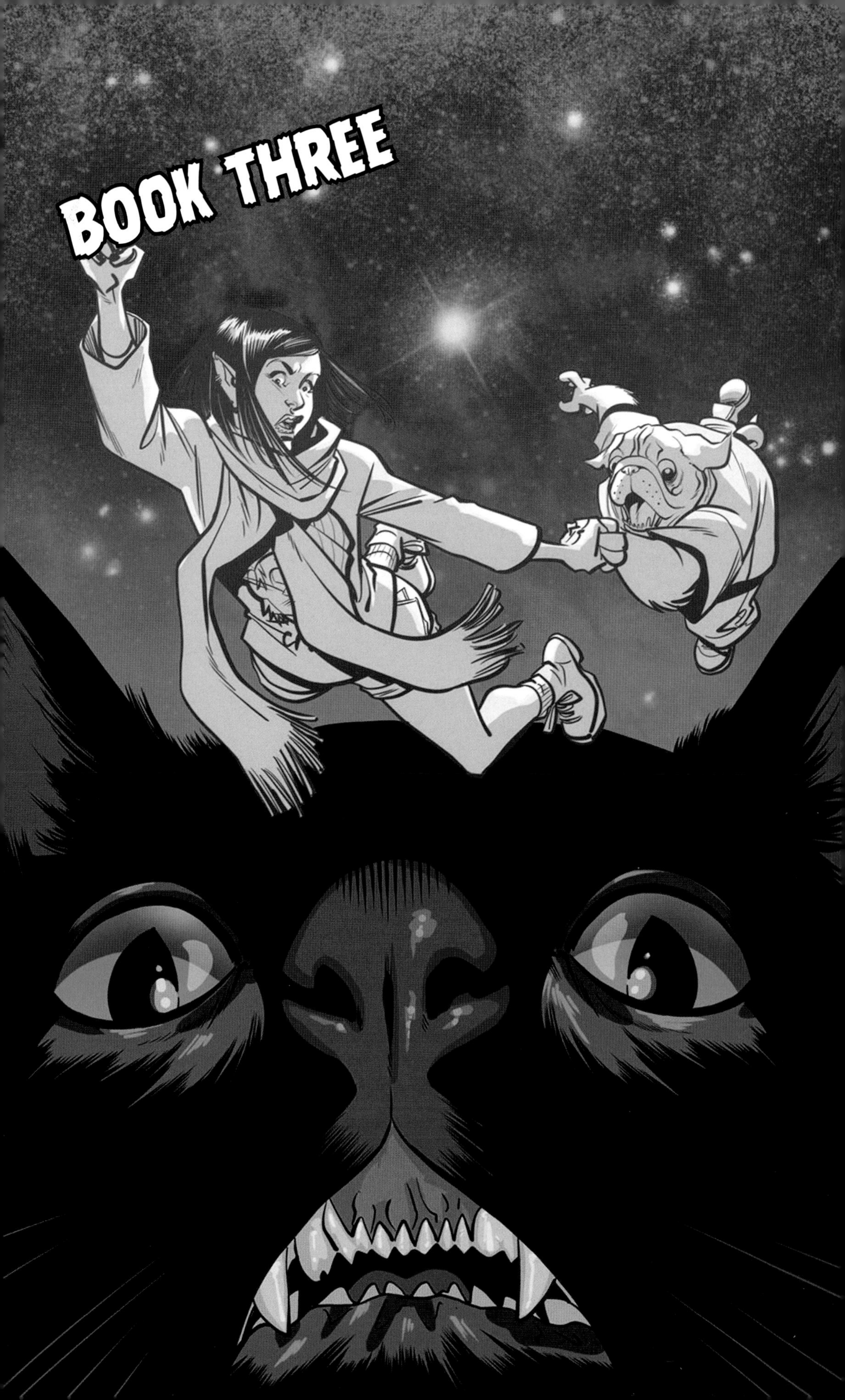
BOOK THREE

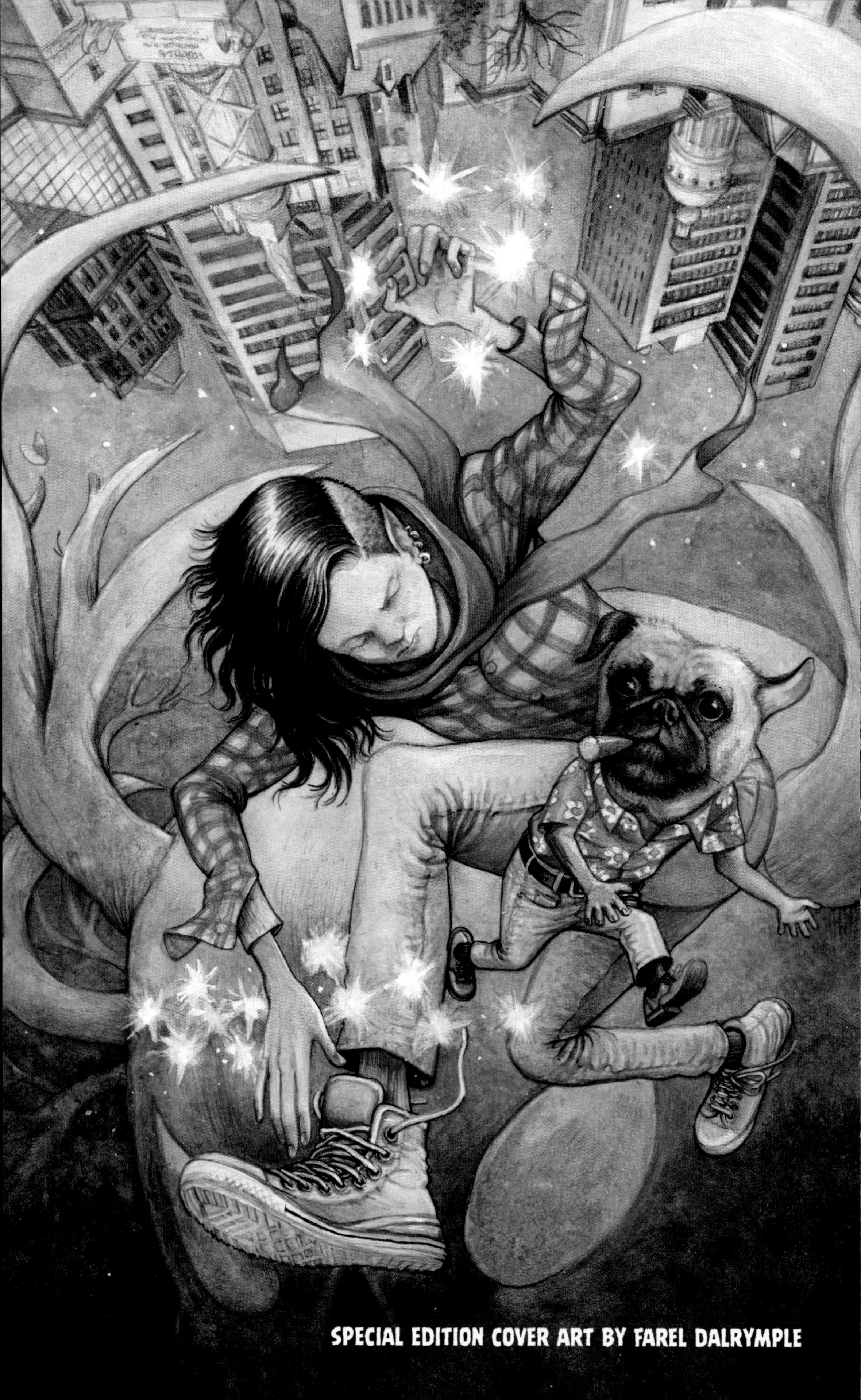

SPECIAL EDITION COVER ART BY FAREL DALRYMPLE

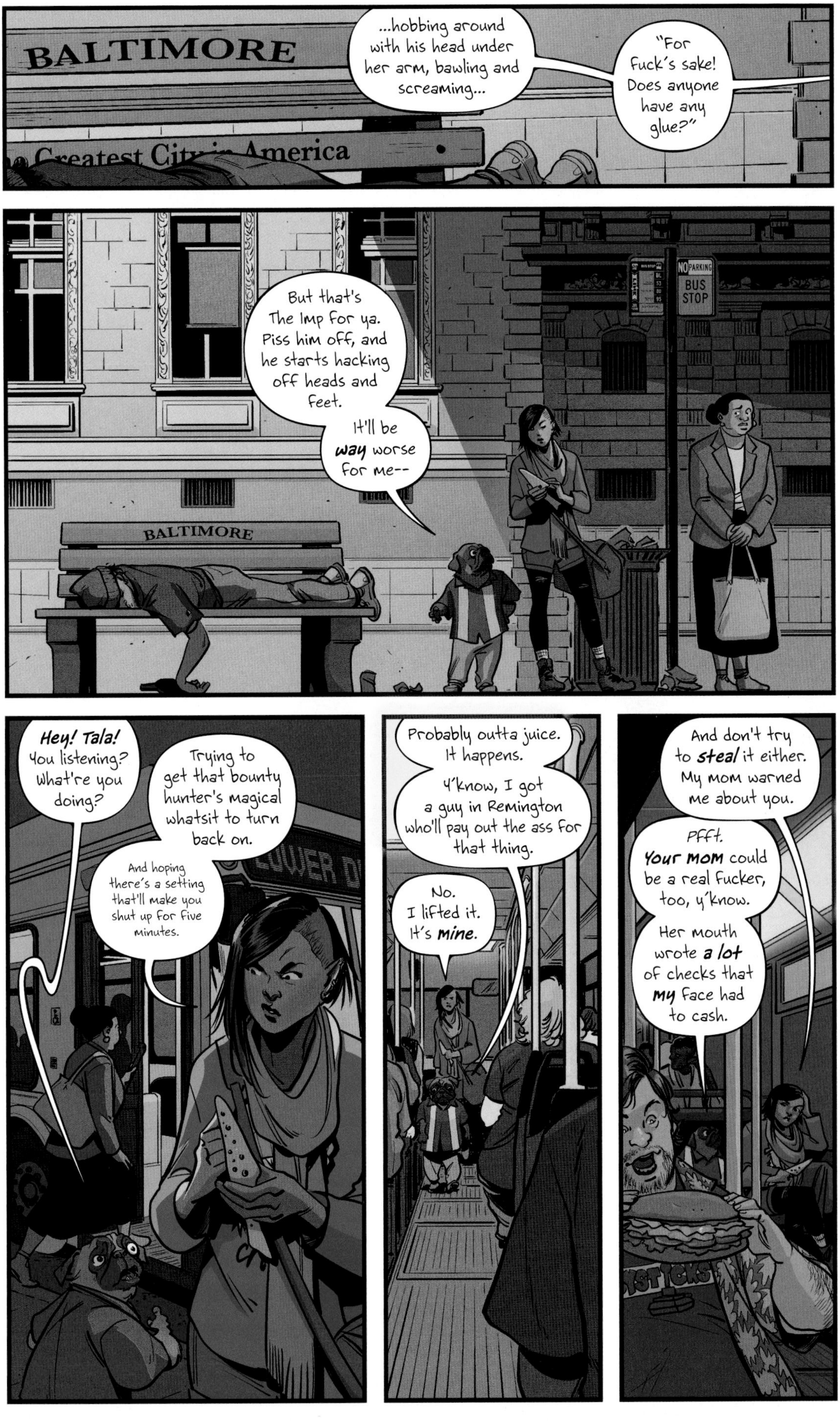
BALTIMORE
...hobbing around with his head under her arm, bawling and screaming...
"For fuck's sake! Does anyone have any glue?"
BALTIMORE
BUS STOP
But that's The Imp for ya. Piss him off, and he starts hacking off heads and feet.
It'll be **way** worse for me--
Hey! Tala! You listening? What're you doing?
Trying to get that bounty hunter's magical whatsit to turn back on.
And hoping there's a setting that'll make you shut up for five minutes.
Probably outta juice. It happens.
Y'know, I got a guy in Remington who'll pay out the ass for that thing.
No. I lifted it. It's **mine**.
And don't try to **steal** it either. My mom warned me about you.
Pfft. **Your mom** could be a real fucker, too, y'know.
Her mouth wrote **a lot** of checks that **my** face had to cash.

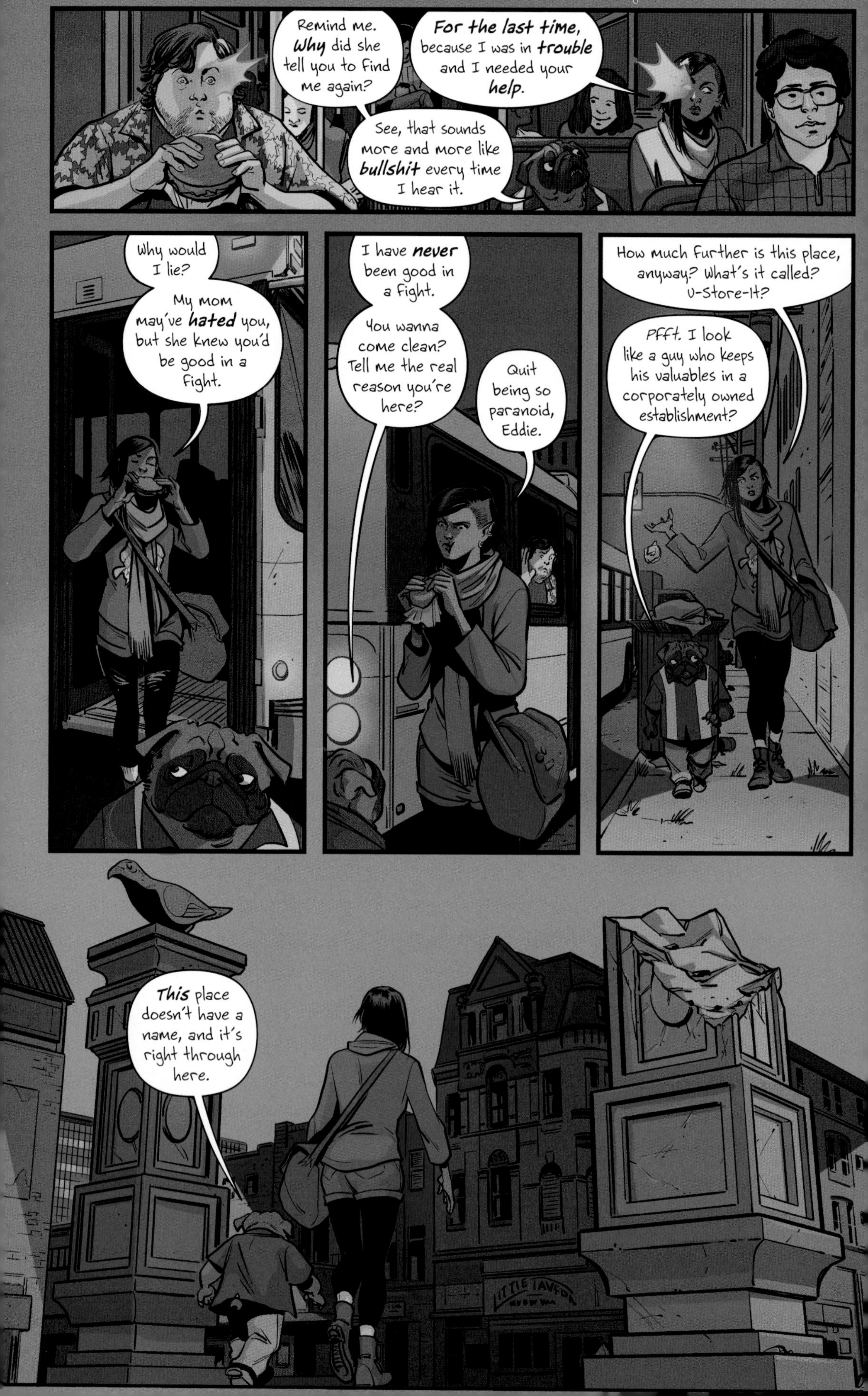
Remind me. **Why** did she tell you to find me again?
For the last time, because I was in **trouble** and I needed your **help.**
See, that sounds more and more like **bullshit** every time I hear it.
Why would I lie?
My mom may've **hated** you, but she knew you'd be good in a fight.
I have **never** been good in a fight.
You wanna come clean? Tell me the real reason you're here?
Quit being so paranoid, Eddie.
How much further is this place, anyway? What's it called? U-Store-It?
Pfft. I look like a guy who keeps his valuables in a corporately owned establishment?
This place doesn't have a name, and it's right through here.
LITTLE TAVERN

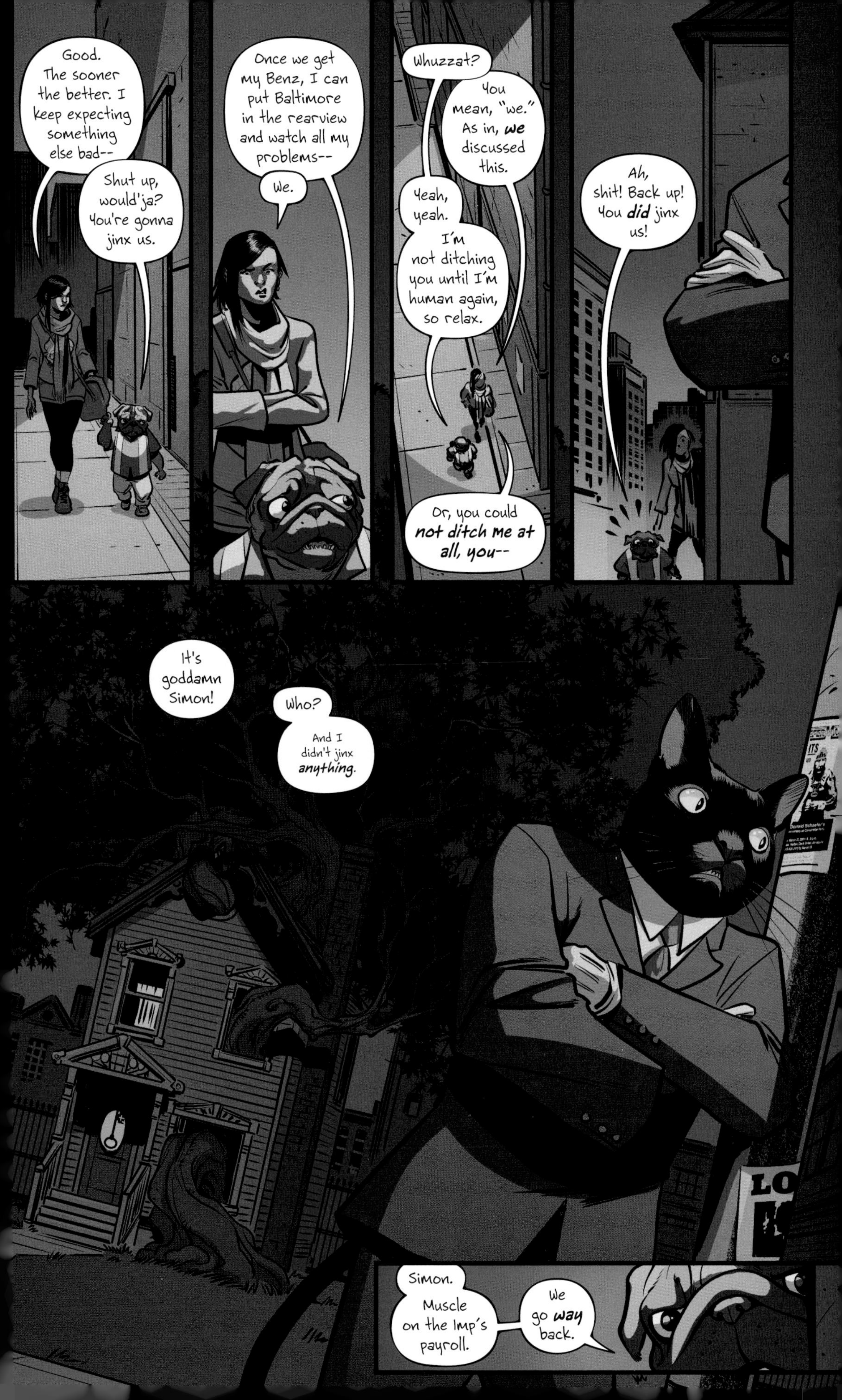

Good. The sooner the better. I keep expecting something else bad--
Shut up, would'ja? You're gonna jinx us.
Once we get my Benz, I can put Baltimore in the rearview and watch all my problems--
We.
Whuzzat?
You mean, "we." As in, **we** discussed this.
Yeah, yeah.
I'm not ditching you until I'm human again, so relax.
Or, you could **not ditch me at all, you--**
Ah, shit! Back up! You ***did*** jinx us!
It's goddamn Simon!
Who?
And I didn't jinx ***anything***.
Simon.
Muscle on the Imp's payroll.
We go ***way*** back.

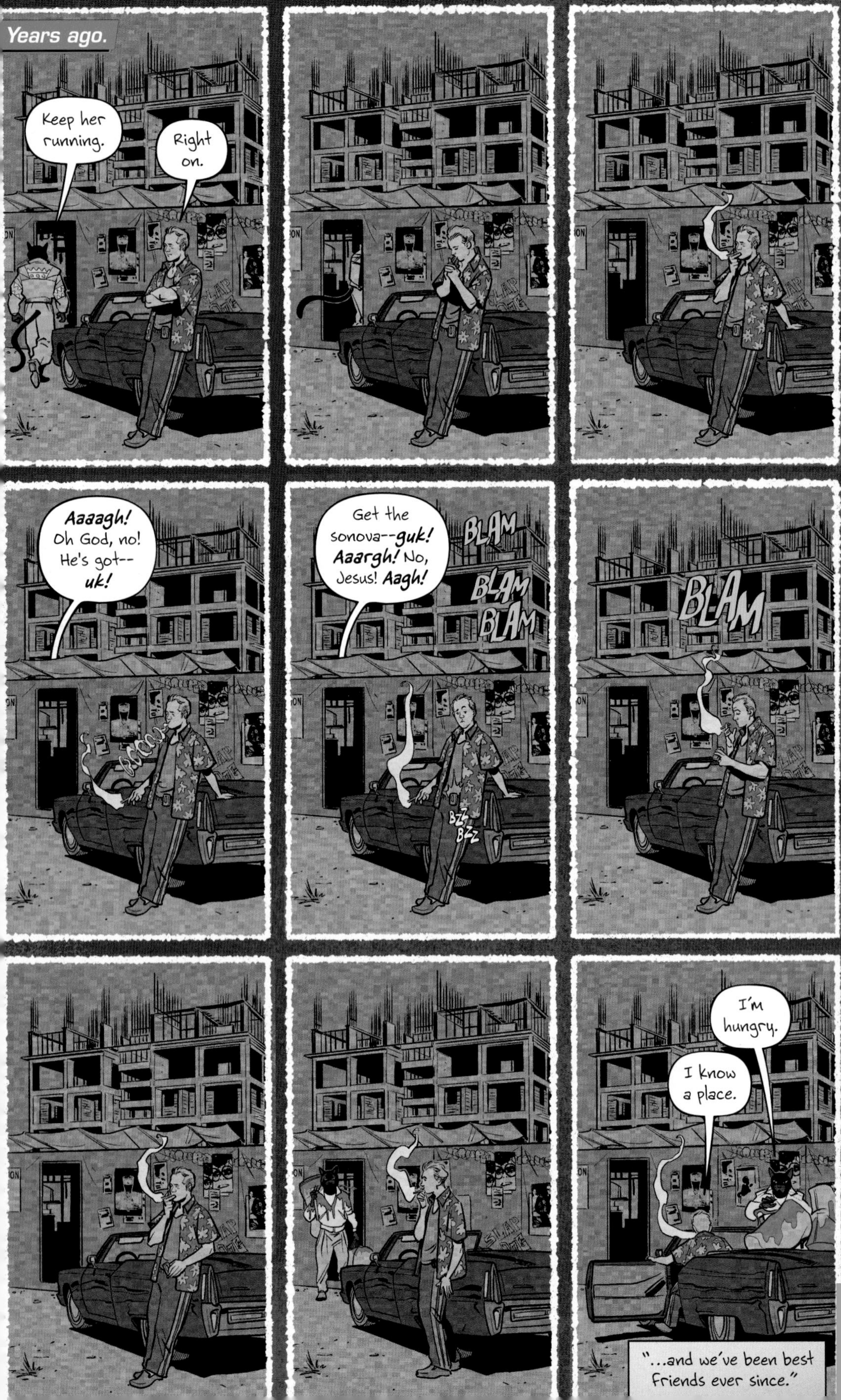
Years ago.
Keep her running.
Right on.
Aaaagh! Oh God, no! He's got-- uk!
Get the sonova--guk! Aaargh! No, Jesus! Aagh!
BLAM
BLAM
BLAM
BZZ BZZ
BLAM
I'm hungry.
I know a place.
"...and we've been best friends ever since."

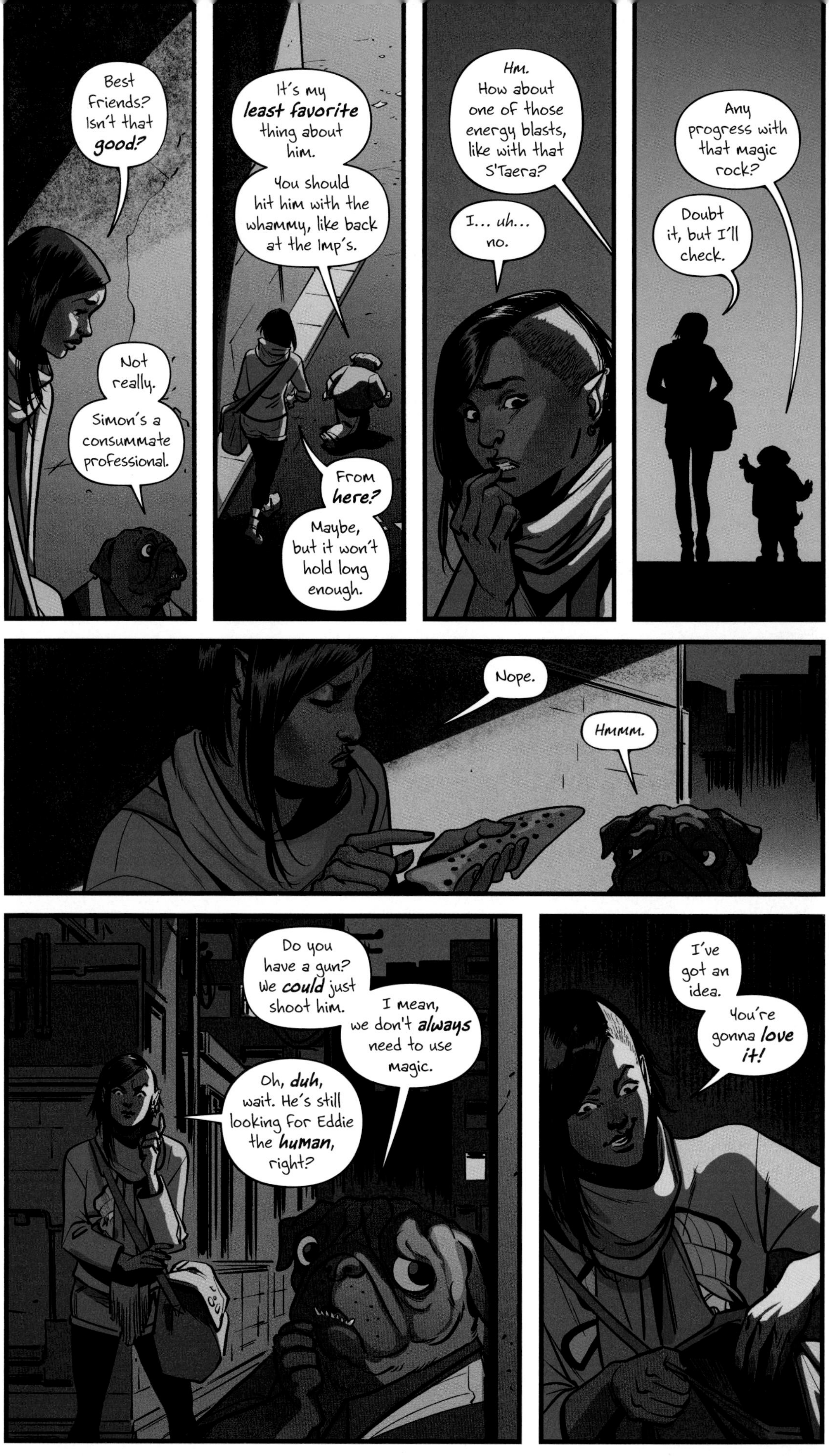
Best Friends? Isn't that good?
Not really.
Simon's a consummate professional.
It's my least favorite thing about him.
You should hit him with the whammy, like back at the Imp's.
From here?
Maybe, but it won't hold long enough.
Hm. How about one of those energy blasts, like with that S'Taera?
I... uh... no.
Any progress with that magic rock?
Doubt it, but I'll check.
Nope.
Hmmm.
Do you have a gun? We could just shoot him.
I mean, we don't always need to use magic.
Oh, duh, wait. He's still looking for Eddie the human, right?
I've got an idea.
You're gonna love it!

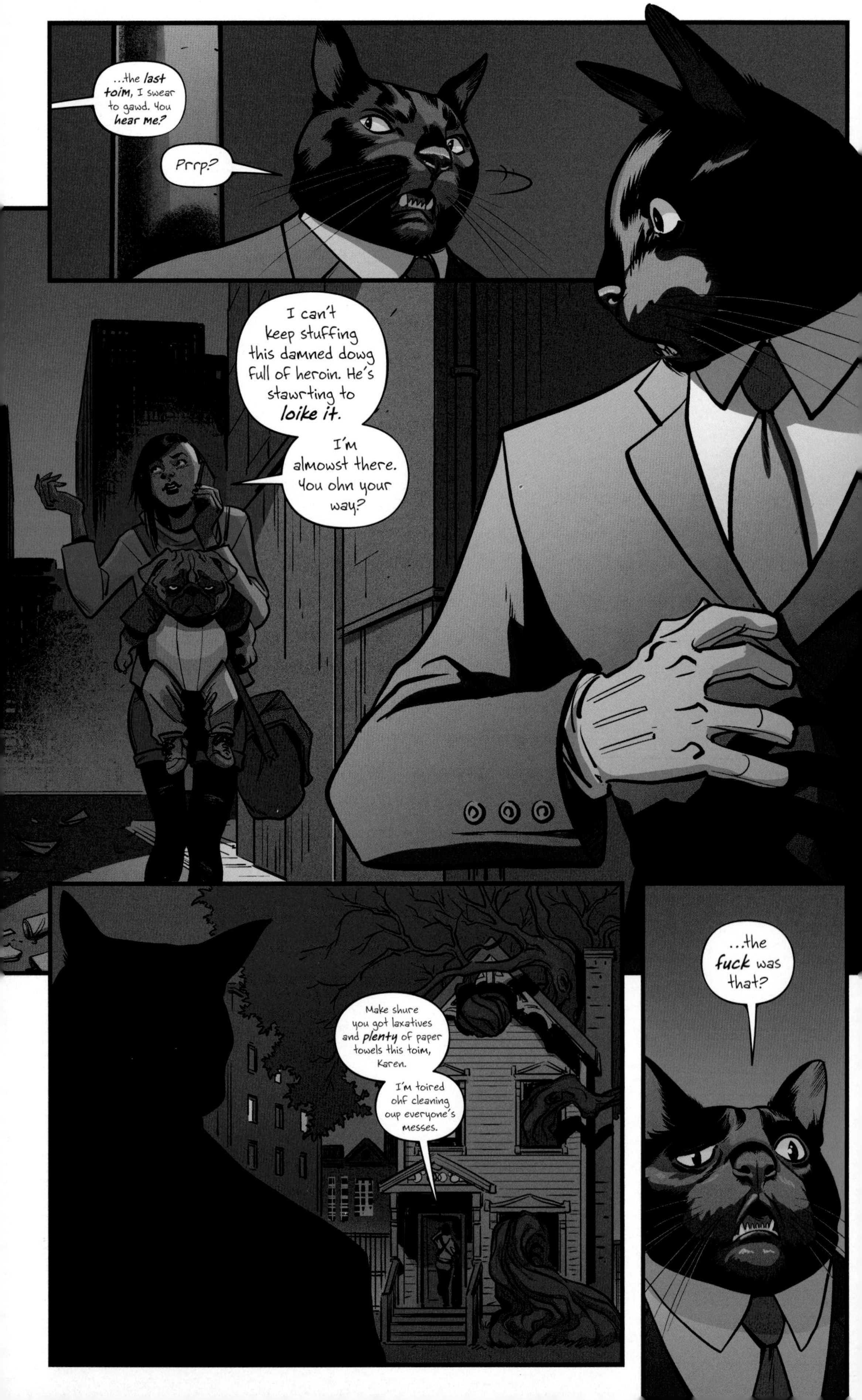
...the *last* *toim*, I swear to gawd. You *hear me?*
Prrp?
I can't keep stuffing this damned dowg full of heroin. He's stawrting to *loike it*.
I'm almowst there. You ohn your way?
Make shure you got laxatives and *plenty* of paper towels this toim, Karen.
I'm toired ohf cleaning oup everyone's messes.
...the *fuck* was that?

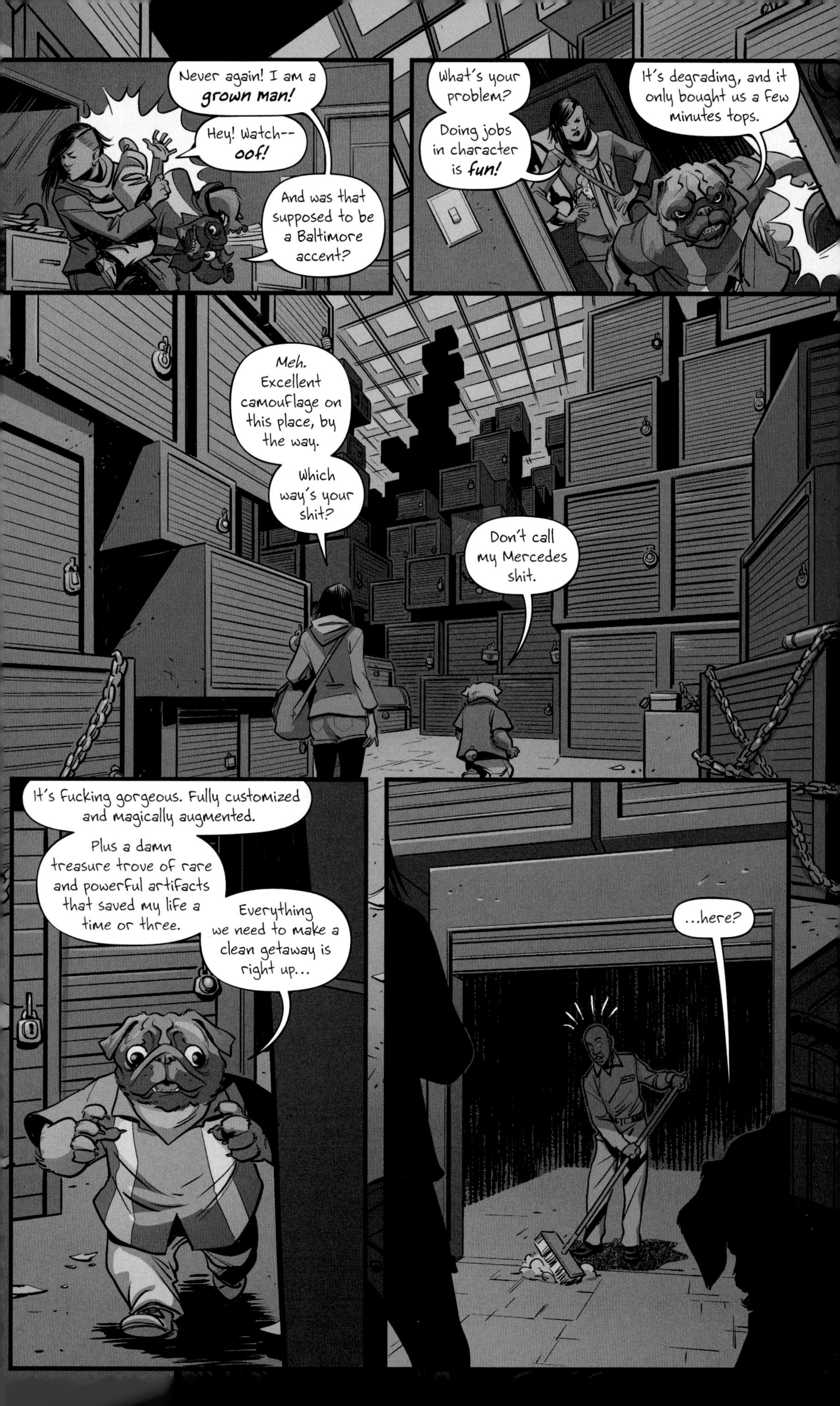
Never again! I am a **grown man!**
Hey! Watch-- **oof!**
And was that supposed to be a Baltimore accent?
What's your problem?
Doing jobs in character is **fun!**
It's degrading, and it only bought us a few minutes tops.
Meh. Excellent camouflage on this place, by the way.
Which way's your shit?
Don't call my Mercedes shit.
It's fucking gorgeous. Fully customized and magically augmented.
Plus a damn treasure trove of rare and powerful artifacts that saved my life a time or three.
Everything we need to make a clean getaway is right up...
...here?

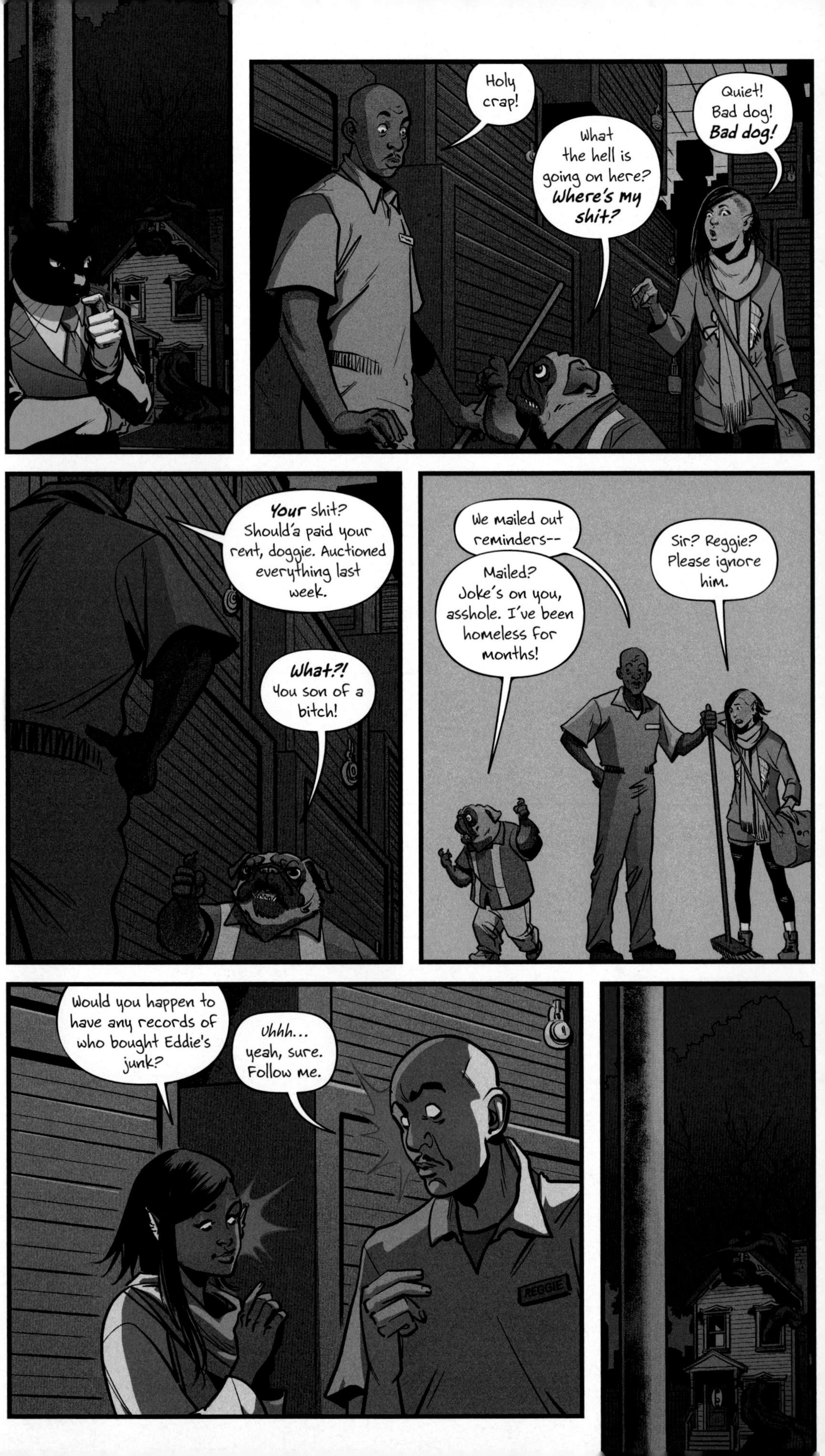
Holy crap!
What the hell is going on here? **Where's my shit?**
Quiet! Bad dog! **Bad dog!**
Your shit? Should'a paid your rent, doggie. Auctioned everything last week.
What?! You son of a bitch!
We mailed out reminders--
Mailed? Joke's on you, asshole. I've been homeless for months!
Sir? Reggie? Please ignore him.
Would you happen to have any records of who bought Eddie's junk?
Uhhh... yeah, sure. Follow me.
REGGIE

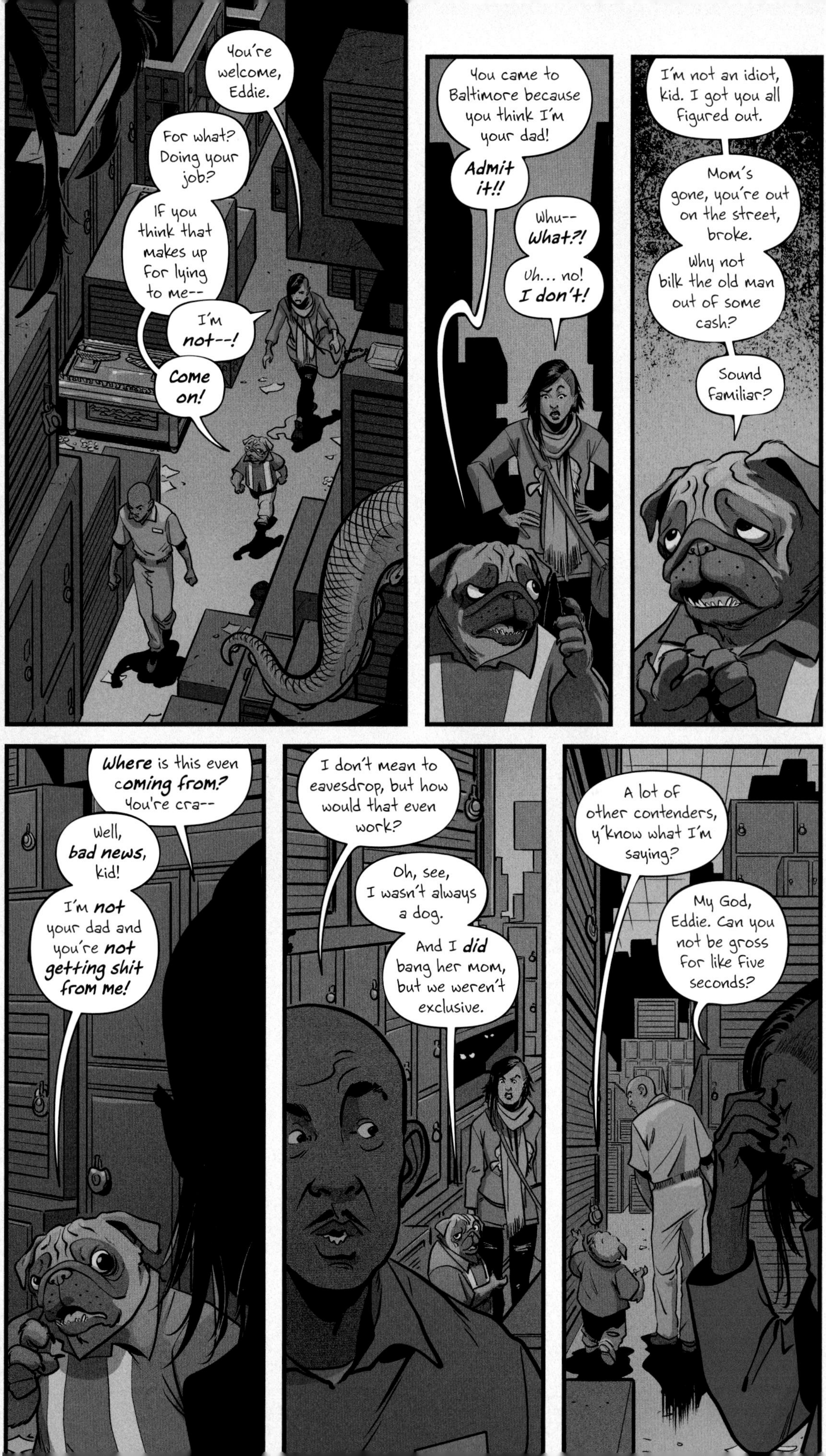
You're welcome, Eddie.
For what? Doing your job?
If you think that makes up for lying to me--
I'm not--!
Come on!
You came to Baltimore because you think I'm your dad!
Admit it!!
Whu-- What?!
Uh... no! I don't!
I'm not an idiot, kid. I got you all figured out.
Mom's gone, you're out on the street, broke.
Why not bilk the old man out of some cash?
Sound familiar?
Where is this even coming from? You're cra--
Well, bad news, kid!
I'm not your dad and you're not getting shit from me!
I don't mean to eavesdrop, but how would that even work?
Oh, see, I wasn't always a dog.
And I did bang her mom, but we weren't exclusive.
A lot of other contenders, y'know what I'm saying?
My God, Eddie. Can you not be gross for like five seconds?

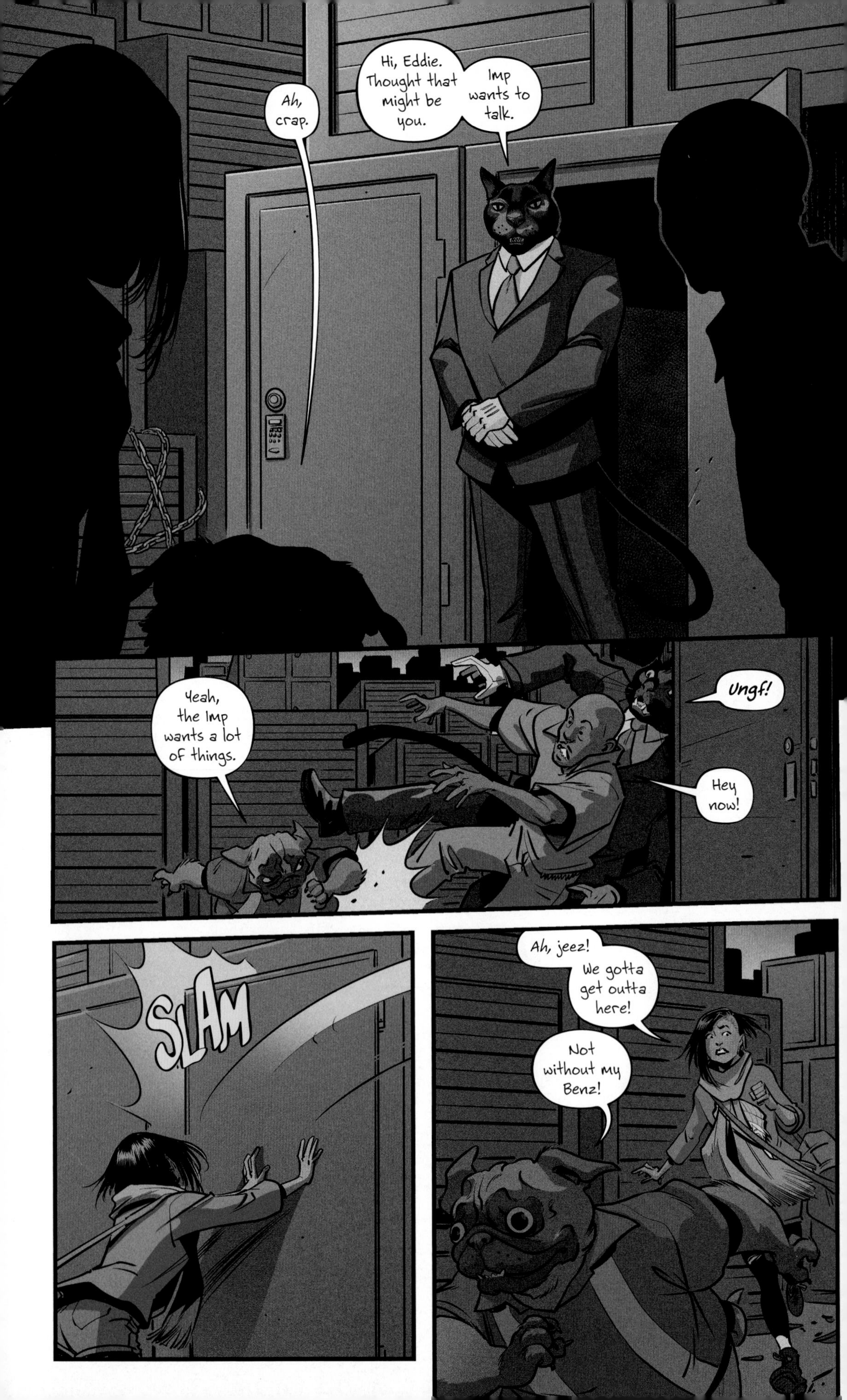
Ah, crap.
Hi, Eddie. Thought that might be you.
Imp wants to talk.
Yeah, the Imp wants a lot of things.
Ungf!
Hey now!
SLAM
Ah, jeez!
We gotta get outta here!
Not without my Benz!

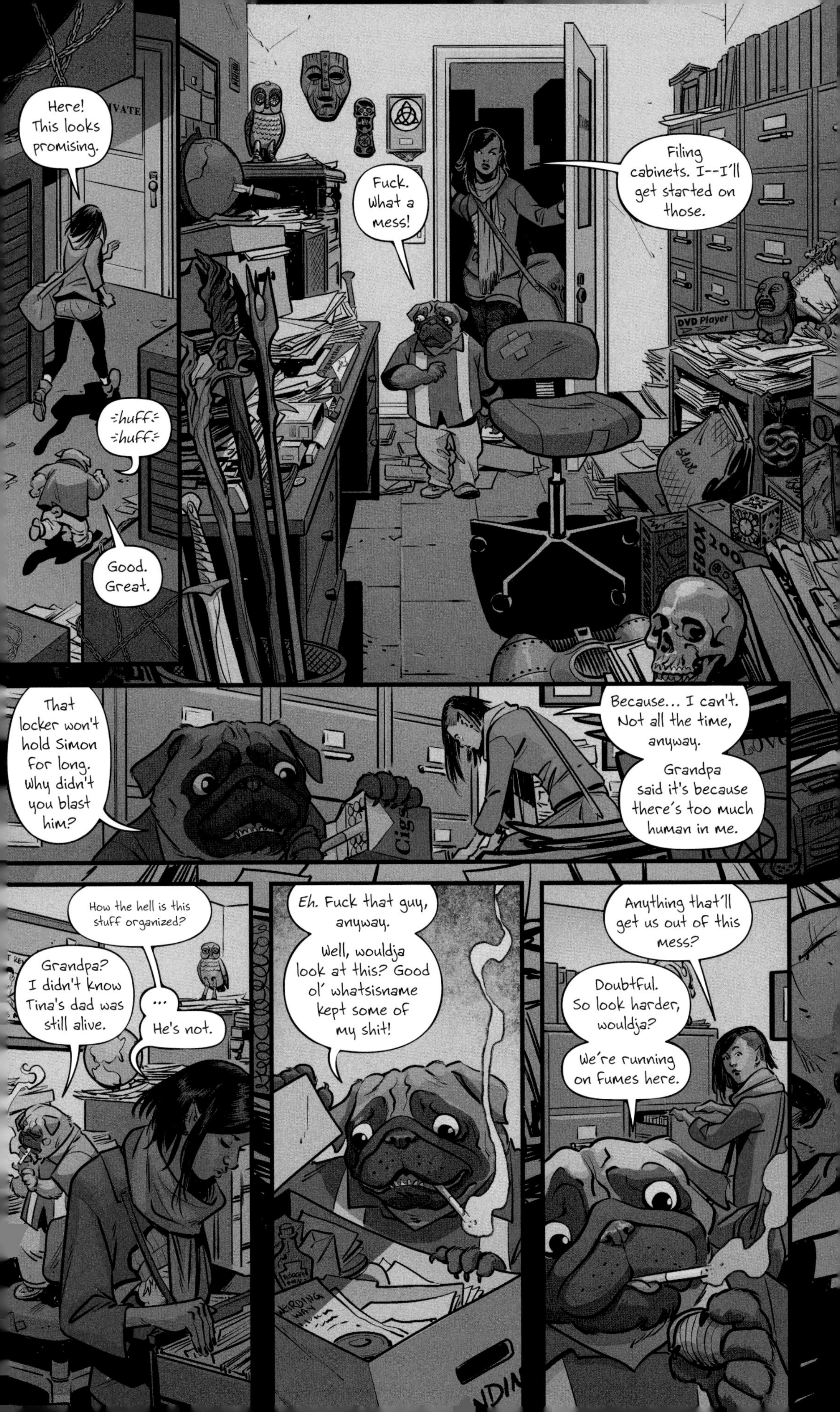
Here! This looks promising.
VATE
Fuck. What a mess!
Filing cabinets. I--I'll get started on those.
DVD Player
-huff-
-huff-
Good. Great.
That locker won't hold Simon for long. Why didn't you blast him?
Cigs
Because... I can't. Not all the time, anyway.
Grandpa said it's because there's too much human in me.
How the hell is this stuff organized?
Grandpa? I didn't know Tina's dad was still alive.
...
He's not.
Eh. Fuck that guy, anyway.
Well, wouldja look at this? Good ol' whatsisname kept some of my shit!
WEIRDING WAY
Anything that'll get us out of this mess?
Doubtful. So look harder, wouldja?
We're running on fumes here.

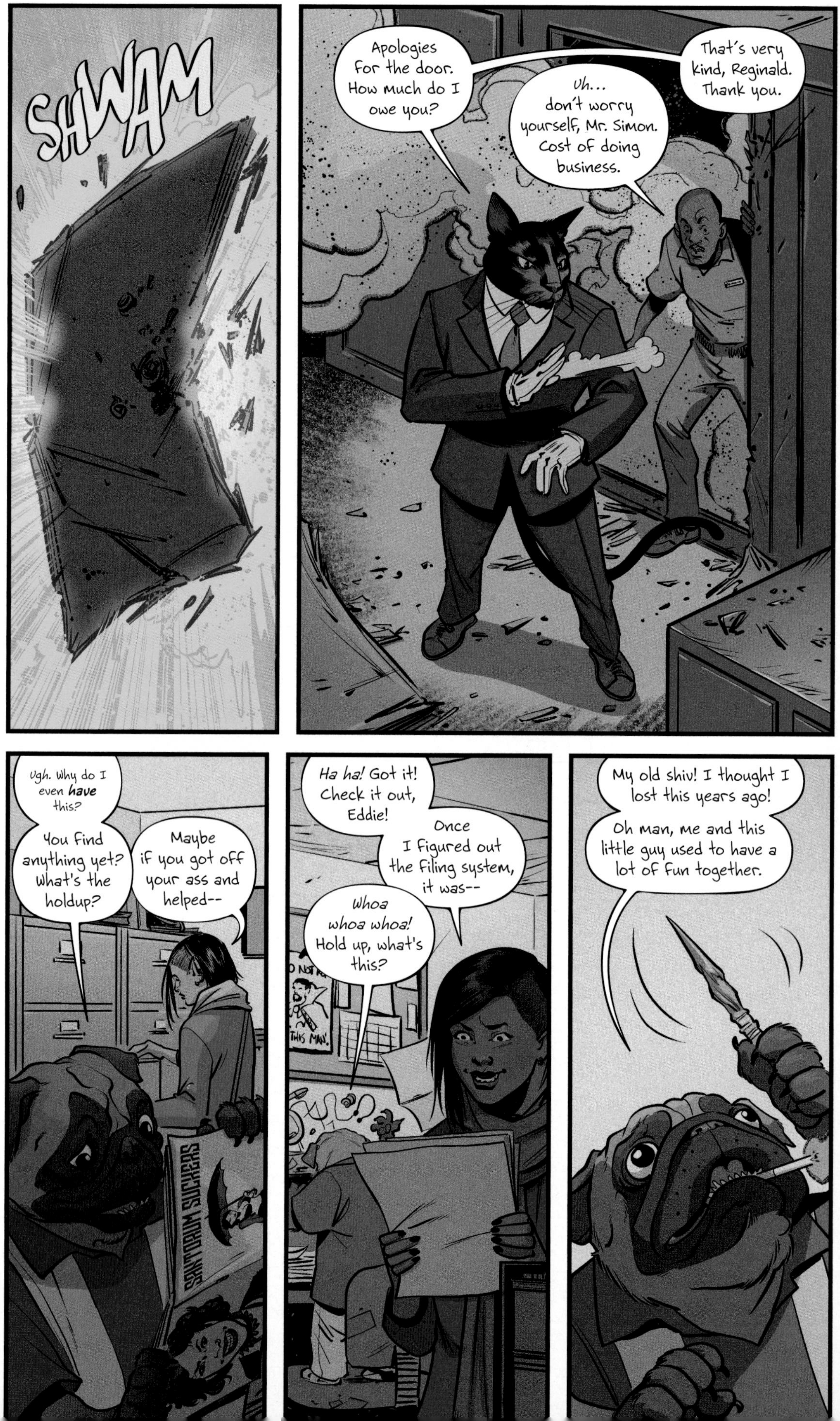
SHWAM
Apologies for the door. How much do I owe you?
Uh... don't worry yourself, Mr. Simon. Cost of doing business.
That's very kind, Reginald. Thank you.
Ugh. Why do I even *have* this?
You find anything yet? What's the holdup?
Maybe if you got off your ass and helped--
SANTORUM SUCKERS
Ha ha! Got it! Check it out, Eddie!
Once I figured out the filing system, it was--
Whoa whoa whoa! Hold up, what's this?
THIS MAN.
My old shiv! I thought I lost this years ago!
Oh man, me and this little guy used to have a lot of fun together.

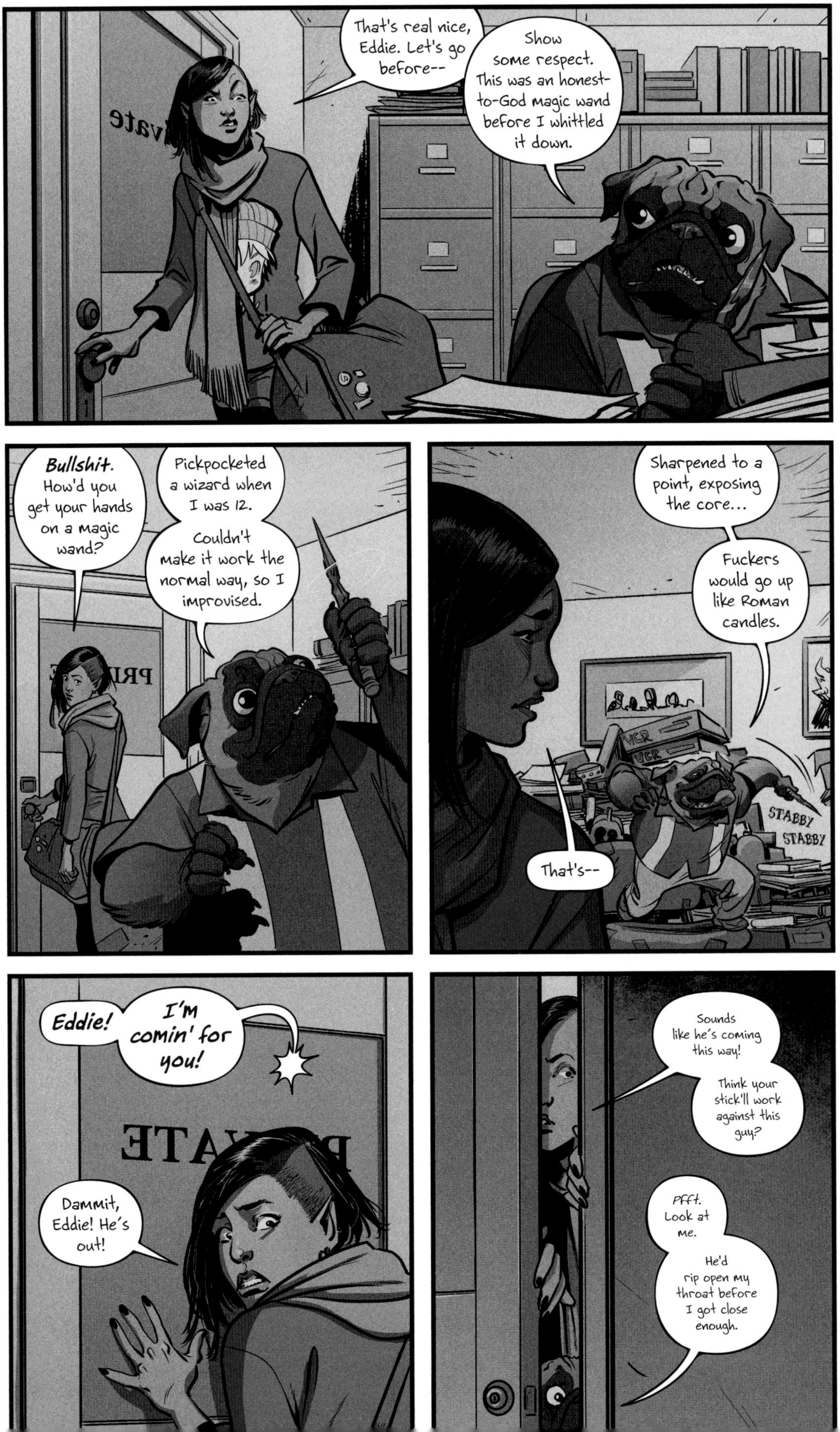

That's real nice, Eddie. Let's go before--
Show some respect. This was an honest-to-God magic wand before I whittled it down.
Bullshit. How'd you get your hands on a magic wand?
Pickpocketed a wizard when I was 12.
Couldn't make it work the normal way, so I improvised.
Sharpened to a point, exposing the core...
Fuckers would go up like Roman candles.
That's--
STABBY STABBY
Eddie!
I'm comin' for you!
Dammit, Eddie! He's out!
Sounds like he's coming this way!
Think your stick'll work against this guy?
Pfft. Look at me.
He'd rip open my throat before I got close enough.

I recognize you too, kid.

Not sure what Tina Palacio's kid is doing hanging out with Eddie Endino, though.

Didn't she ever tell you **why** she left Baltimore?

She **must** have told you how Eddie **fucked her over?**

Don't listen to him--

Shush.

Your mom actually **loved** the stupid asshole, you believe that?

And he throws her under the bus with Sideways Joe to save his own ass. Broke her heart and nearly got her killed.

Official

Animal Pens

Cold Storage/ Cryogenics

Hazardous Material Storage

I got no beef with you, young lady.

I just want Eddie.

Tala. Kid. I can explain.

Shut up.

I have **another** idea.

You're gonna **hate** it.

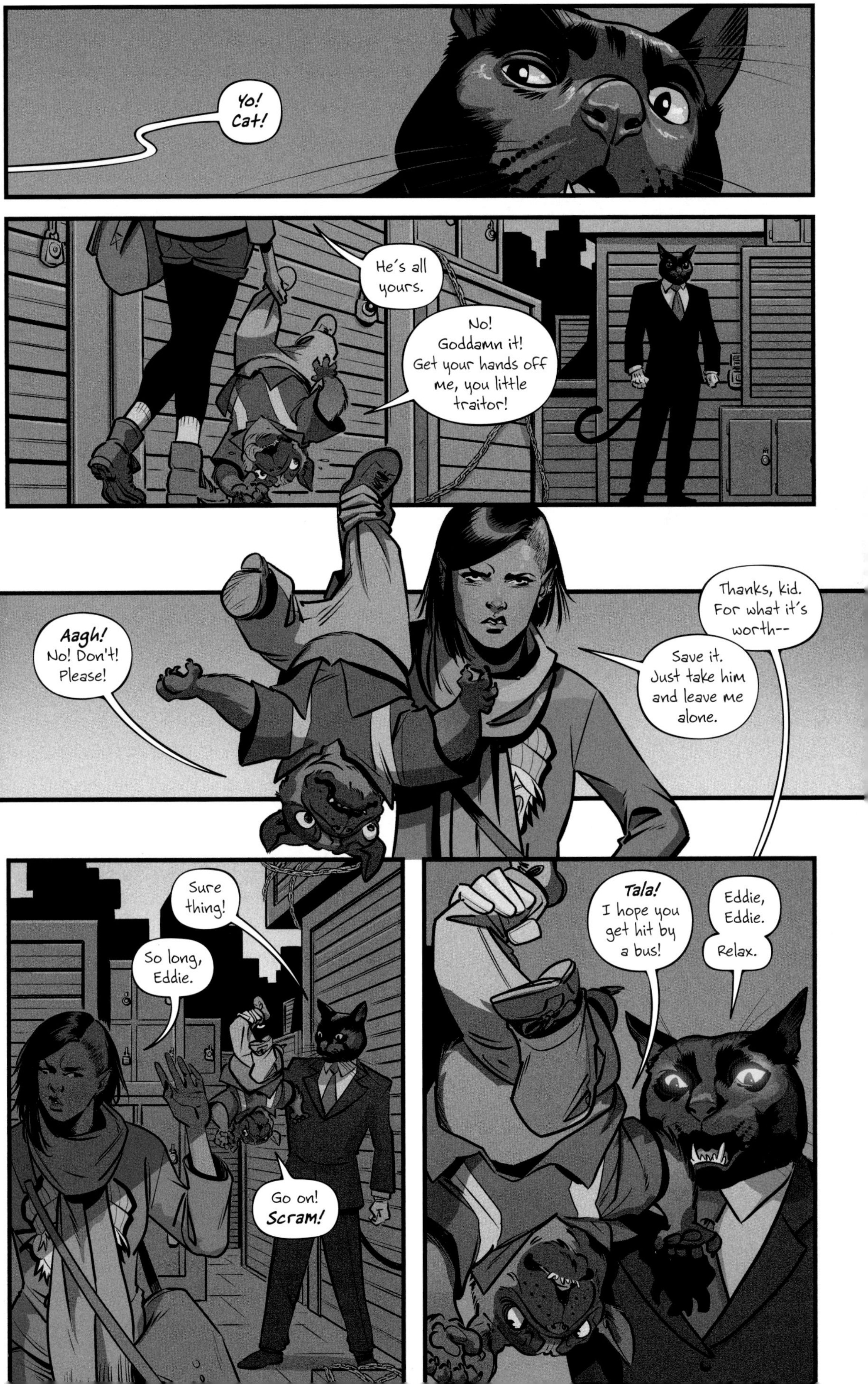

Yo! Cat!
He's all yours.
No! Goddamn it! Get your hands off me, you little traitor!
Aagh! No! Don't! Please!
Thanks, kid. For what it's worth--
Save it. Just take him and leave me alone.
Sure thing!
So long, Eddie.
Go on! Scram!
Tala! I hope you get hit by a bus!
Eddie, Eddie.
Relax.

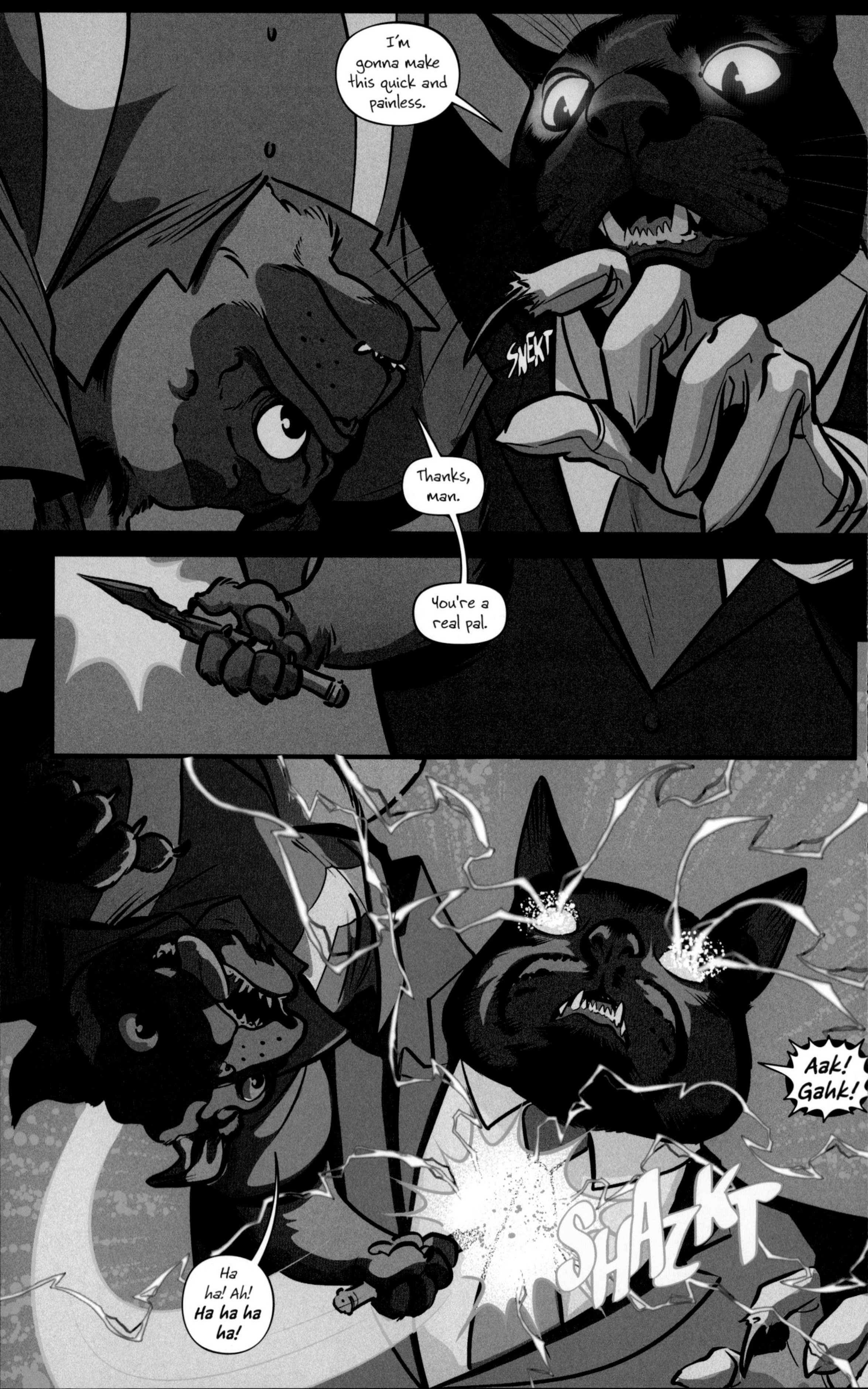
I'm gonna make this quick and painless.
SNEKT
Thanks, man.
You're a real pal.
Aak! Gahk!
SHAZKT
Ha ha! Ah! **Ha ha ha ha!**

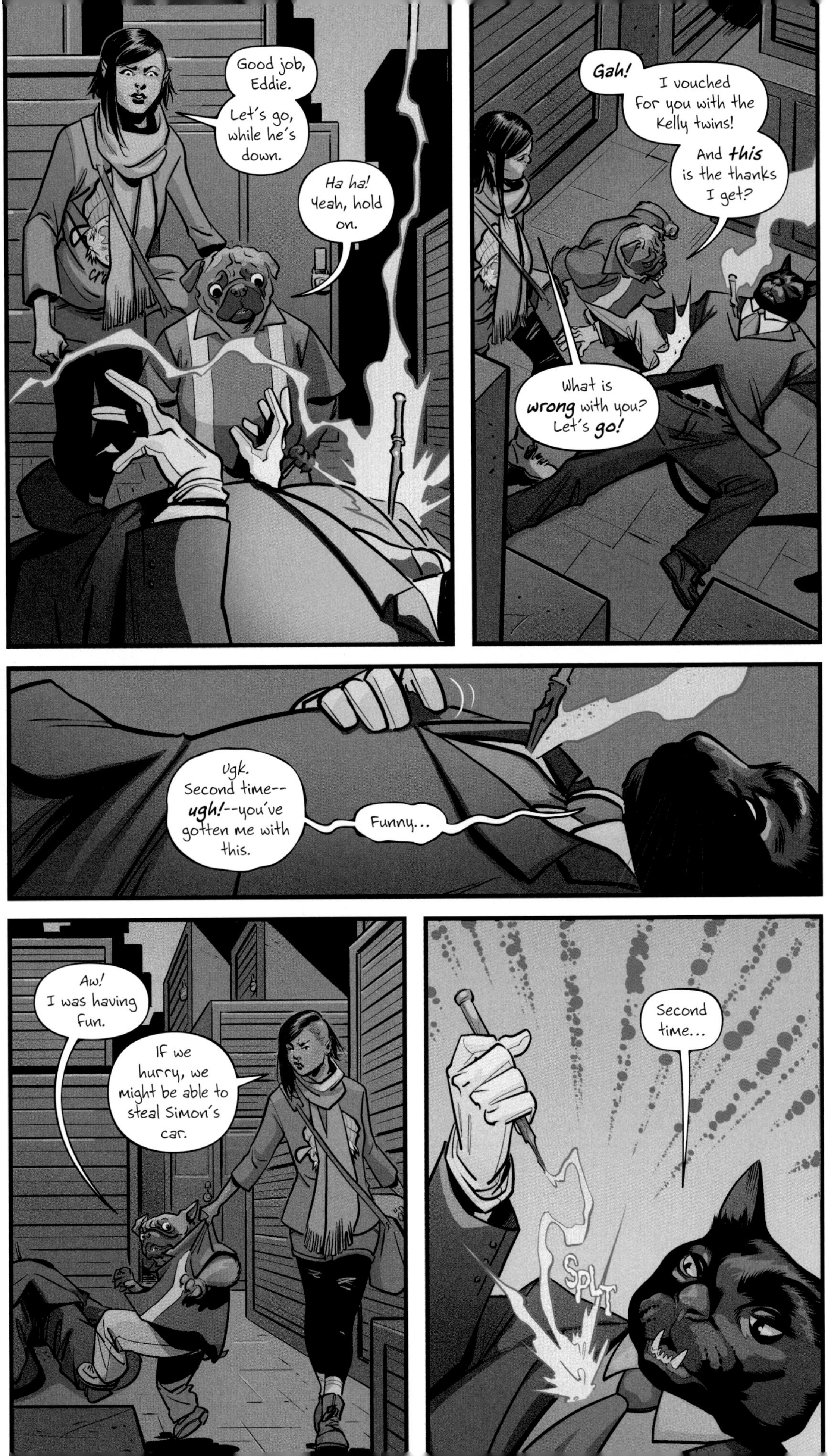
Good job, Eddie.
Let's go, while he's down.
Ha ha! Yeah, hold on.
Gah!
I vouched for you with the Kelly twins!
And this is the thanks I get?
What is wrong with you? Let's go!
Ugk. Second time--ugh!--you've gotten me with this.
Funny...
Aw! I was having fun.
If we hurry, we might be able to steal Simon's car.
Second time...
SPLT

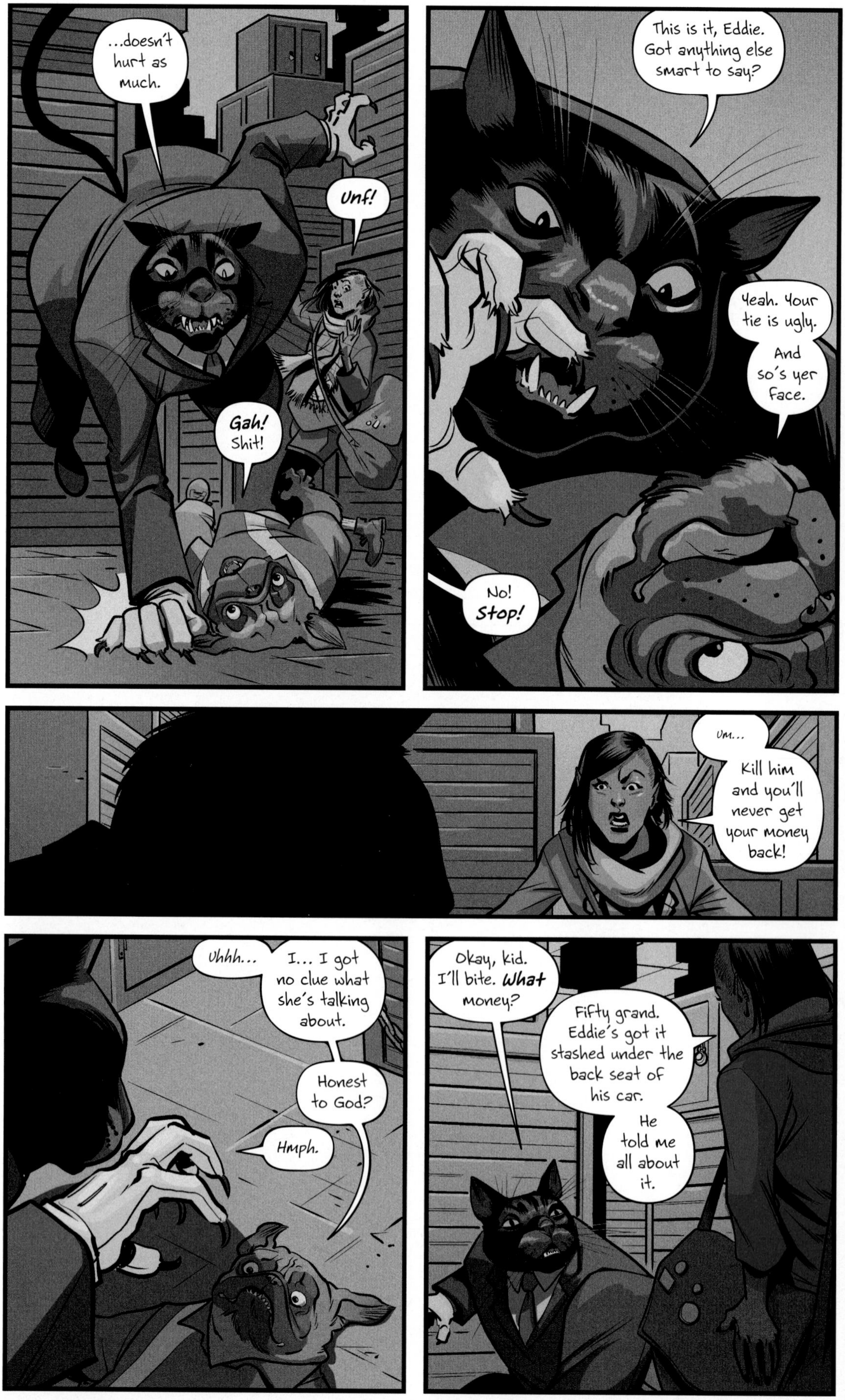
...doesn't hurt as much.
Unf!
Gah! Shit!
This is it, Eddie. Got anything else smart to say?
Yeah. Your tie is ugly.
And so's yer face.
No! Stop!
Um...
Kill him and you'll never get your money back!
Uhhh...
I... I got no clue what she's talking about.
Honest to God?
Hmph.
Okay, kid. I'll bite. What money?
Fifty grand. Eddie's got it stashed under the back seat of his car.
He told me all about it.

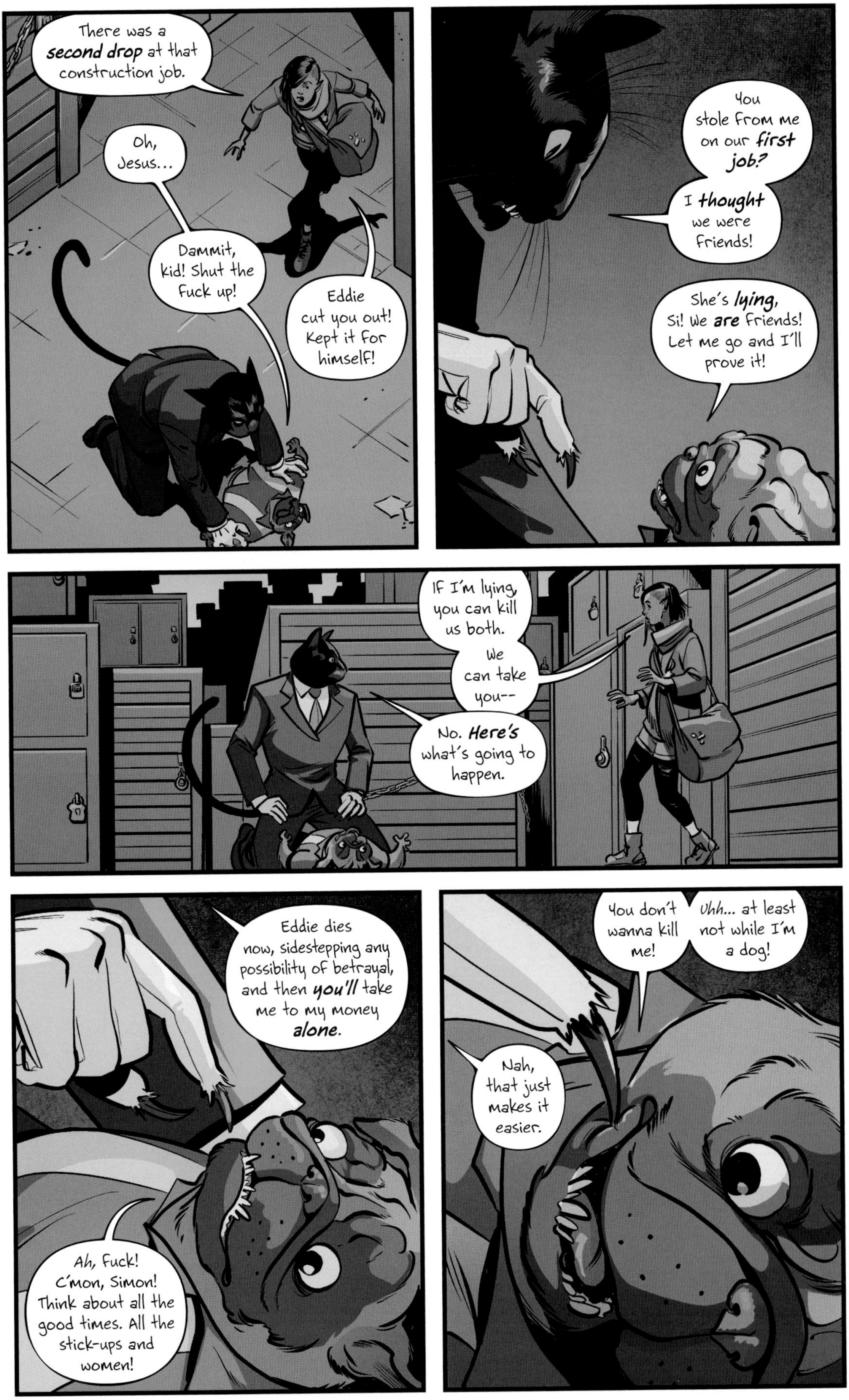
There was a second drop at that construction job.
Oh, Jesus...
Dammit, kid! Shut the fuck up!
Eddie cut you out! Kept it for himself!
You stole from me on our first job?
I thought we were friends!
She's lying, Si! We are friends! Let me go and I'll prove it!
If I'm lying, you can kill us both.
We can take you--
No. Here's what's going to happen.
Eddie dies now, sidestepping any possibility of betrayal, and then you'll take me to my money alone.
Ah, Fuck! C'mon, Simon! Think about all the good times. All the stick-ups and women!
You don't wanna kill me!
Uhh... at least not while I'm a dog!
Nah, that just makes it easier.

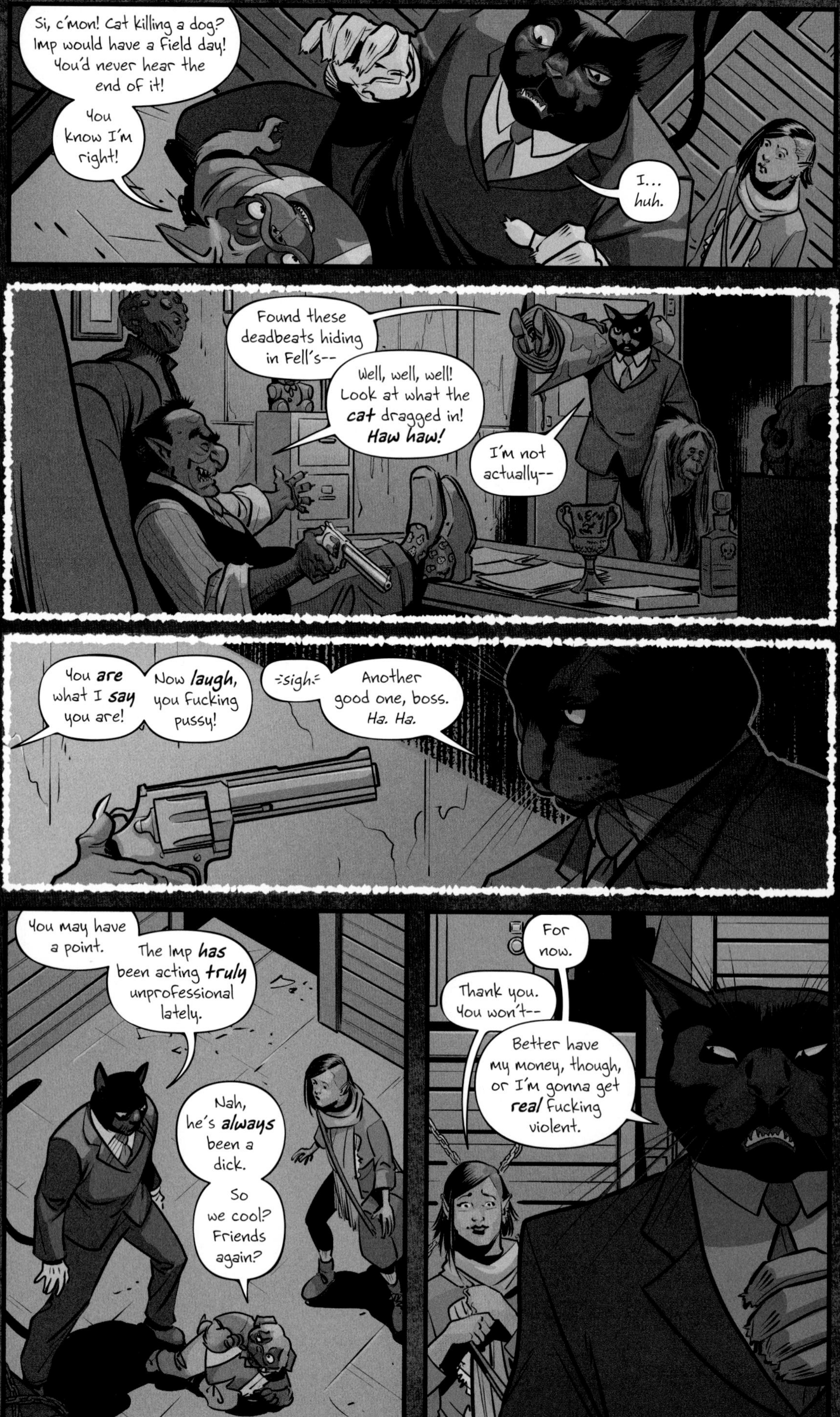

Si, c'mon! Cat killing a dog? Imp would have a field day! You'd never hear the end of it!
You know I'm right!
I... huh.
Found these deadbeats hiding in Fell's--
Well, well, well! Look at what the cat dragged in! Haw haw!
I'm not actually--
You are what I say you are!
Now laugh, you fucking pussy!
sigh
Another good one, boss. Ha. Ha.
You may have a point.
The Imp has been acting truly unprofessional lately.
Nah, he's always been a dick.
So we cool? Friends again?
For now.
Thank you. You won't--
Better have my money, though, or I'm gonna get real fucking violent.

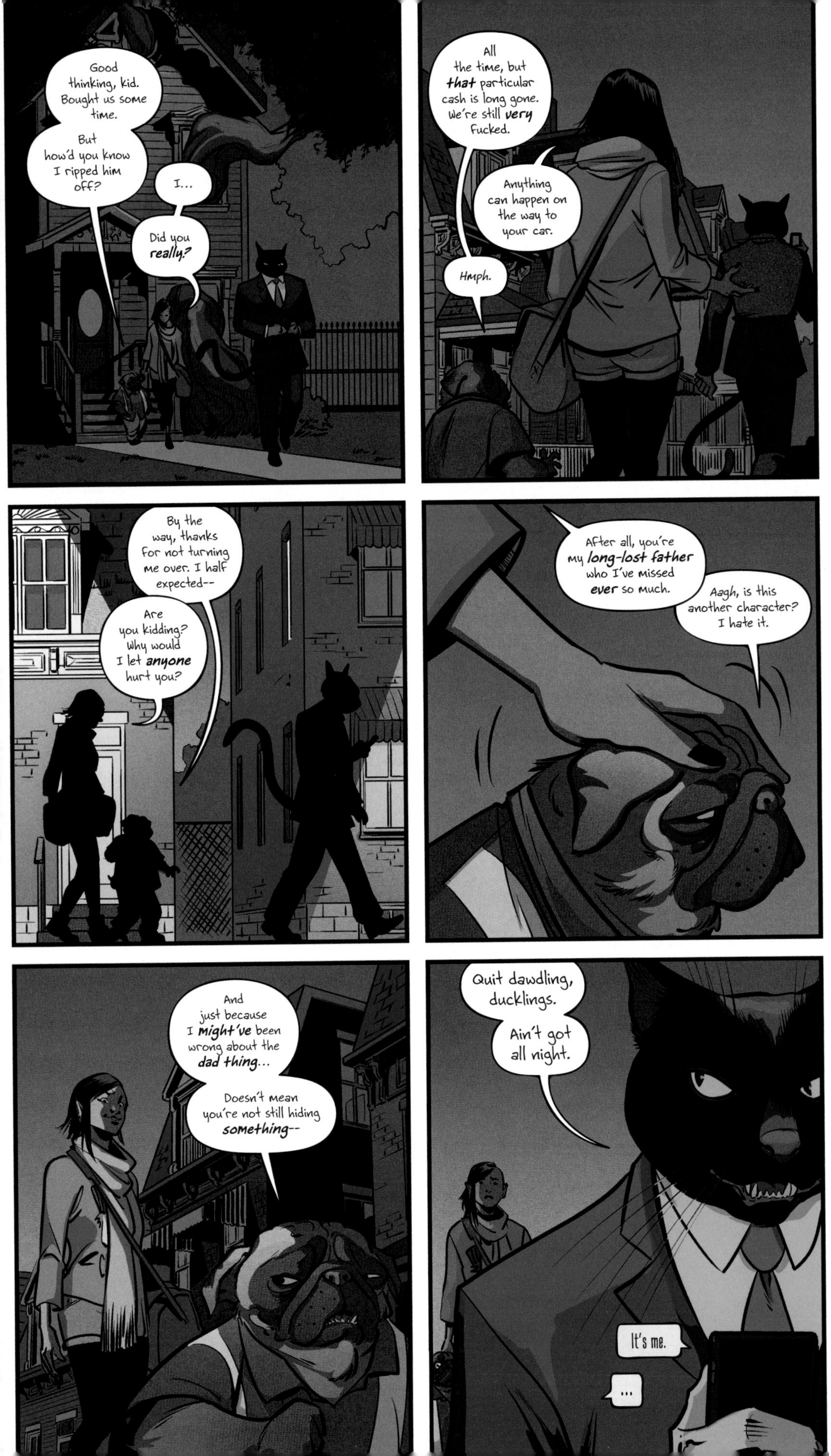
Good thinking, kid. Bought us some time.
But how'd you know I ripped him off?
I...
Did you *really?*
All the time, but ***that*** particular cash is long gone. We're still ***very*** fucked.
Anything can happen on the way to your car.
Hmph.
By the way, thanks for not turning me over. I half expected--
Are you kidding? Why would I let ***anyone*** hurt you?
After all, you're my ***long-lost father*** who I've missed ***ever*** so much.
Aagh, is this another character? I hate it.
And just because I ***might've*** been wrong about the ***dad thing...***
Doesn't mean you're not still hiding ***something--***
Quit dawdling, ducklings.
Ain't got all night.
It's me.
...

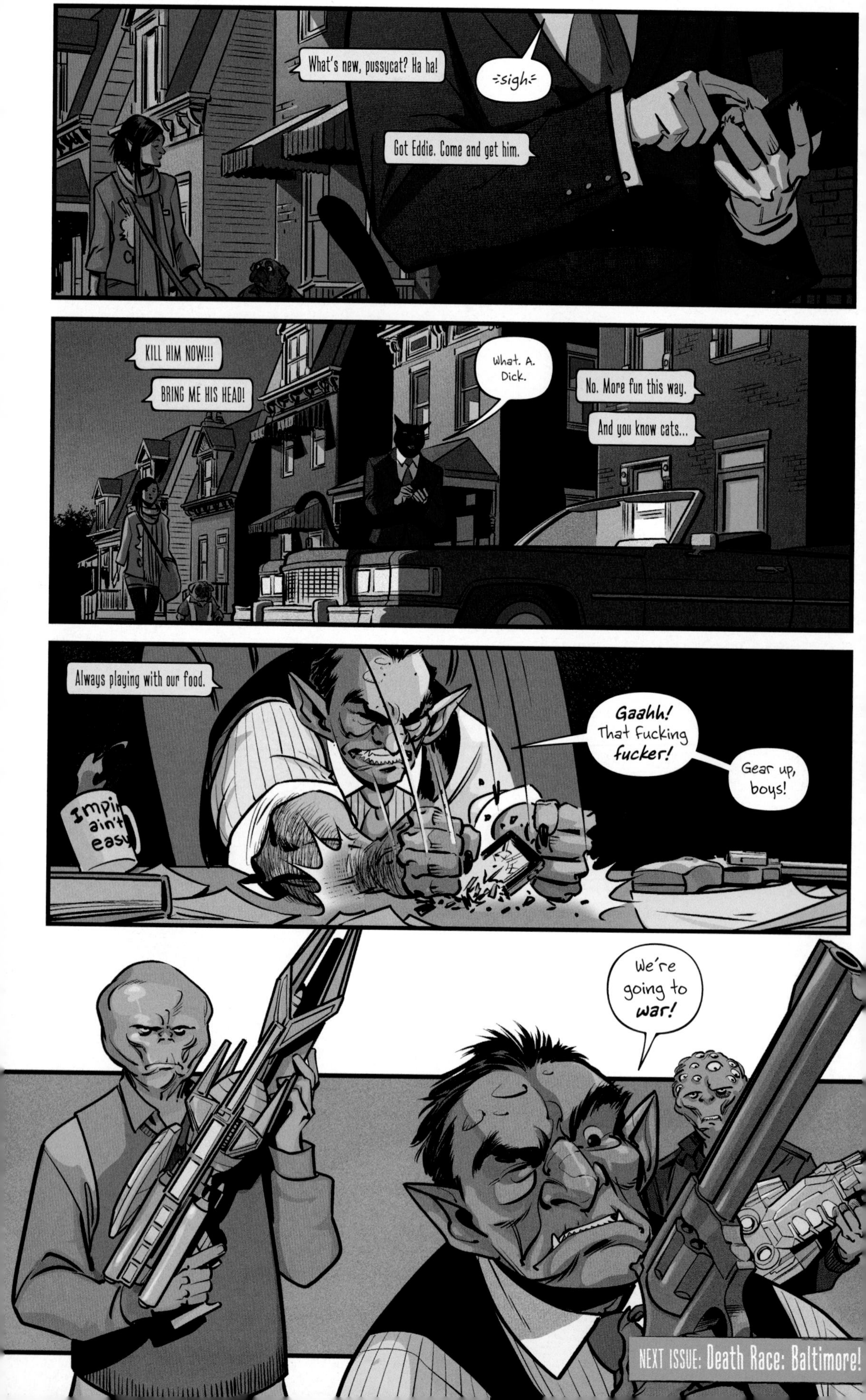
What's new, pussycat? Ha ha!
=sigh=
Got Eddie. Come and get him.
KILL HIM NOW!!!
BRING ME HIS HEAD!
What. A. Dick.
No. More fun this way.
And you know cats...
Always playing with our food.
Impin ain't easy
Gaahh! That fucking fucker!
Gear up, boys!
We're going to war!
NEXT ISSUE: Death Race: Baltimore!

BOOK FOUR

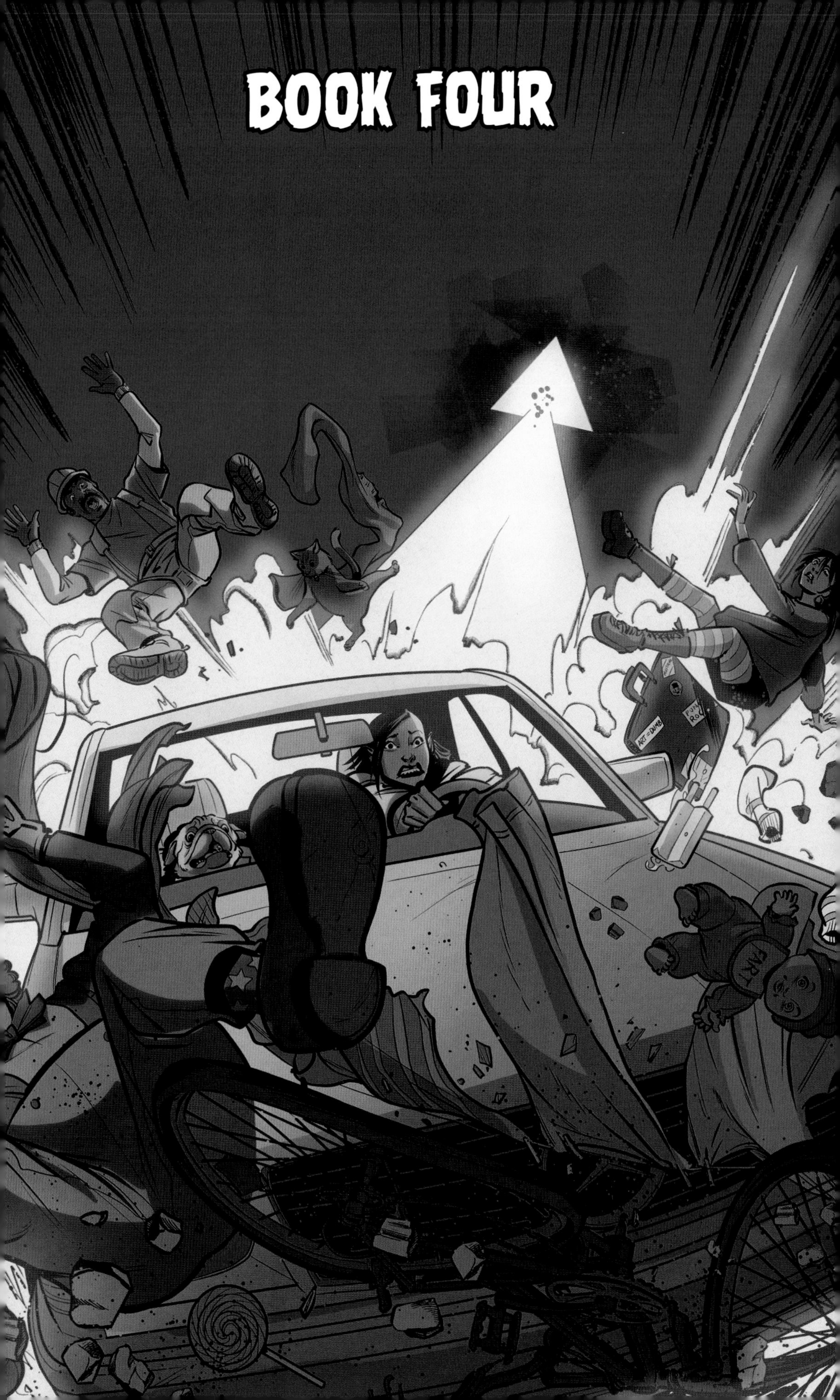
ART=DUMB
FART

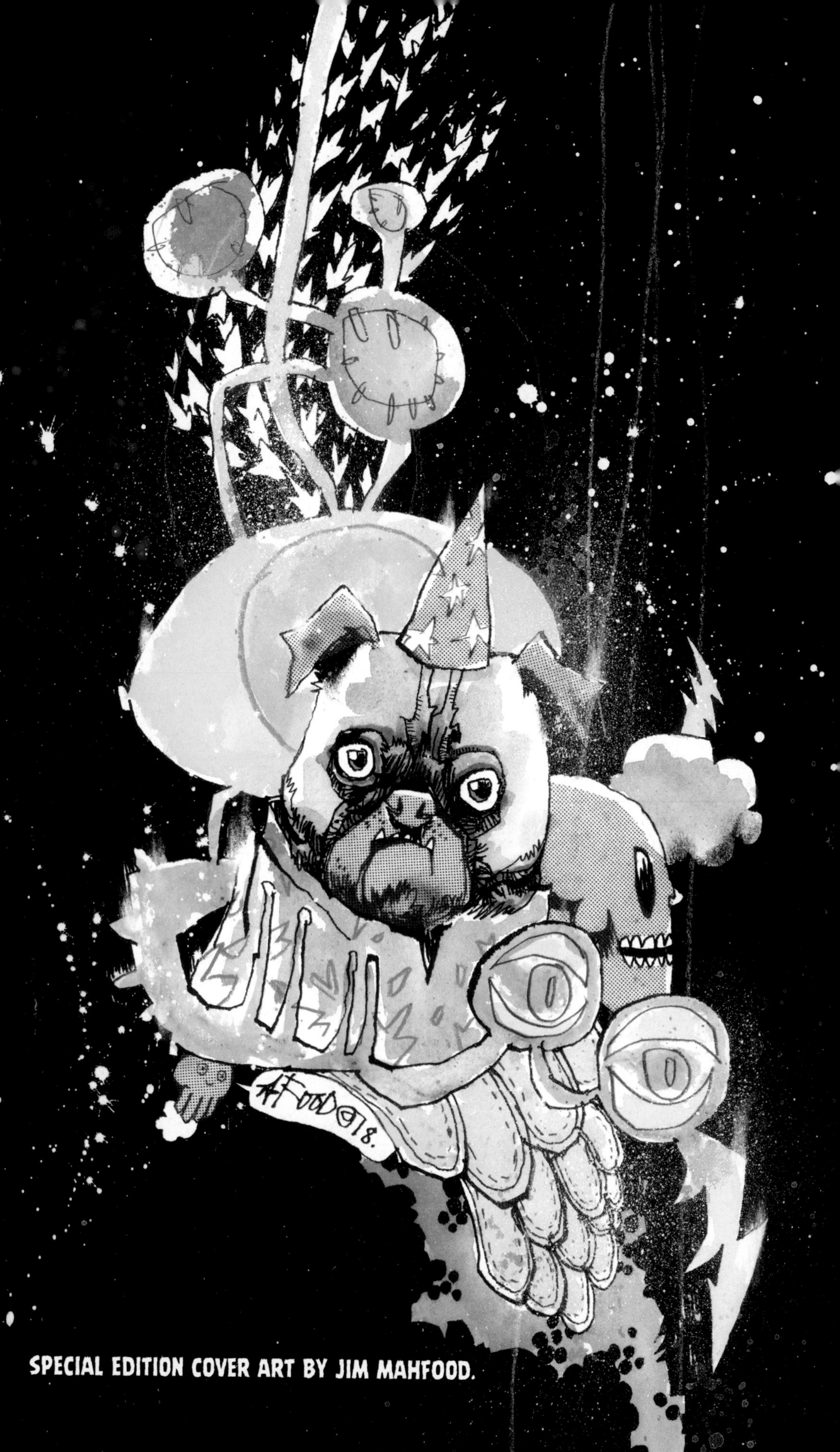

SPECIAL EDITION COVER ART BY JIM MAHFOOD.

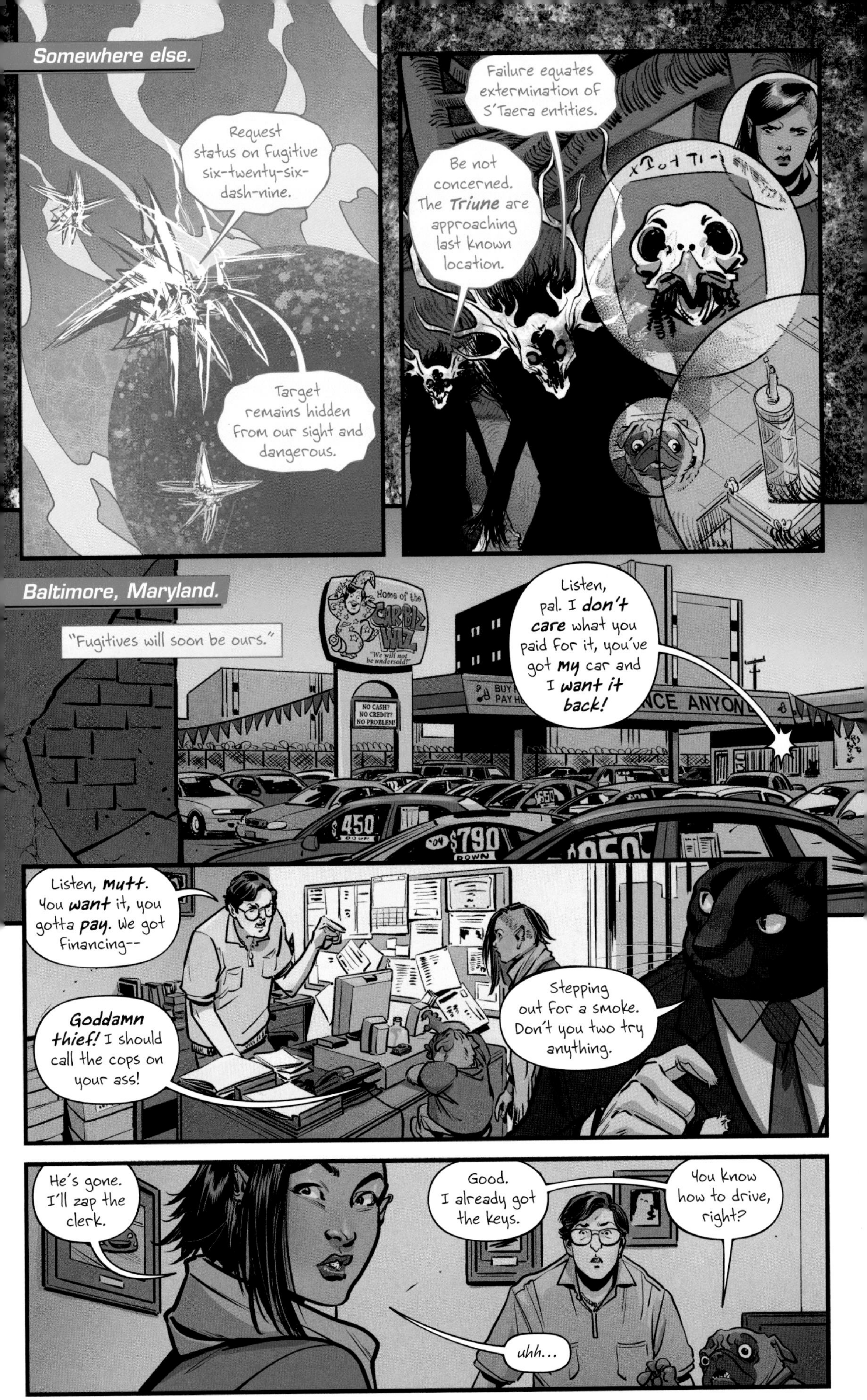
Somewhere else.
Request status on fugitive six-twenty-six-dash-nine.
Target remains hidden from our sight and dangerous.
Failure equates extermination of S'Taera entities.
Be not concerned. The Triune are approaching last known location.
Baltimore, Maryland.
"Fugitives will soon be ours."
Home of the CAR BIZ WIZ "We will not be undersold!"
NO CASH? NO CREDIT? NO PROBLEM!
BUY H PAY H
NCE ANYON
Listen, pal. I don't care what you paid for it, you've got my car and I want it back!
$450 DOWN
'04 $790 DOWN
Listen, mutt. You want it, you gotta pay. We got financing--
Goddamn thief! I should call the cops on your ass!
Stepping out for a smoke. Don't you two try anything.
He's gone. I'll zap the clerk.
Good. I already got the keys.
You know how to drive, right?
uhh...

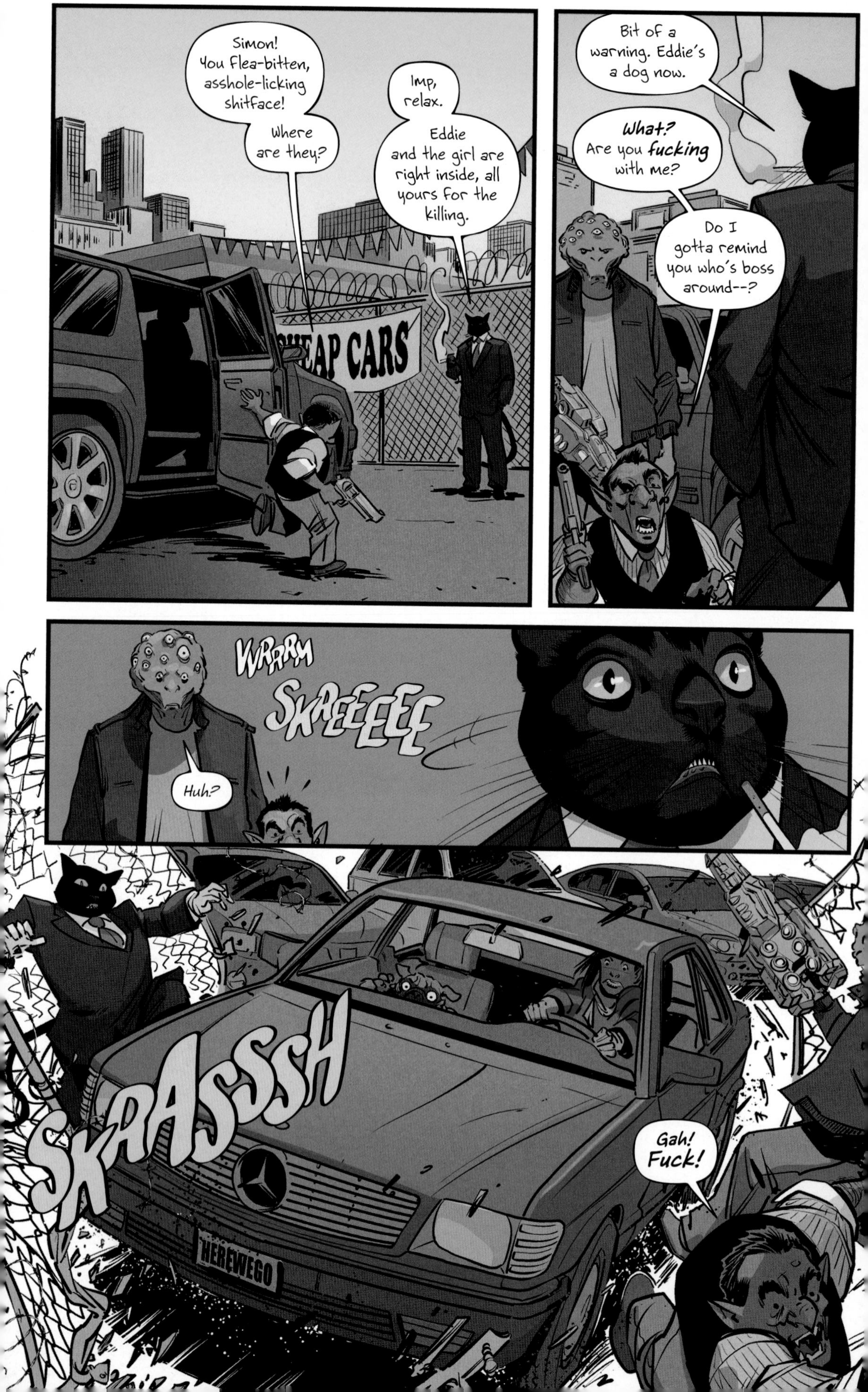
Simon! You flea-bitten, asshole-licking shitface!
Where are they?
Imp, relax.
Eddie and the girl are right inside, all yours for the killing.
CHEAP CARS
Bit of a warning. Eddie's a dog now.
What? Are you fucking with me?
Do I gotta remind you who's boss around--?
VRRRM
SKREEEEE
Huh?
SKRASSSH
HEREWEGO
Gah! Fuck!

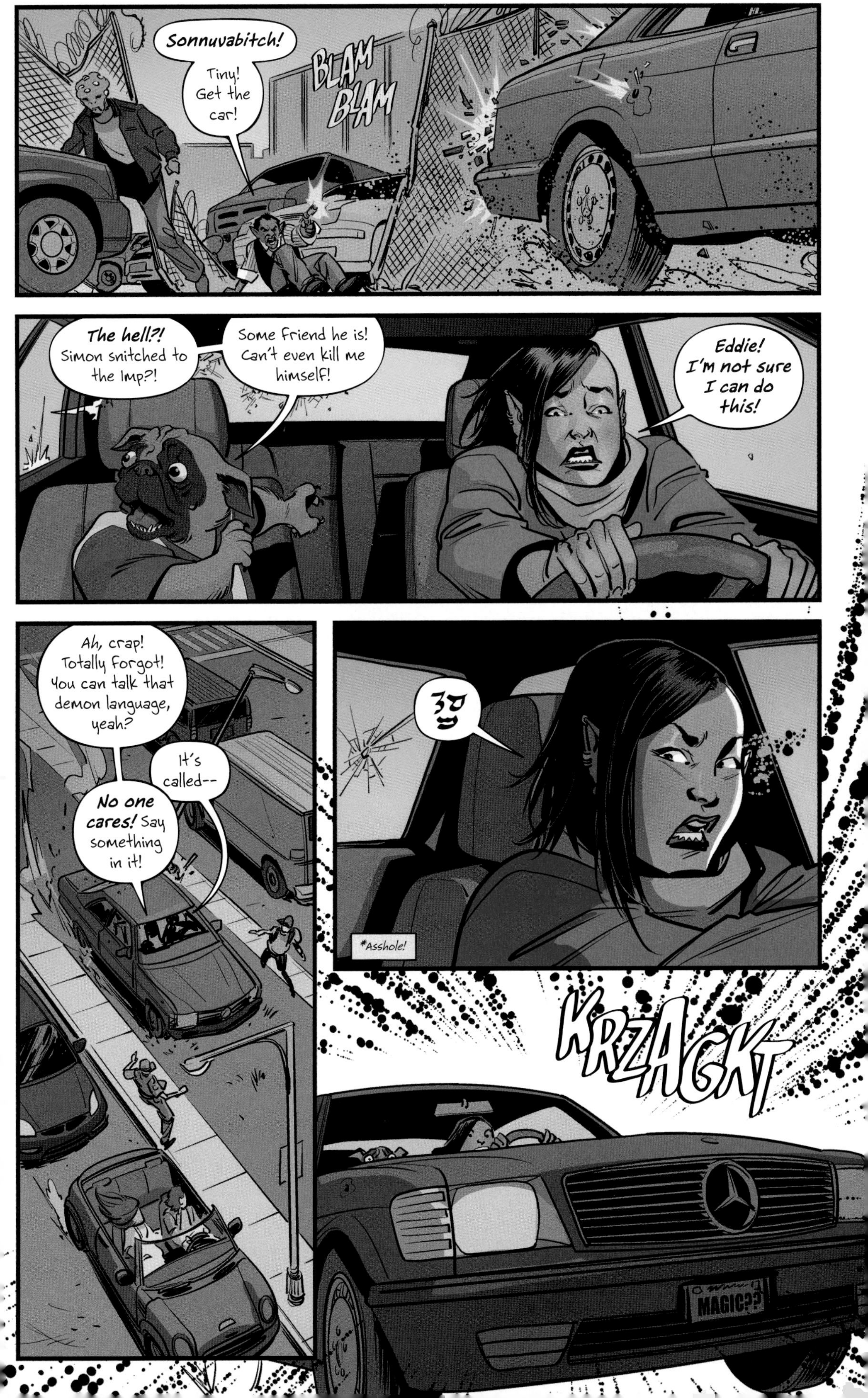
Sonnuvabitch!
Tiny! Get the car!
BLAM BLAM
The hell?! Simon snitched to the Imp?!
Some friend he is! Can't even kill me himself!
Eddie! I'm not sure I can do this!
Ah, crap! Totally forgot! You can talk that demon language, yeah?
It's called--
No one cares! Say something in it!
*Asshole!
KRZAGKT
MAGIC??

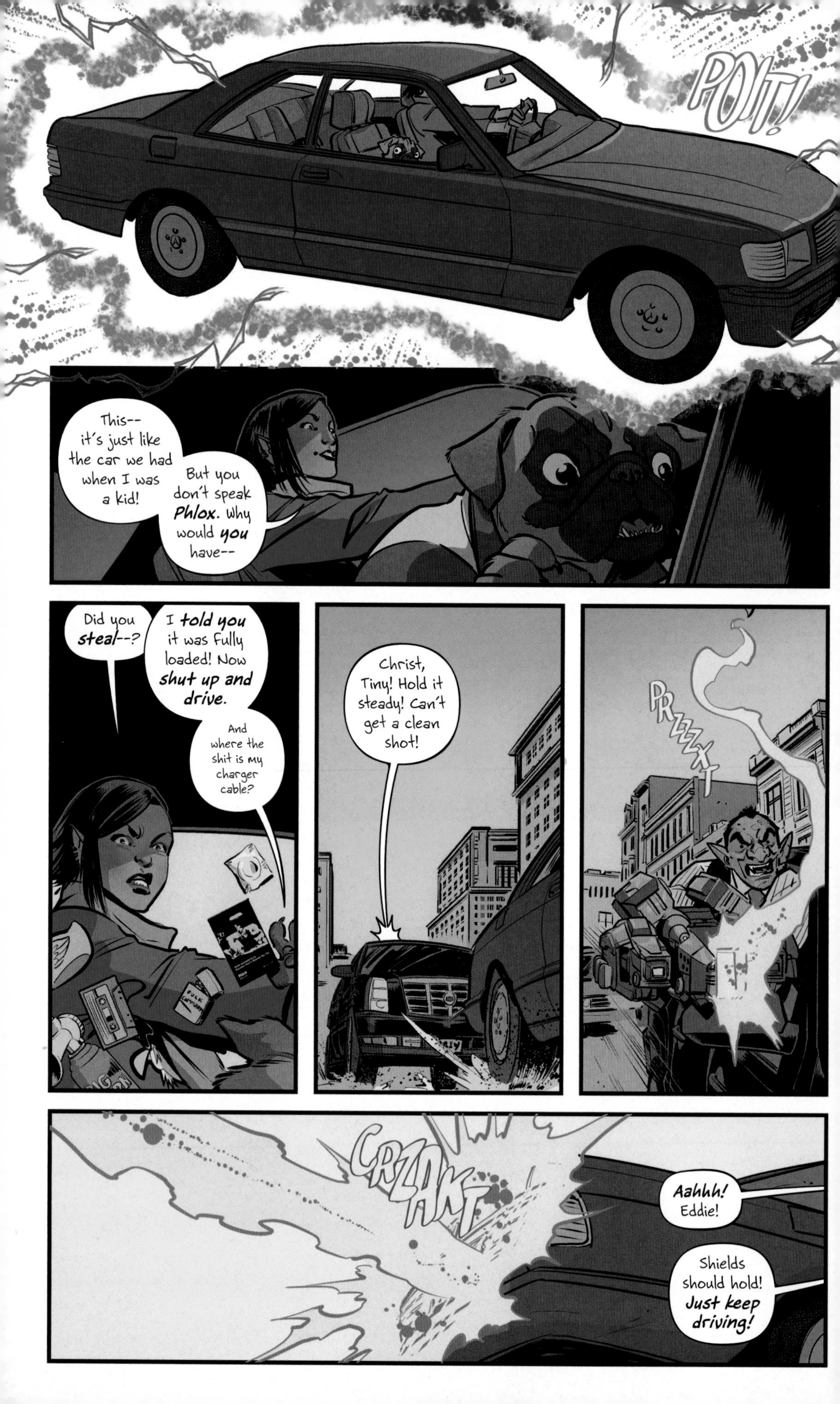

POIT!
This-- it's just like the car we had when I was a kid!
But you don't speak Phlox. Why would you have--
Did you steal--?
I told you it was fully loaded! Now shut up and drive.
And where the shit is my charger cable?
Christ, Tiny! Hold it steady! Can't get a clean shot!
PRZZZXT
CRZAKT
Aahhh! Eddie!
Shields should hold! Just keep driving!

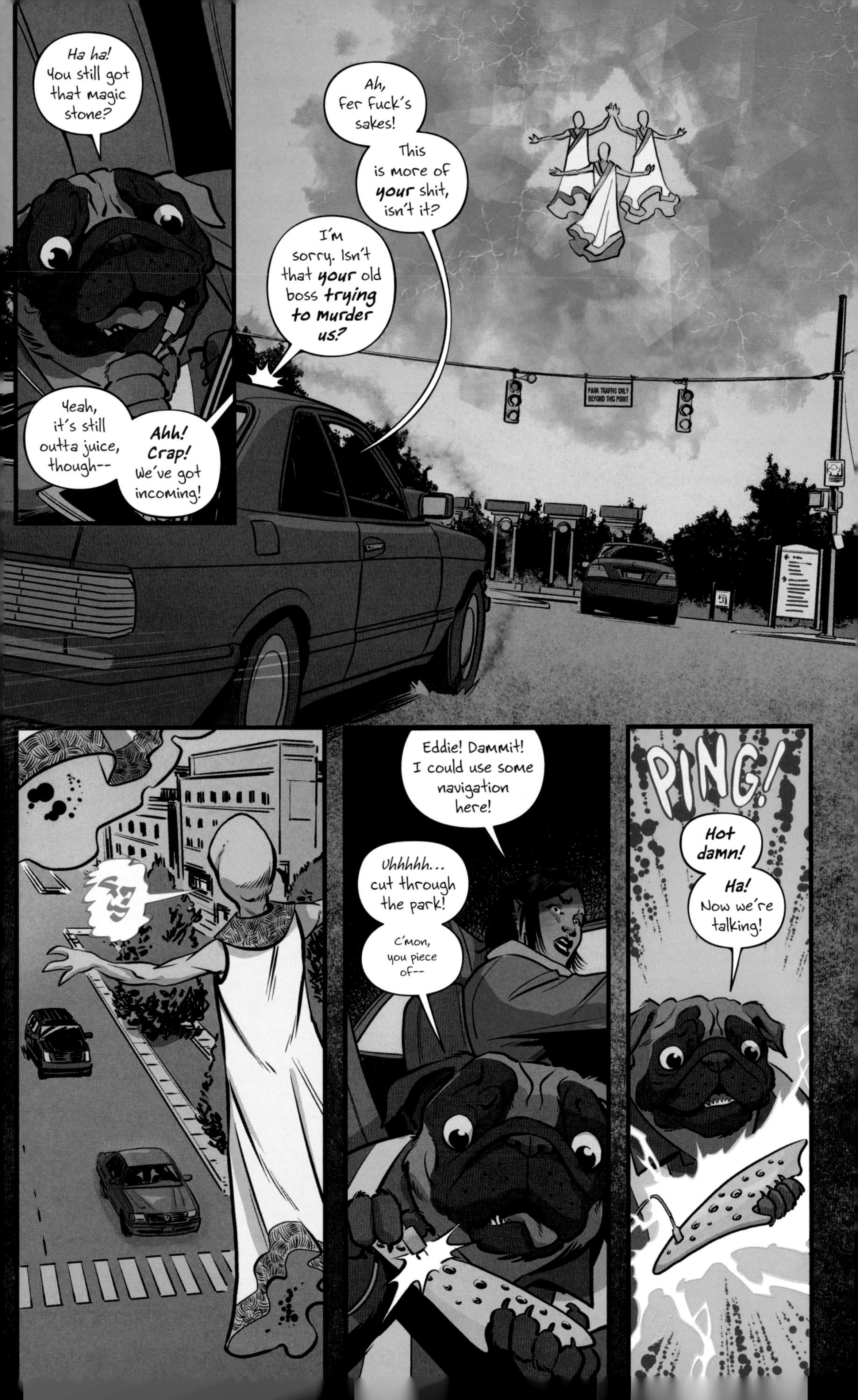
Ha ha! You still got that magic stone?
Yeah, it's still outta juice, though--
Ahh! Crap! We've got incoming!
Ah, fer fuck's sakes!
This is more of your shit, isn't it?
I'm sorry. Isn't that your old boss trying to murder us?
PARK TRAFFIC ONLY BEYOND THIS POINT
Eddie! Dammit! I could use some navigation here!
Uhhhhh... cut through the park!
C'mon, you piece of--
PING!
Hot damn!
Ha! Now we're talking!

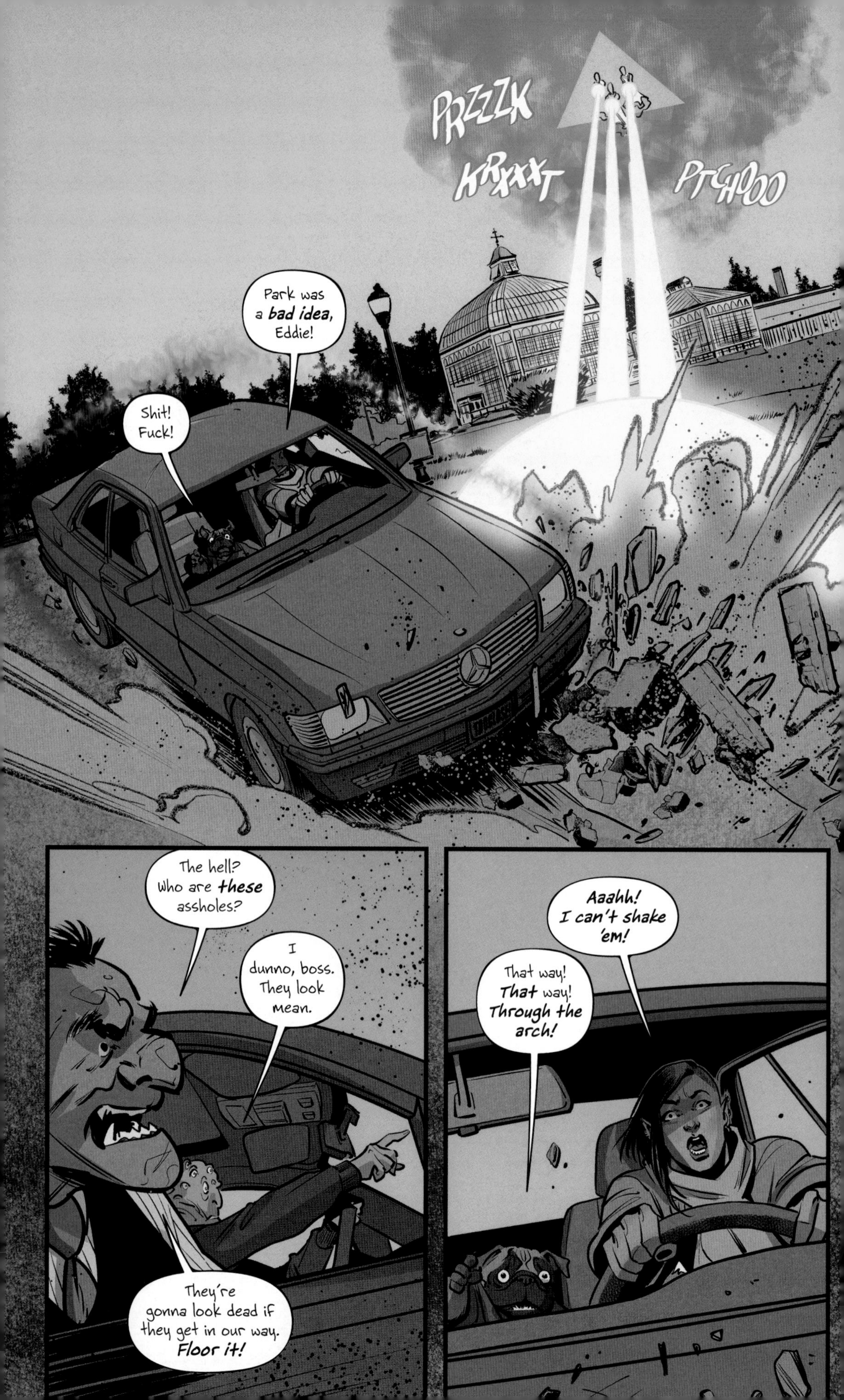
PRZZZK
KRXXXT
PTCHOOO
Park was a *bad idea*, Eddie!
Shit! Fuck!
The hell? Who are *these* assholes?
I dunno, boss. They look mean.
They're gonna look dead if they get in our way. *Floor it!*
Aaahh! I can't shake 'em!
That way! *That* way! Through the arch!

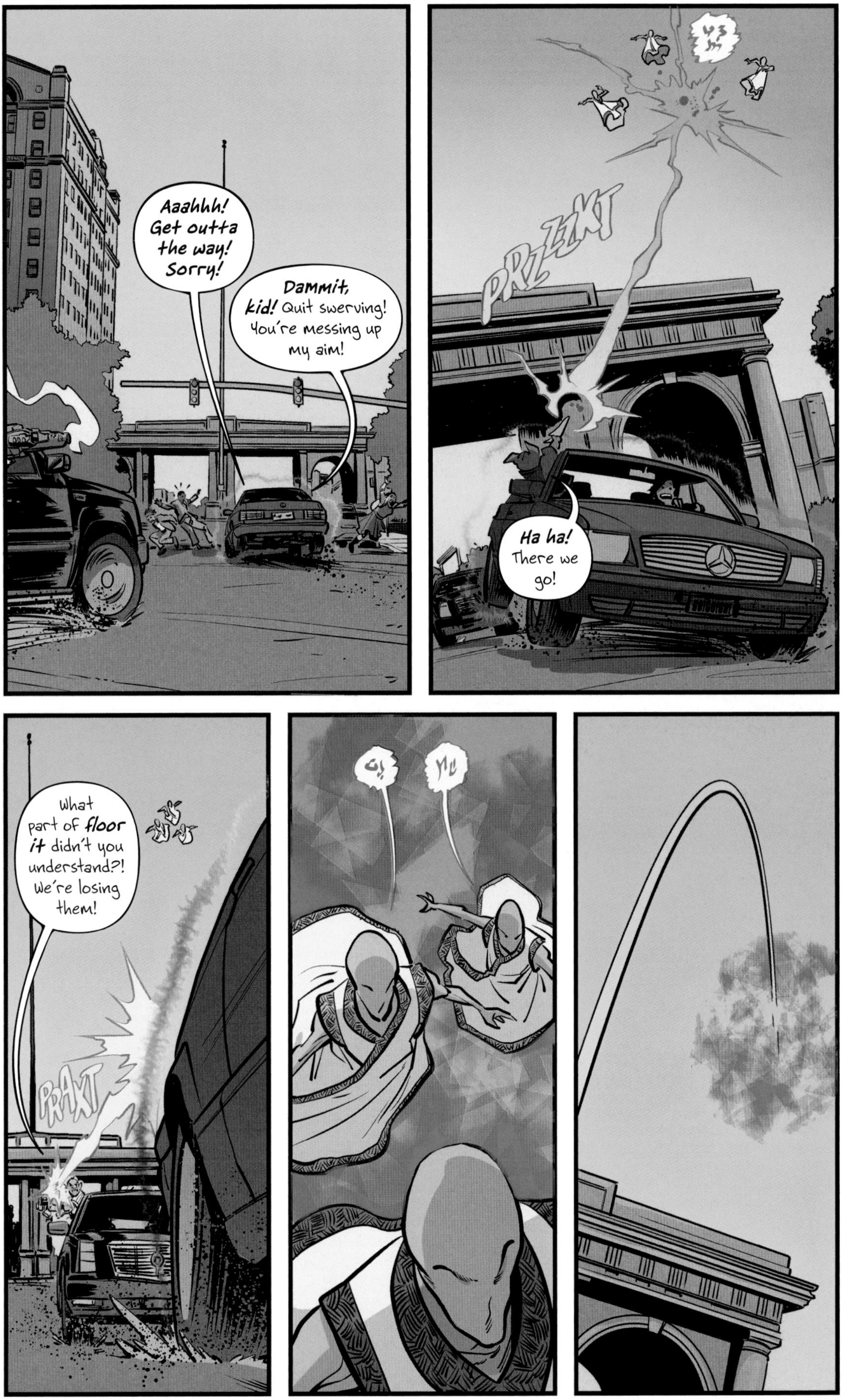
Aaahhh! Get outta the way! Sorry!
Dammit, kid! Quit swerving! You're messing up my aim!
PRZZZKT
Ha ha! There we go!
What part of floor it didn't you understand?! We're losing them!
PRAKT

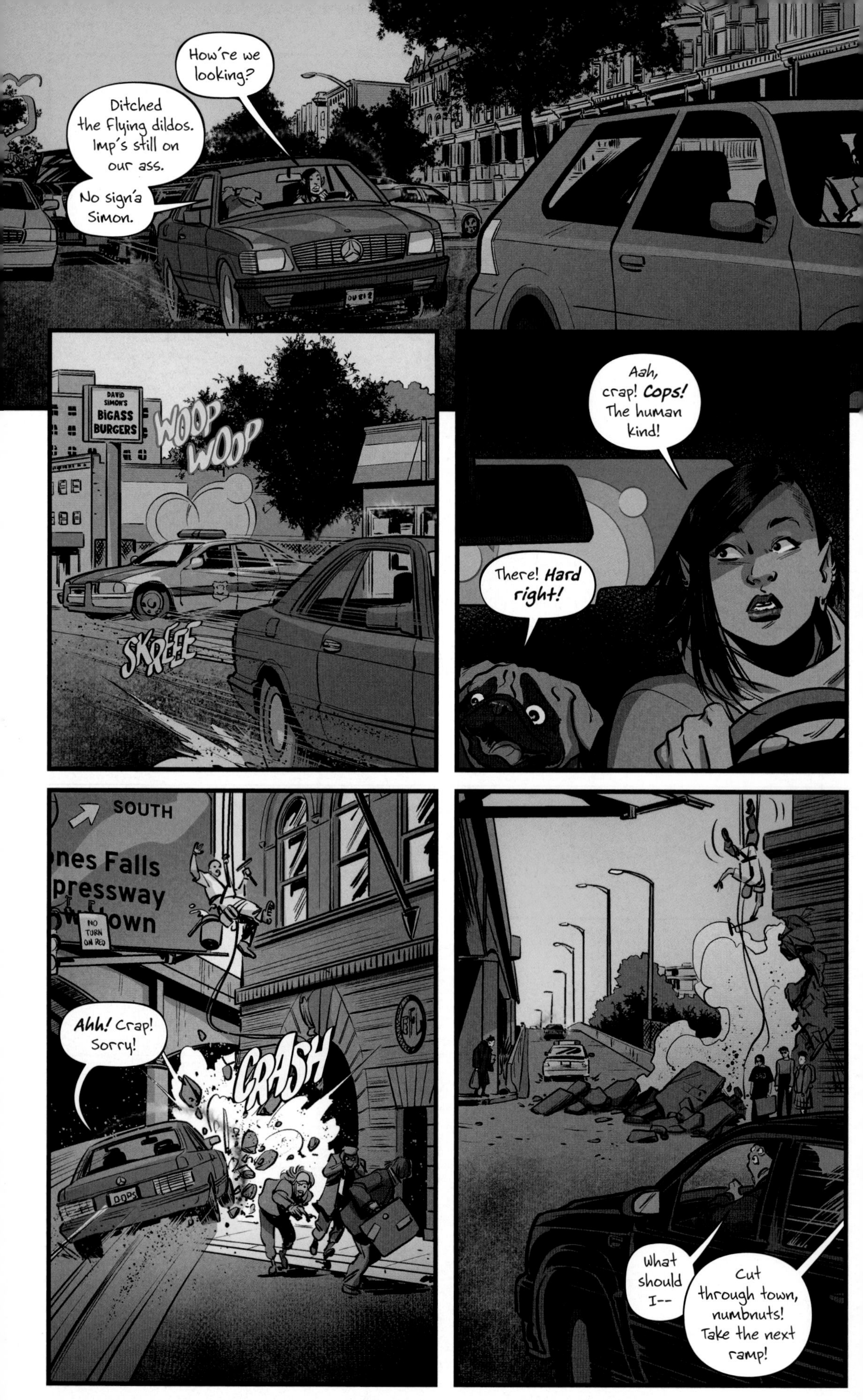
How're we looking?
Ditched the flying dildos. Imp's still on our ass.
No sign'a Simon.
DAVID SIMON'S BIGASS BURGERS
WOOP WOOP
SKREEE
Aah, crap! Cops! The human kind!
There! Hard right!
SOUTH
nes Falls
pressway
own
NO TURN ON RED
Ahh! Crap! Sorry!
CRASH
What should I--
Cut through town, numbnuts! Take the next ramp!

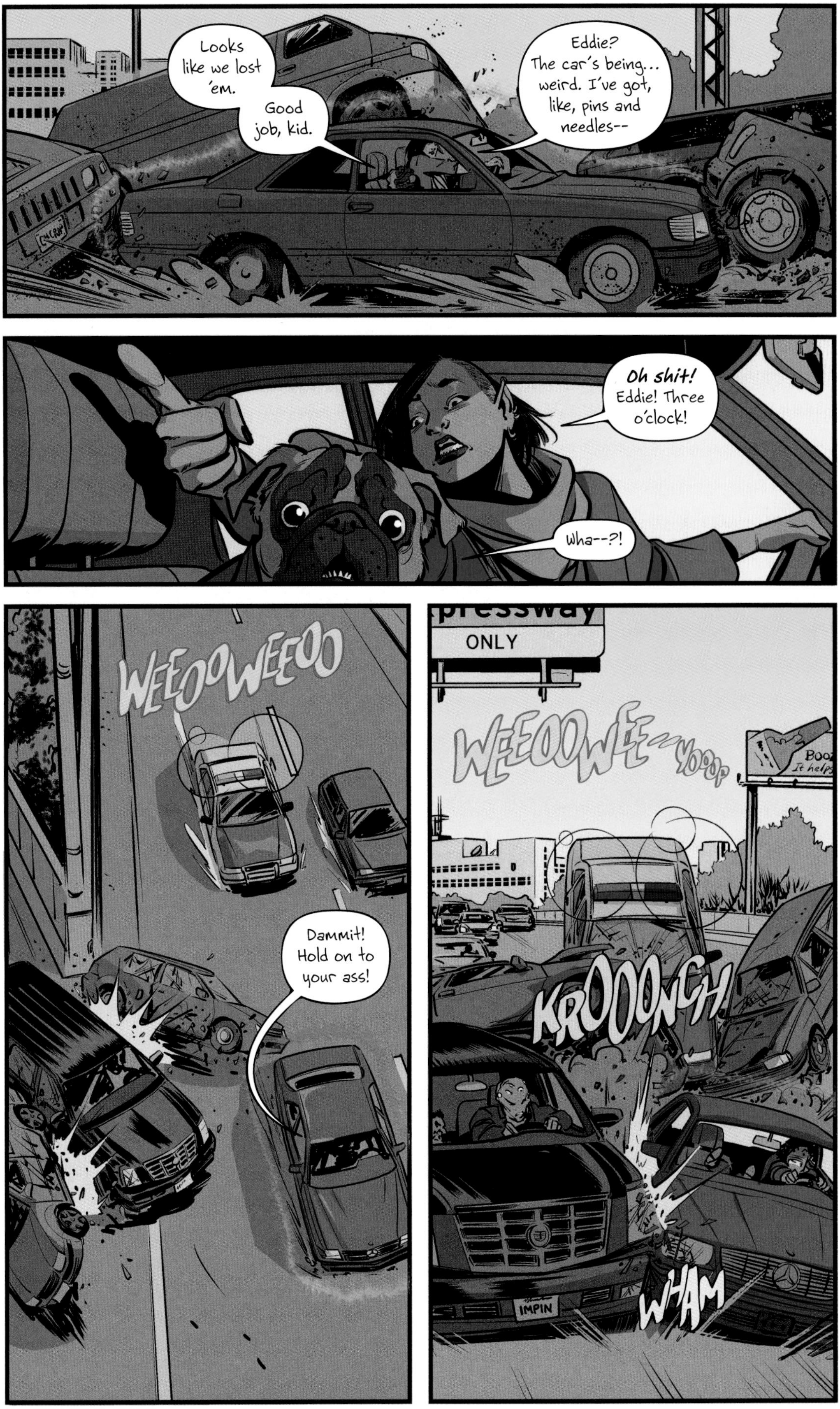

Looks like we lost 'em.
Good job, kid.
Eddie? The car's being... weird. I've got, like, pins and needles--
Oh shit! Eddie! Three o'clock!
Wha--?!
WEEOOWEEOO
Dammit! Hold on to your ass!
ONLY
WEEOOWEE--yooop
KROOOONCH
IMPIN
WHAM

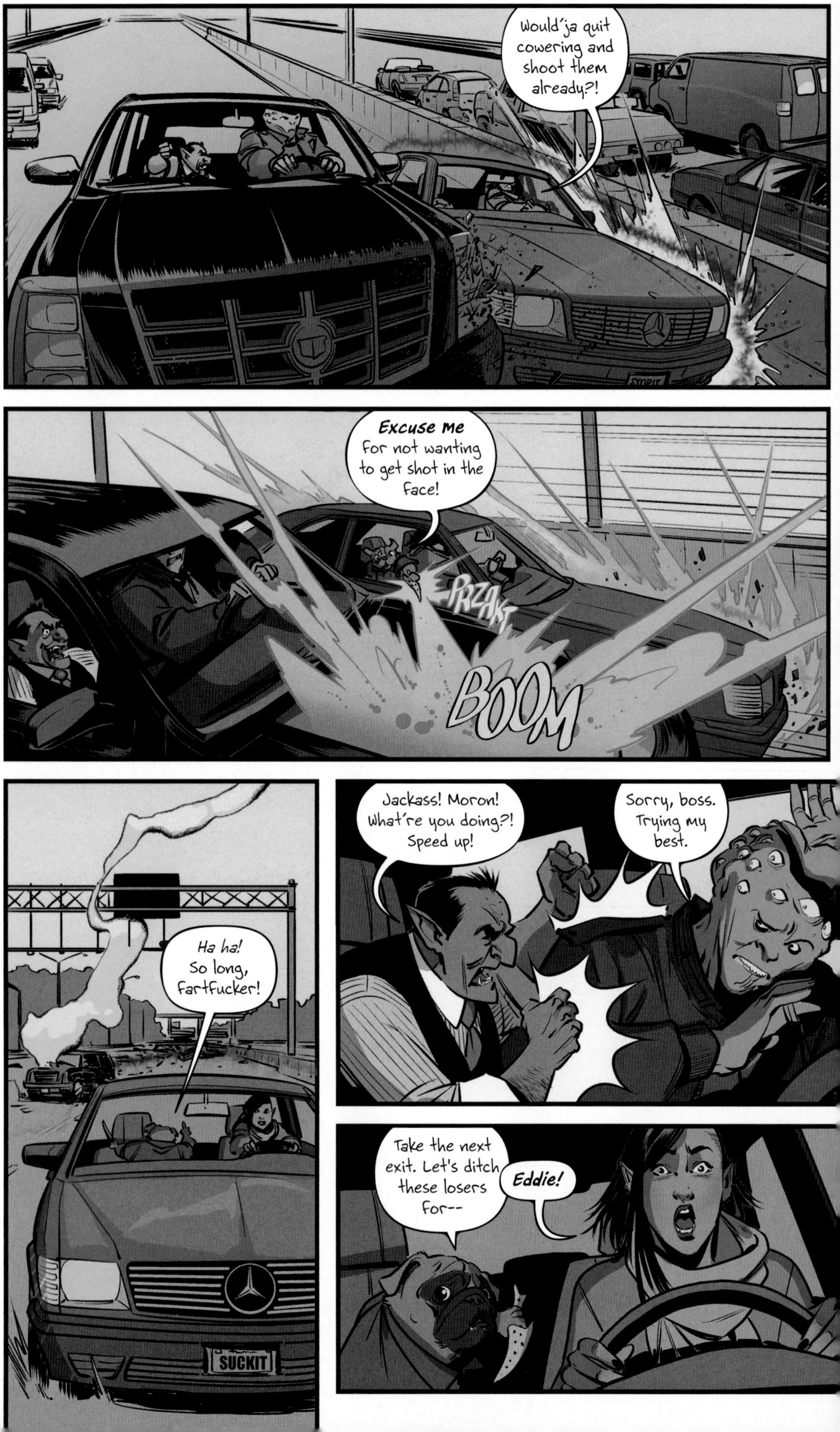

Would'ja quit cowering and shoot them already?!
STOPIT
Excuse me for not wanting to get shot in the face!
PRZAKT
BOOM
Ha ha! So long, Fartfucker!
SUCKIT
Jackass! Moron! What're you doing?! Speed up!
Sorry, boss. Trying my best.
Take the next exit. Let's ditch these losers for--
Eddie!

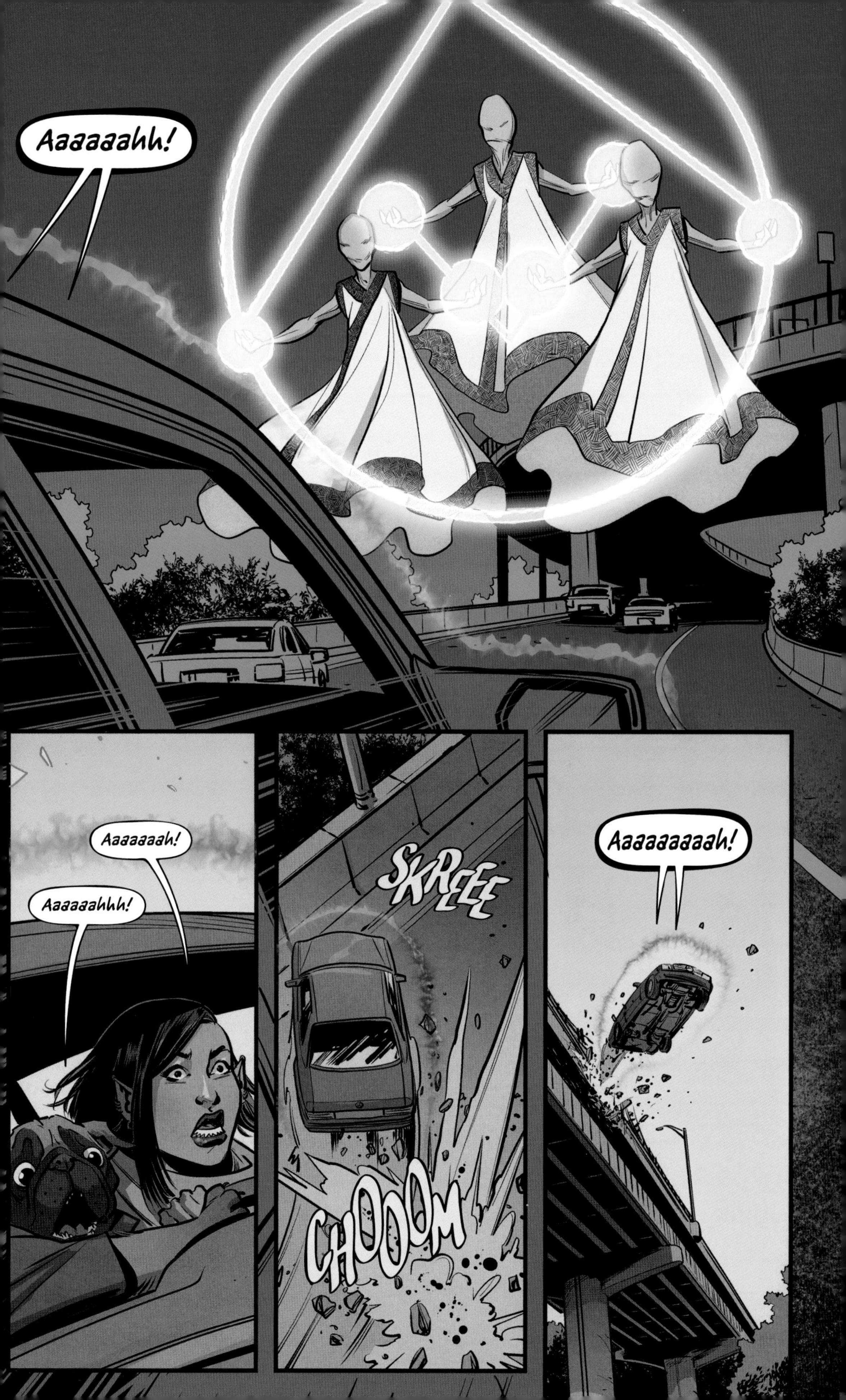
Aaaaaaahh!
Aaaaaaah!
Aaaaaahhh!
SKREEE
CHOOOM
Aaaaaaaaah!

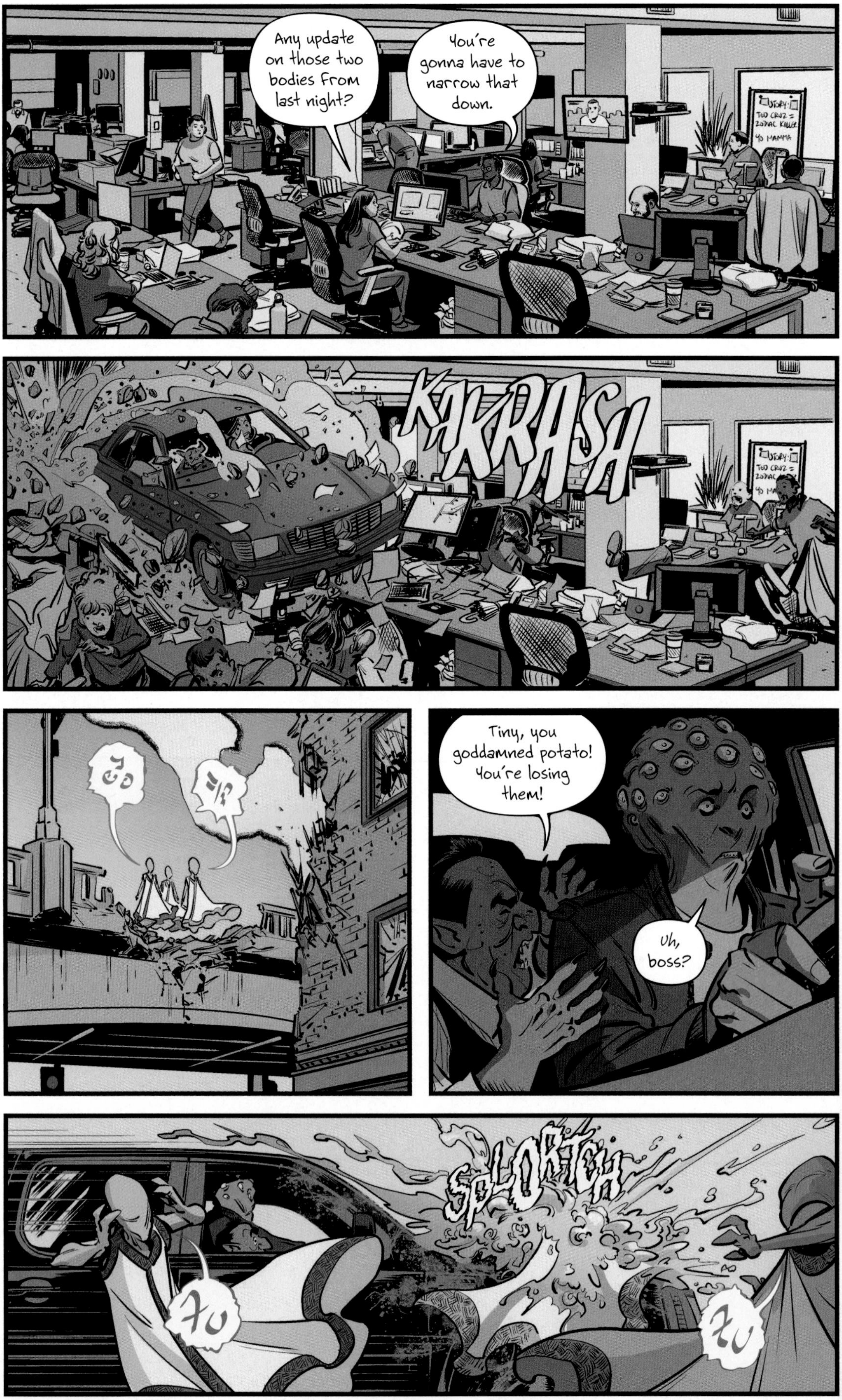
Any update on those two bodies from last night?
You're gonna have to narrow that down.
STORY:
TED CRUZ = ZODIAC KILLER
YO MAMMA
KAKRASH
Tiny, you goddamned potato! You're losing them!
Uh, boss?
SPLORTCH

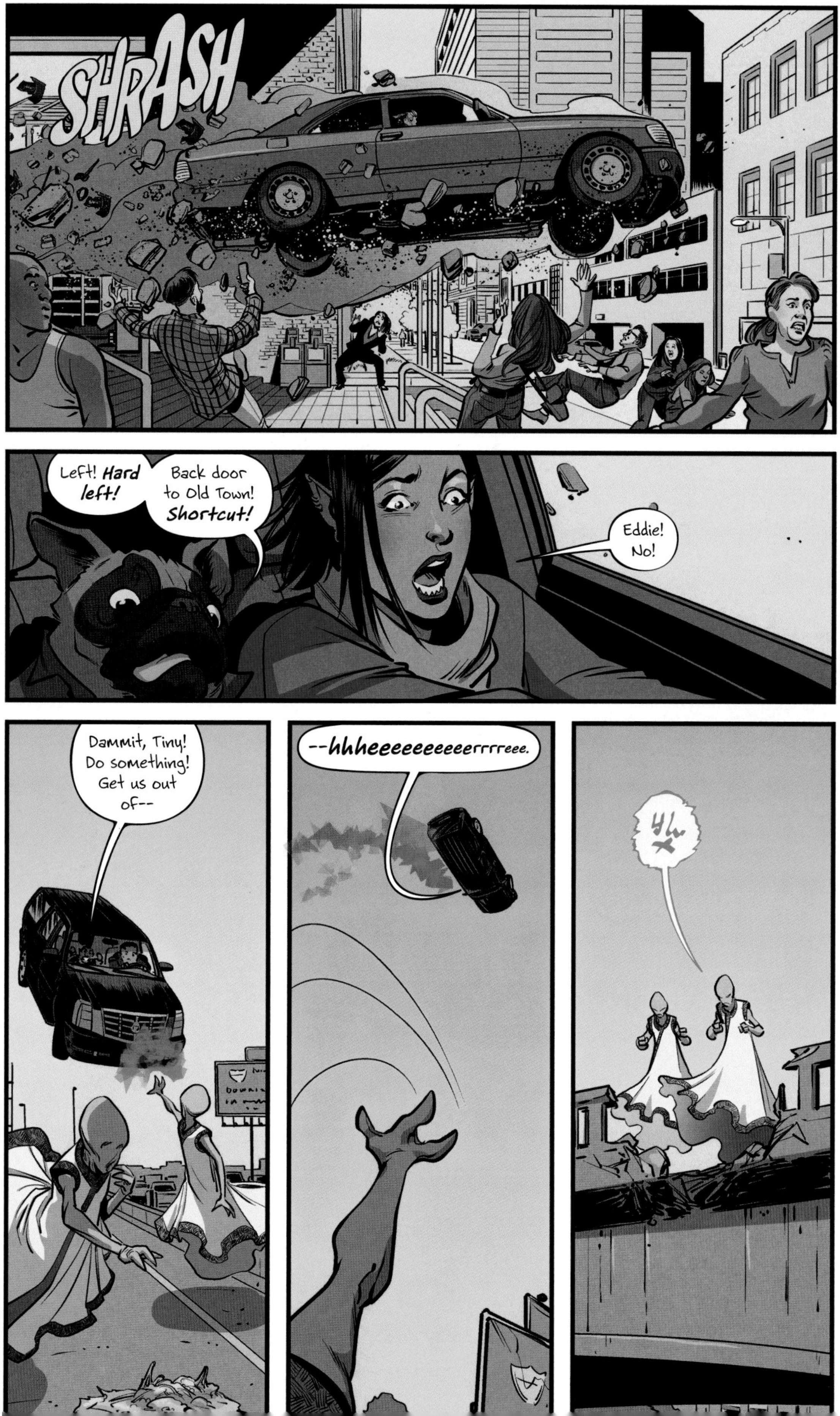
SHRASH
Left! Hard left!
Back door to Old Town! Shortcut!
Eddie! No!
Dammit, Tiny! Do something! Get us out of--
--hhheeeeeeeeeerrrreee.

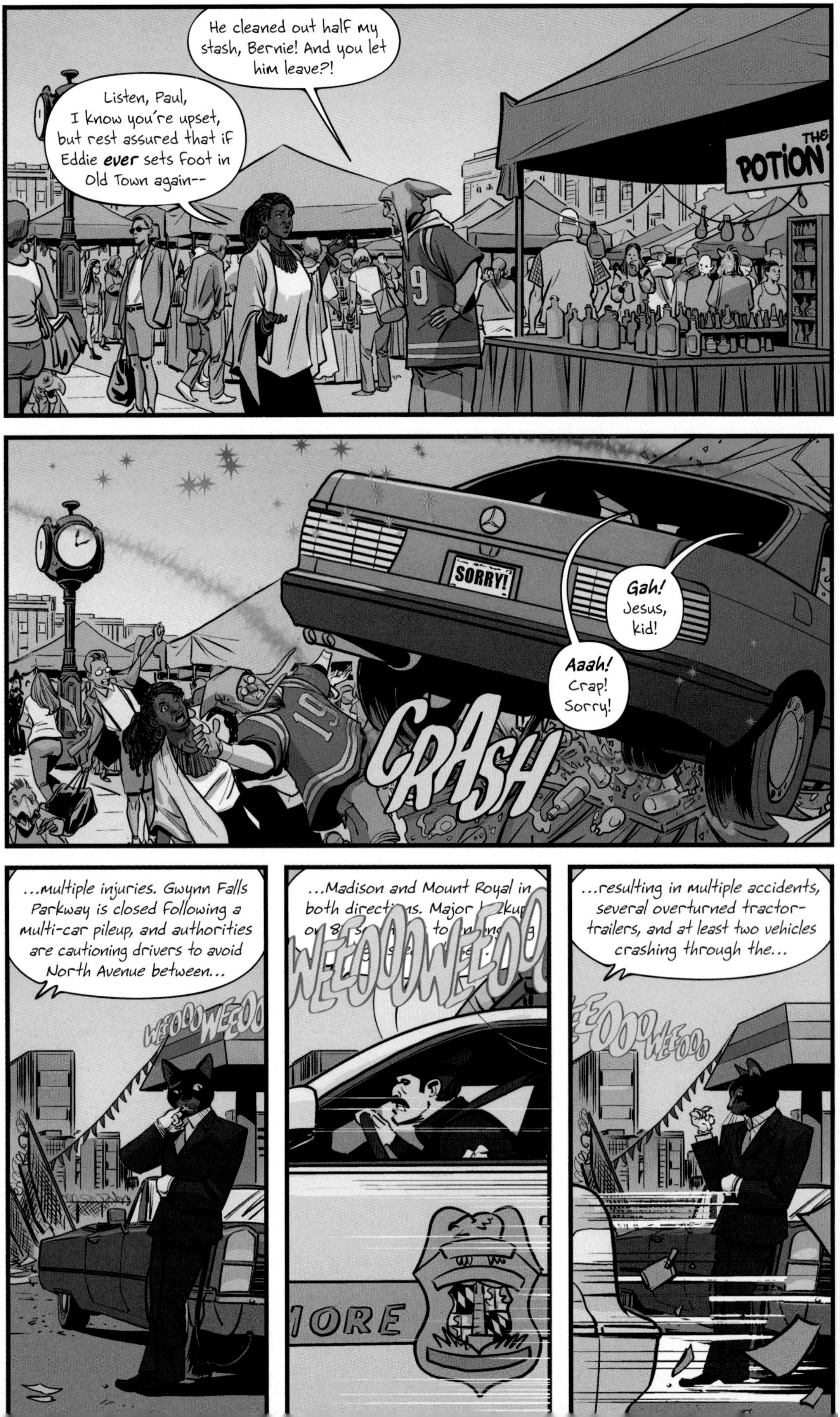
THE POTION
He cleaned out half my stash, Bernie! And you let him leave?!
Listen, Paul, I know you're upset, but rest assured that if Eddie **ever** sets foot in Old Town again--
SORRY!
Gah! Jesus, kid!
Aaah! Crap! Sorry!
CRASH
...multiple injuries. Gwynn Falls Parkway is closed following a multi-car pileup, and authorities are cautioning drivers to avoid North Avenue between...
...Madison and Mount Royal in both
...resulting in multiple accidents, several overturned tractor-trailers, and at least two vehicles crashing through the...

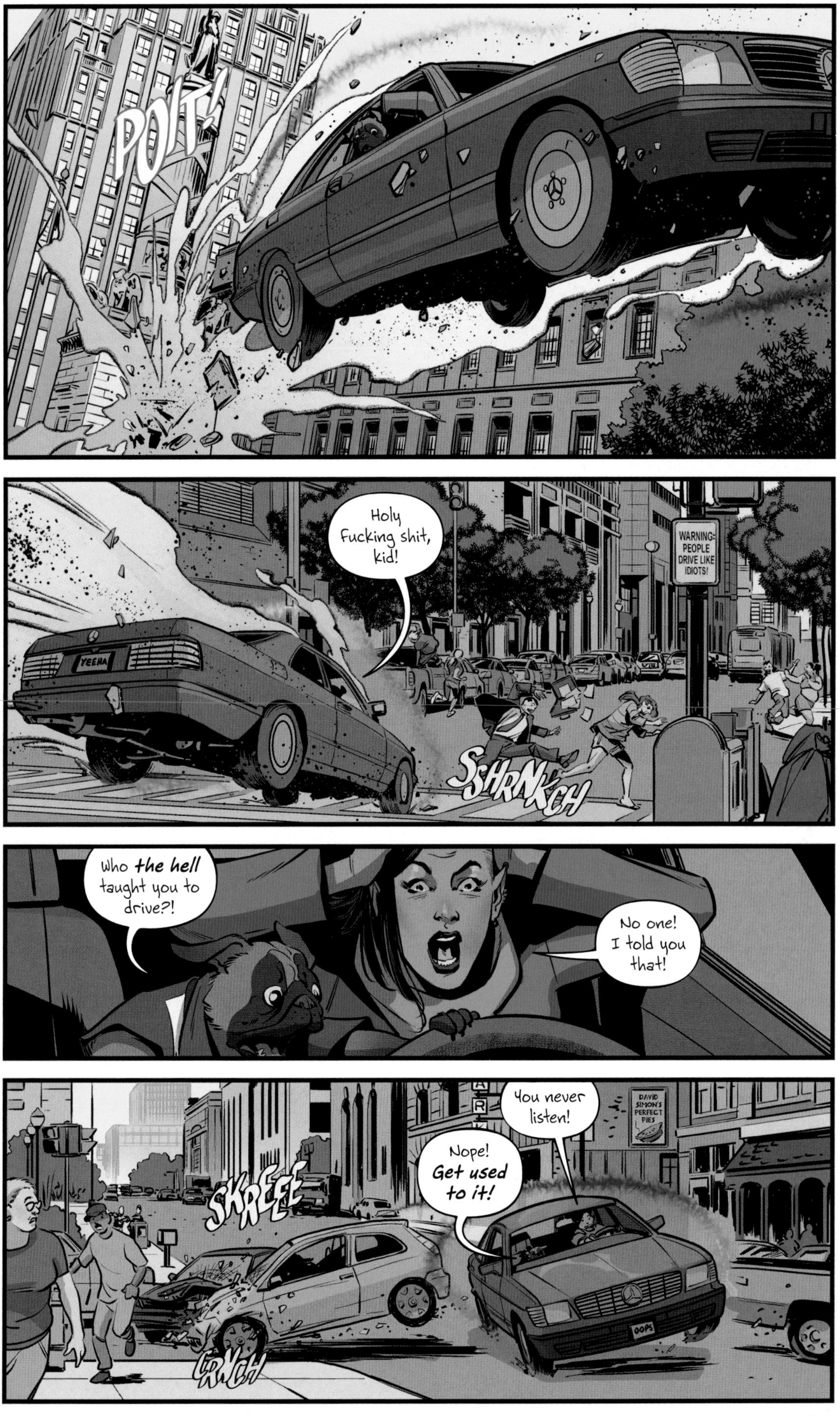
POIT!
Holy Fucking shit, kid!
YEEHA
WARNING: PEOPLE DRIVE LIKE IDIOTS!
SSHRNKCH
Who **the hell** taught you to drive?!
No one! I told you that!
DAVID SIMON'S PERFECT PIES
You never listen!
Nope! **Get used to it!**
SKREEE
OOPS
CRNCH

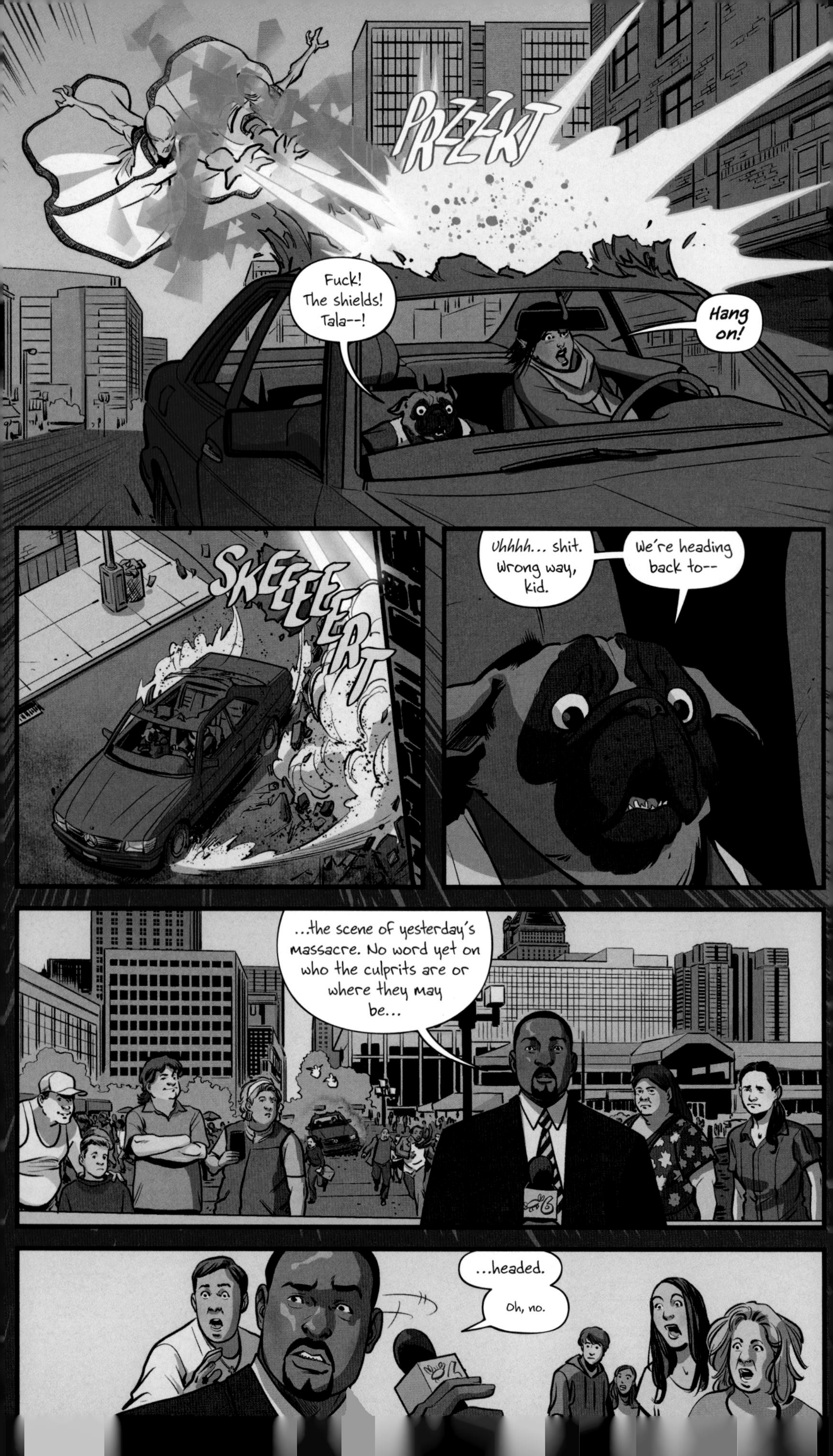
PRZZZKT
Fuck! The shields! Tala--!
Hang on!
SKEEEEERT
Uhhhh... shit. Wrong way, kid.
We're heading back to--
...the scene of yesterday's massacre. No word yet on who the culprits are or where they may be...
...headed.
Oh, no.

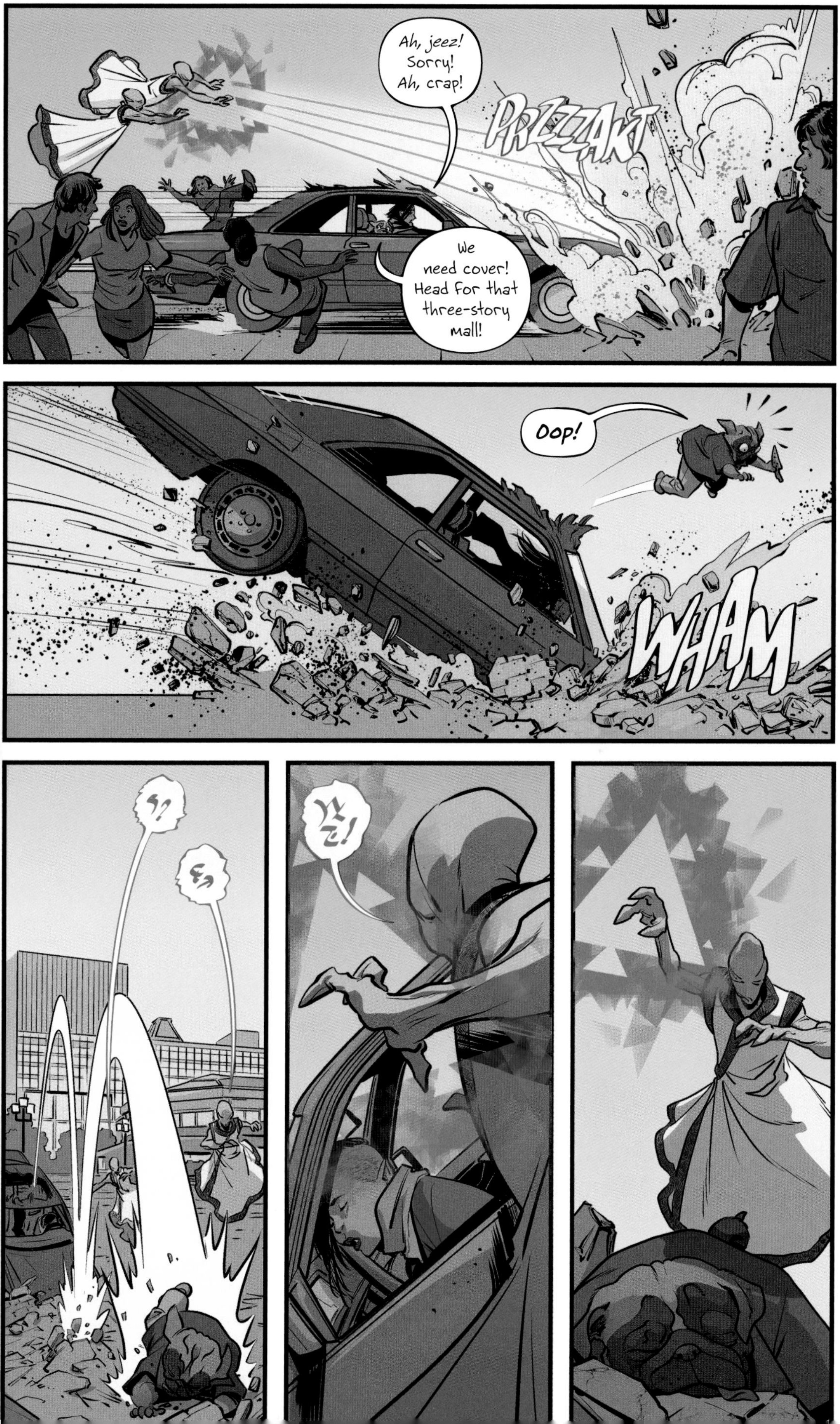
Ah, jeez! Sorry! Ah, crap!
PRZZZAKT
We need cover! Head for that three-story mall!
Oop!
WHAM

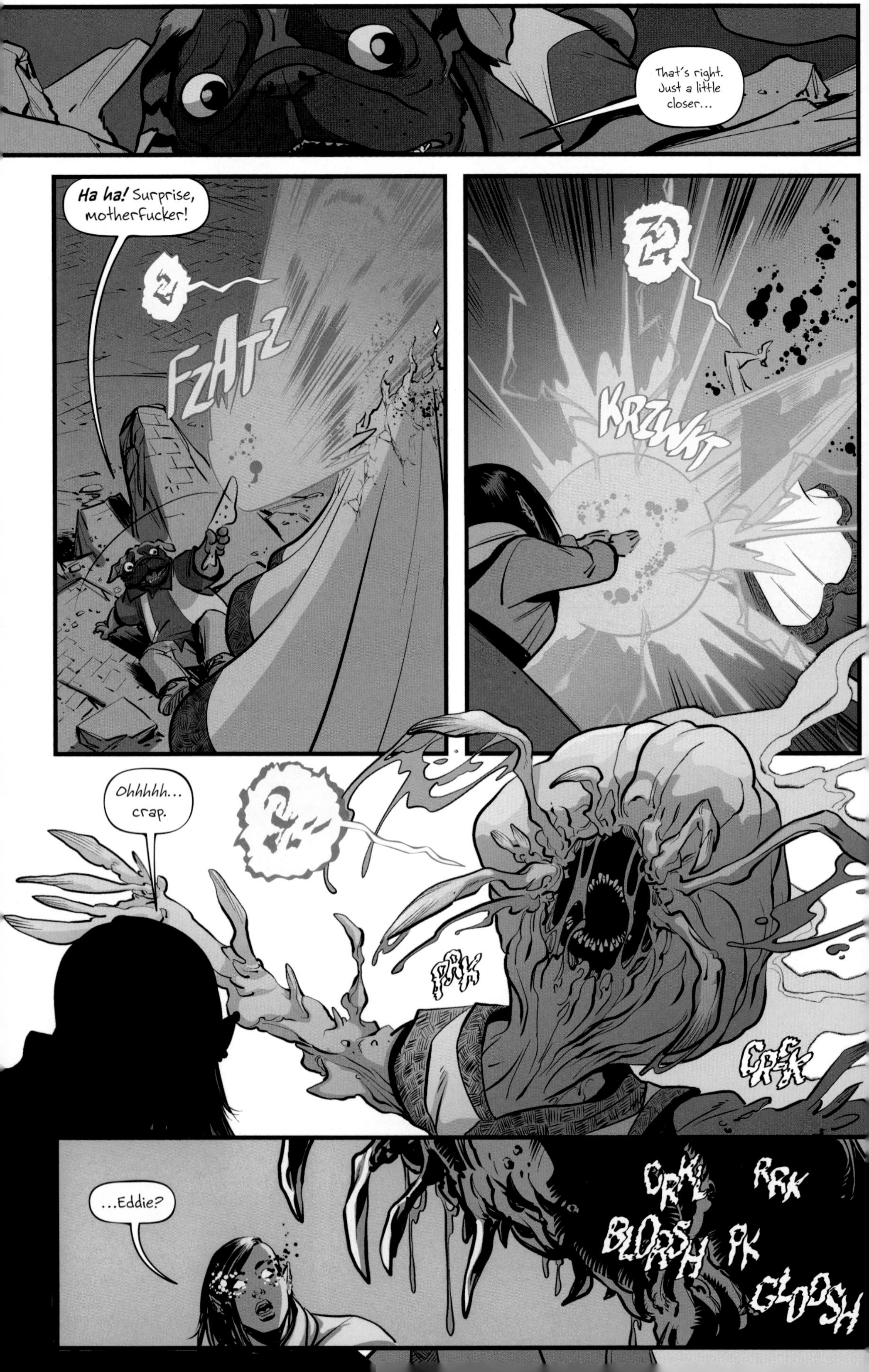
That's right. Just a little closer...
Ha ha! Surprise, motherfucker!
FZATZ
KRZWKT
Ohhhhh... crap.
RRK
CREEK
...Eddie?
CRKL
RRK
BLOOSH
PK
GLOOSH

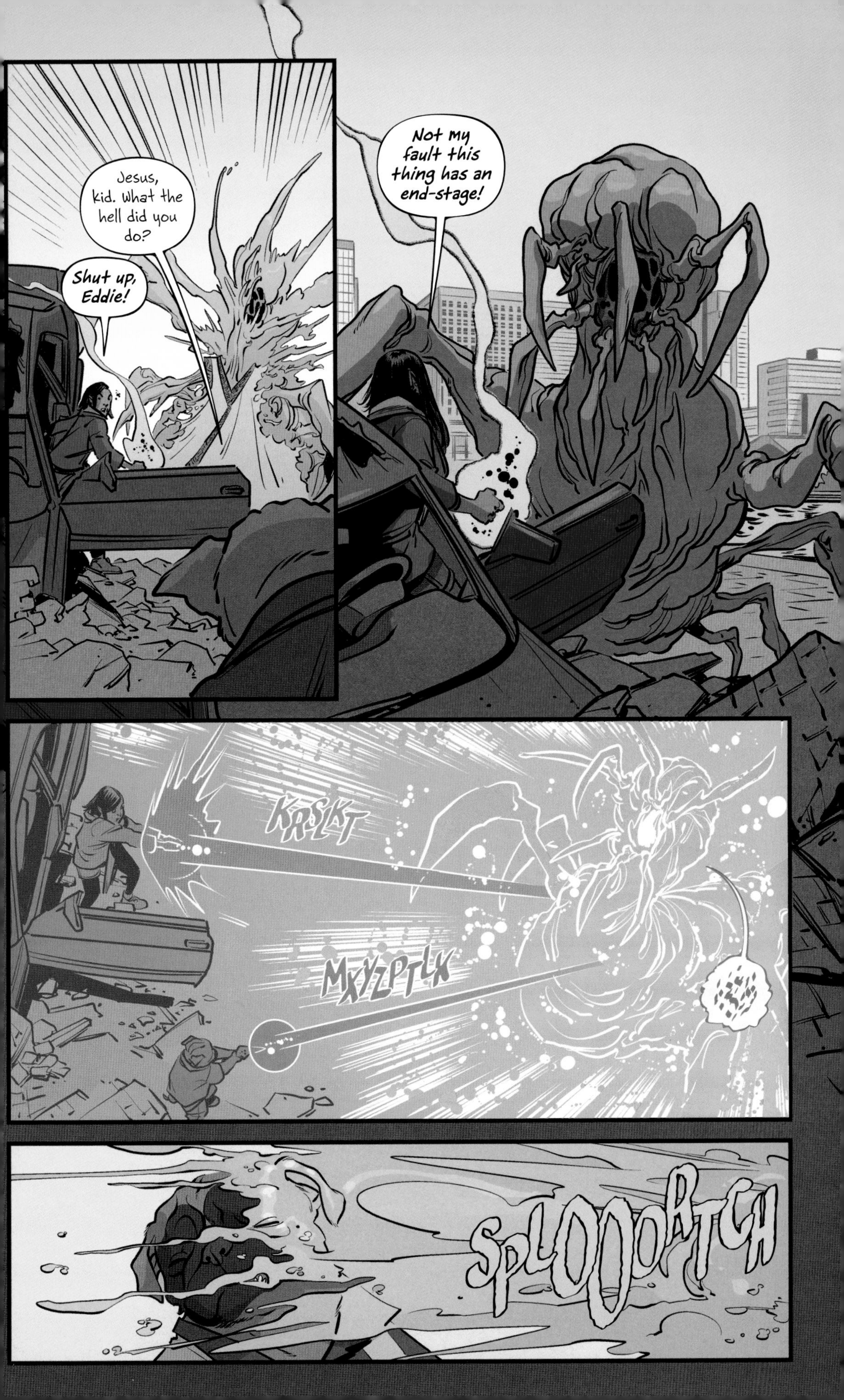
Jesus, kid. What the hell did you do?
Shut up, Eddie!
Not my fault this thing has an end-stage!
KRSLKT
MXYZPTLK
SPLOOOORTCH

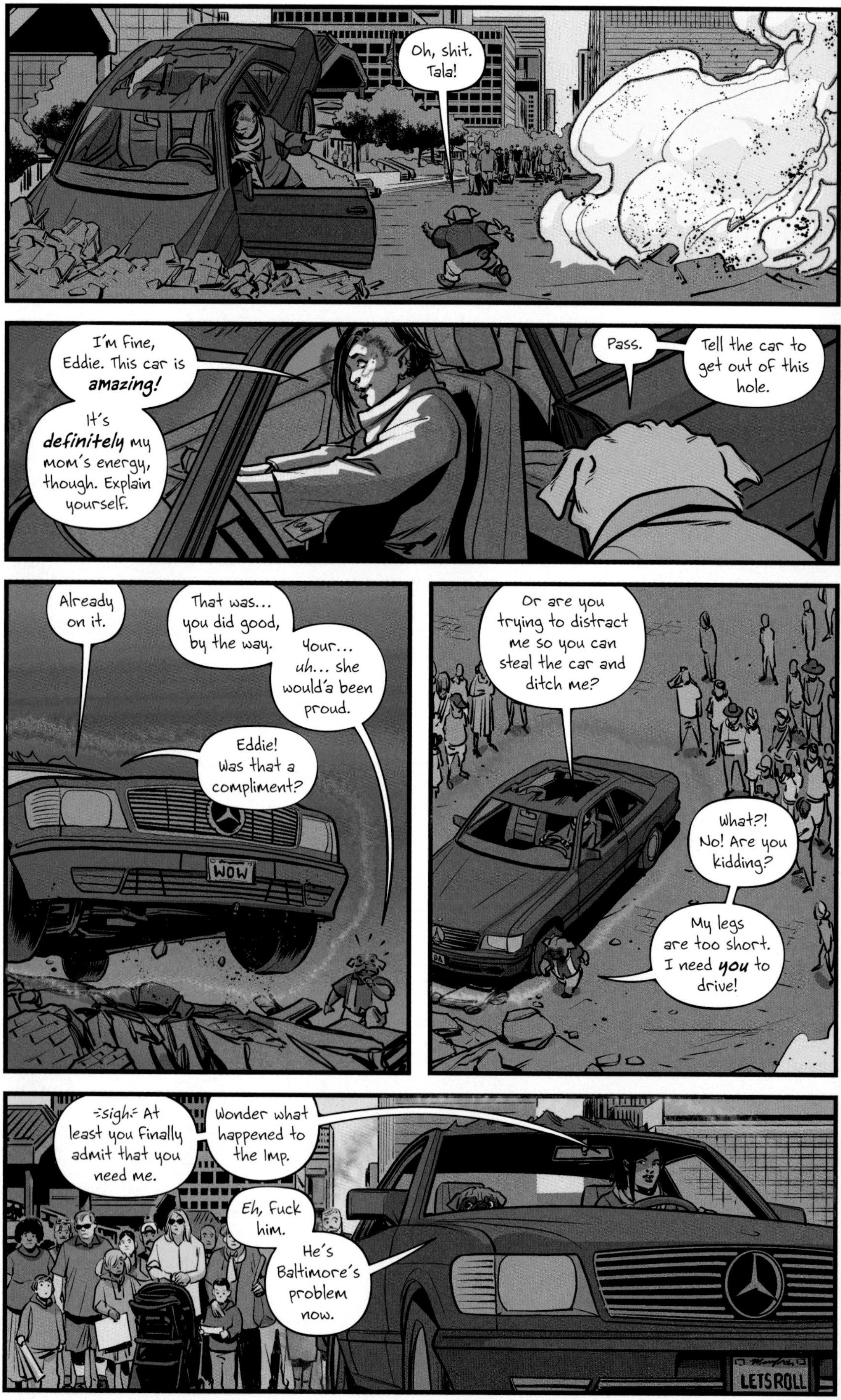
Oh, shit. Tala!
I'm fine, Eddie. This car is **amazing!**
It's **definitely** my mom's energy, though. Explain yourself.
Pass.
Tell the car to get out of this hole.
Already on it.
That was... you did good, by the way.
Your... uh... she would'a been proud.
Eddie! Was that a compliment?
WOW
Or are you trying to distract me so you can steal the car and ditch me?
What?! No! Are you kidding?
My legs are too short. I need **you** to drive!
=sigh= At least you finally admit that you need me.
Wonder what happened to the Imp.
Eh, fuck him.
He's Baltimore's problem now.
LETSROLL

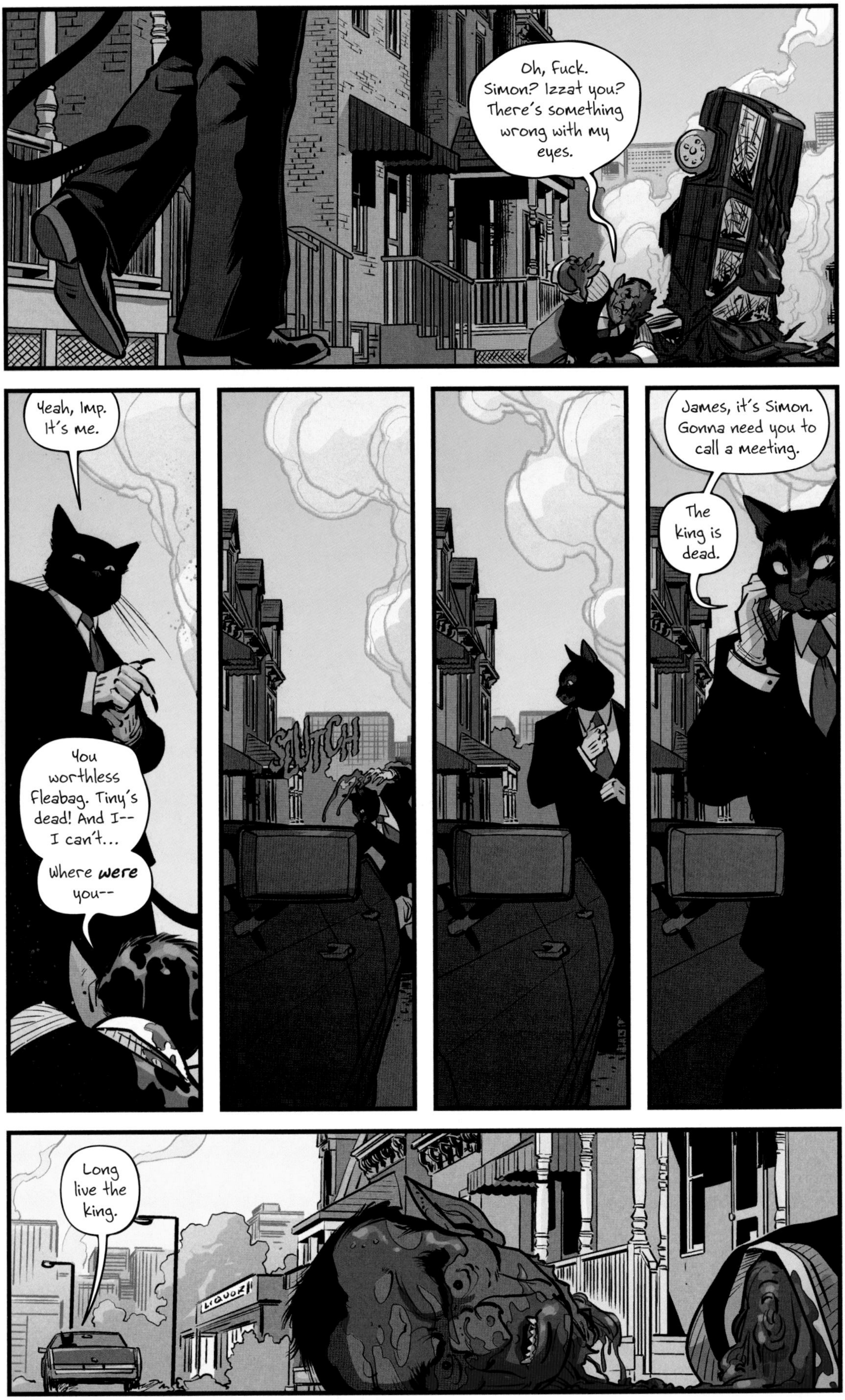
Oh, Fuck. Simon? Izzat you? There's something wrong with my eyes.
Yeah, Imp. It's me.
You worthless Fleabag. Tiny's dead! And I-- I can't...
Where **were** you--
SLUTCH
James, it's Simon. Gonna need you to call a meeting.
The king is dead.
Long live the king.
LIQUOR

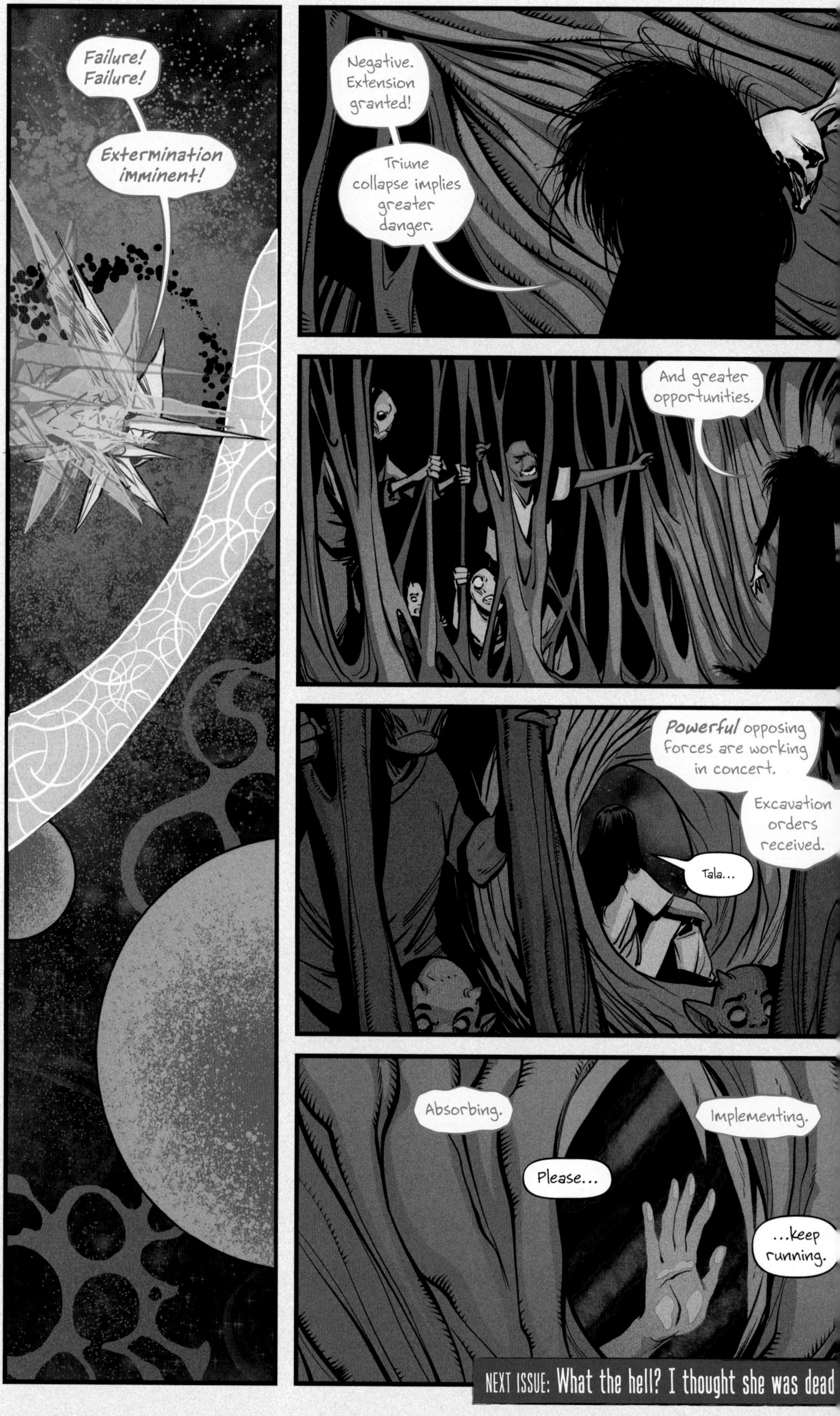
Failure! Failure!
Extermination imminent!
Negative. Extension granted!
Triune collapse implies greater danger.
And greater opportunities.
Powerful opposing forces are working in concert.
Excavation orders received.
Tala...
Absorbing.
Implementing.
Please...
...keep running.
NEXT ISSUE: What the hell? I thought she was dead

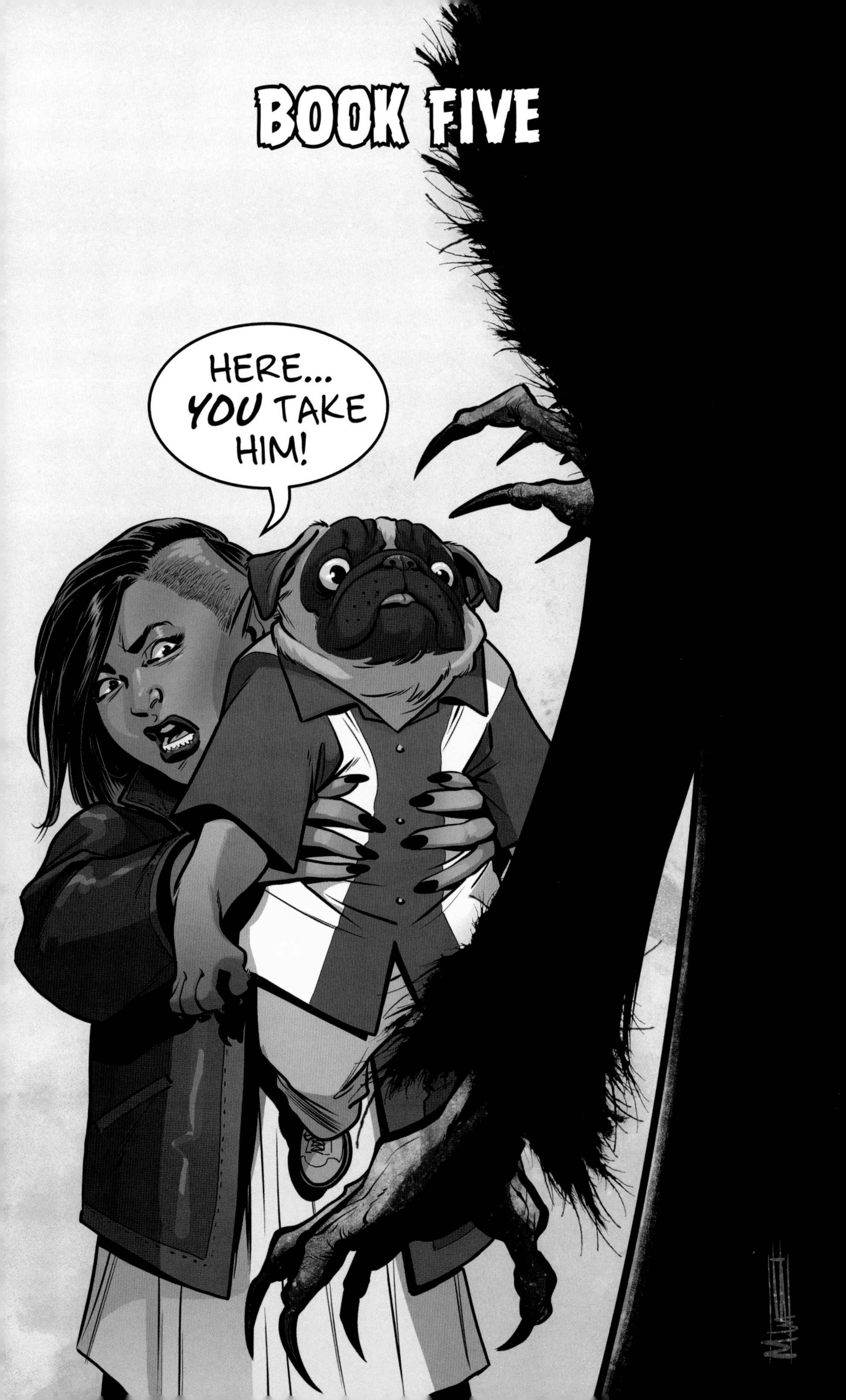
BOOK FIVE
HERE... YOU TAKE HIM!

SPECIAL EDITION COVER ART BY EVAN DORKIN & ADDISON DUKE.

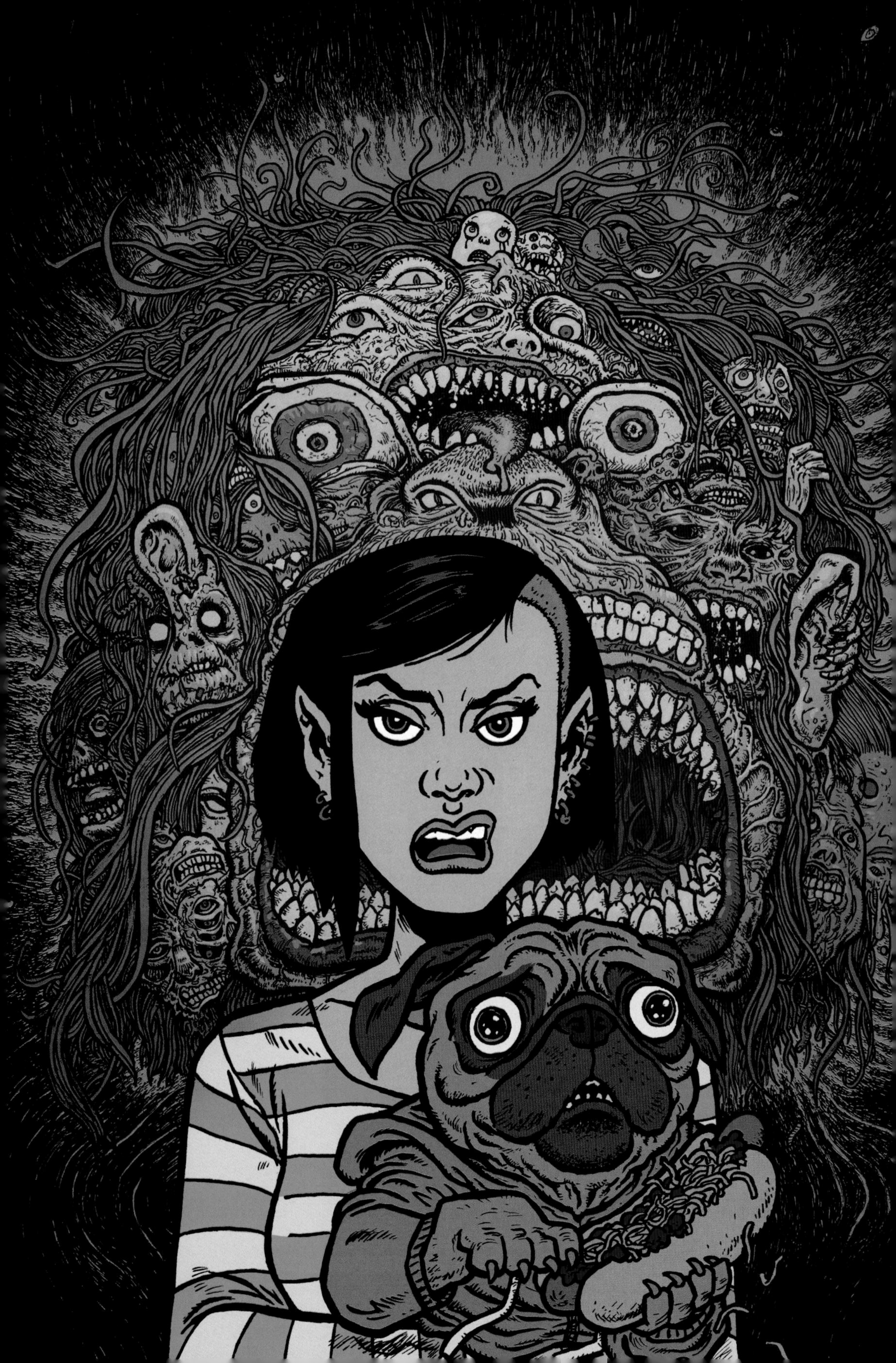

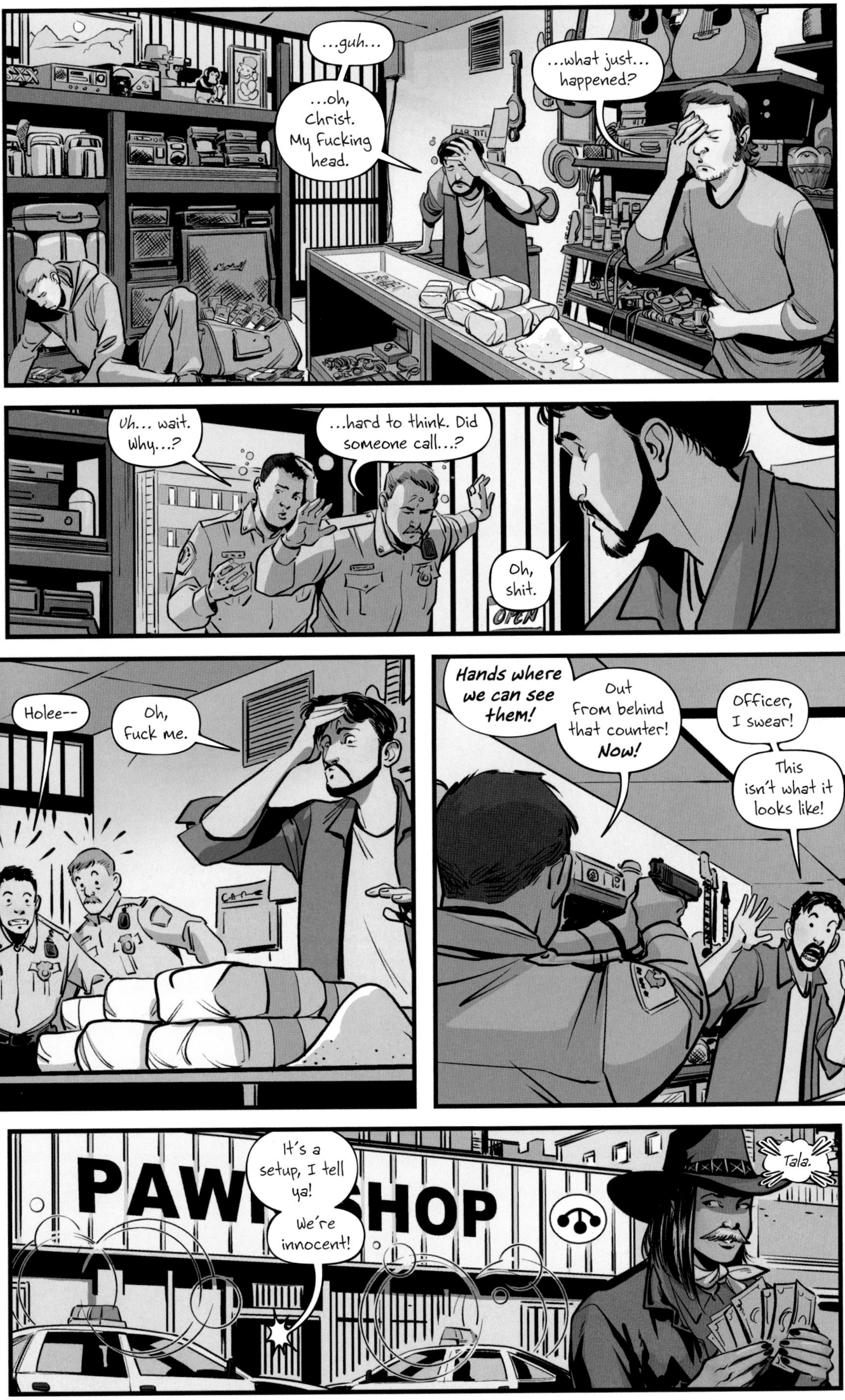
...guh...
...oh, Christ. My fucking head.
...what just... happened?
Uh... wait. Why...?
...hard to think. Did someone call...?
Oh, shit.
OPEN
Holee--
Oh, fuck me.
Hands where we can see them!
Out from behind that counter! **Now!**
Officer, I swear!
This isn't what it looks like!
PAWN SHOP
It's a setup, I tell ya!
We're innocent!
Tala.

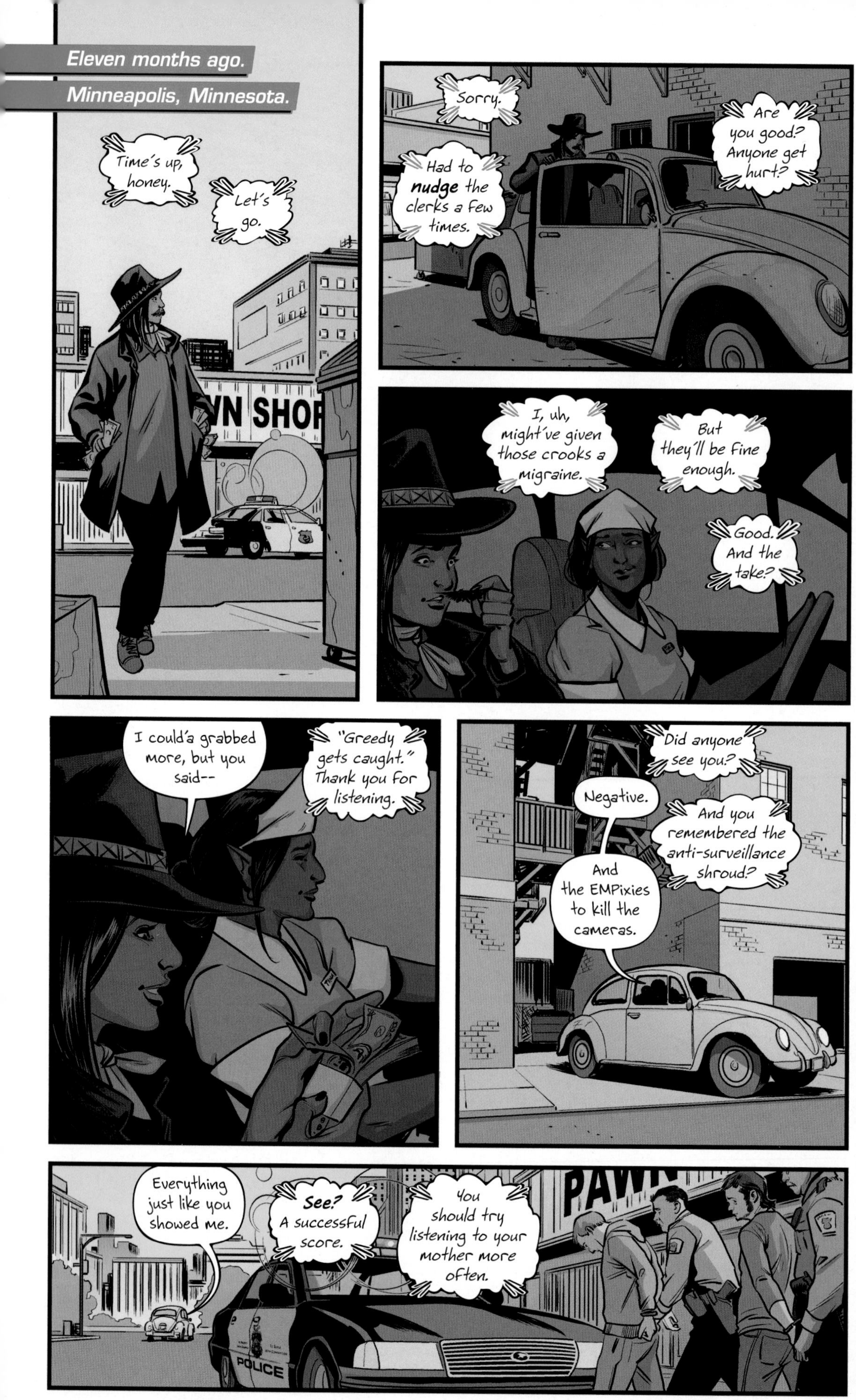
Eleven months ago.
Minneapolis, Minnesota.
Time's up, honey.
Let's go.
PAWN SHOP
Sorry.
Had to **nudge** the clerks a few times.
Are you good? Anyone get hurt?
I, uh, might've given those crooks a migraine.
But they'll be fine enough.
Good. And the take?
I could'a grabbed more, but you said--
"Greedy gets caught." Thank you for listening.
Did anyone see you?
Negative.
And you remembered the anti-surveillance shroud?
And the EMPixies to kill the cameras.
Everything just like you showed me.
See? A successful score.
You should try listening to your mother more often.
PAWN
POLICE

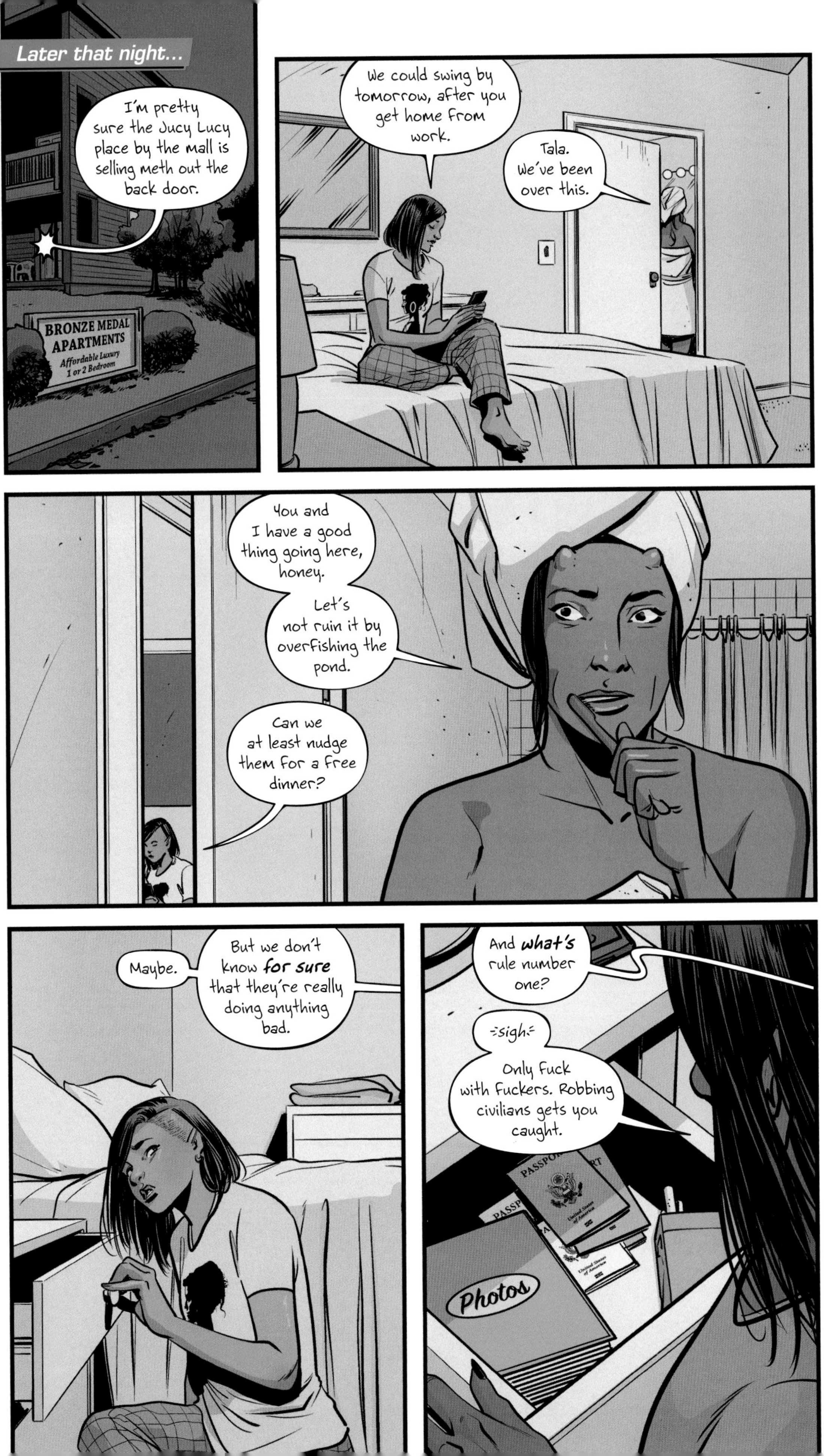
Later that night...
I'm pretty sure the Jucy Lucy place by the mall is selling meth out the back door.
BRONZE MEDAL APARTMENTS
Affordable Luxury
1 or 2 Bedroom
We could swing by tomorrow, after you get home from work.
Tala. We've been over this.
You and I have a good thing going here, honey.
Let's not ruin it by overfishing the pond.
Can we at least nudge them for a free dinner?
Maybe.
But we don't know *for sure* that they're really doing anything bad.
And ***what's*** rule number one?
sigh
Only fuck with fuckers. Robbing civilians gets you caught.
PASSPORT
Photos

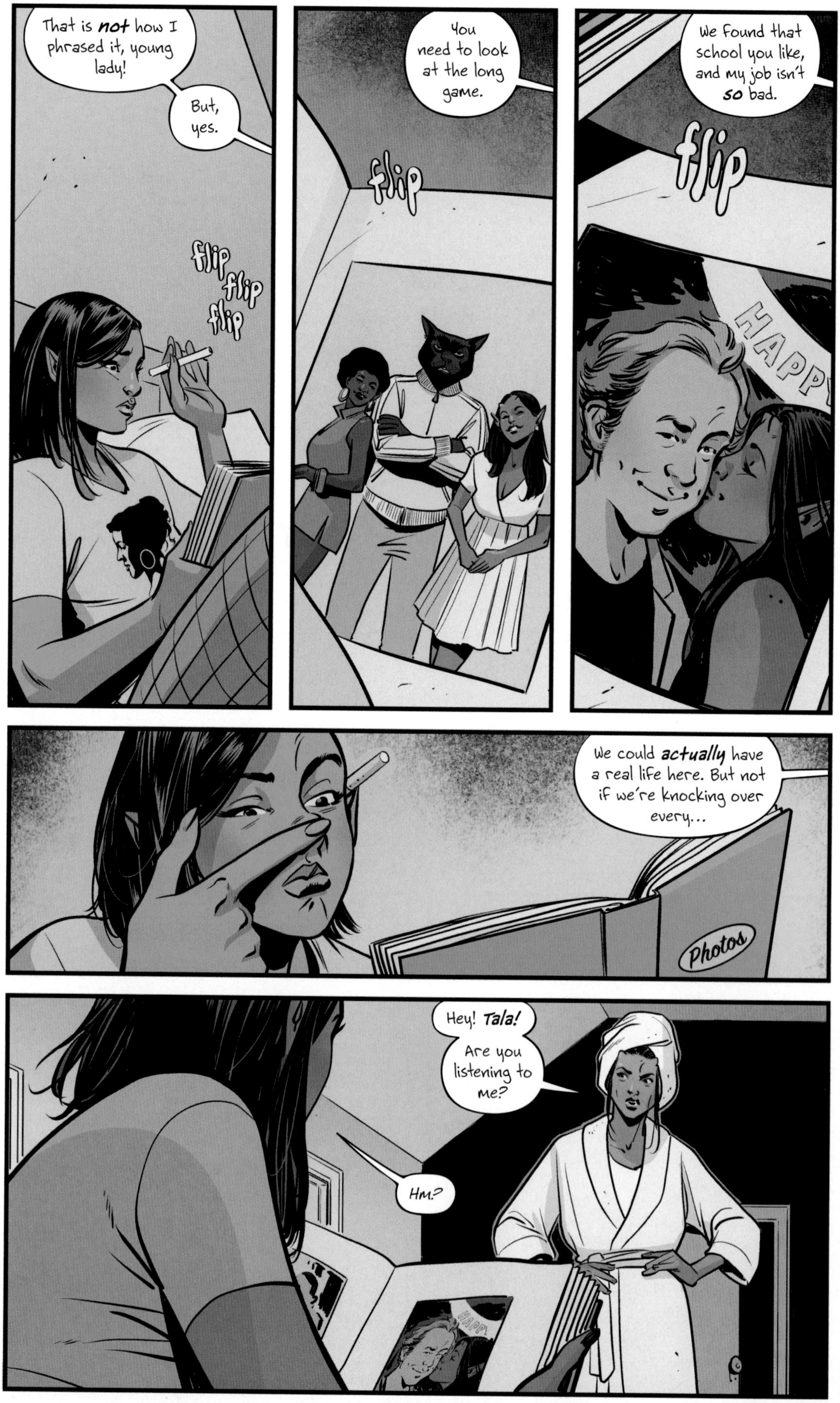
That is **not** how I phrased it, young lady!
But, yes.
flip flip flip
You need to look at the long game.
flip
We found that school you like, and my job isn't **so** bad.
flip
HAPPY
We could **actually** have a real life here. But not if we're knocking over every...
Photos
Hey! *Tala!*
Are you listening to me?
Hm?
HAPPY

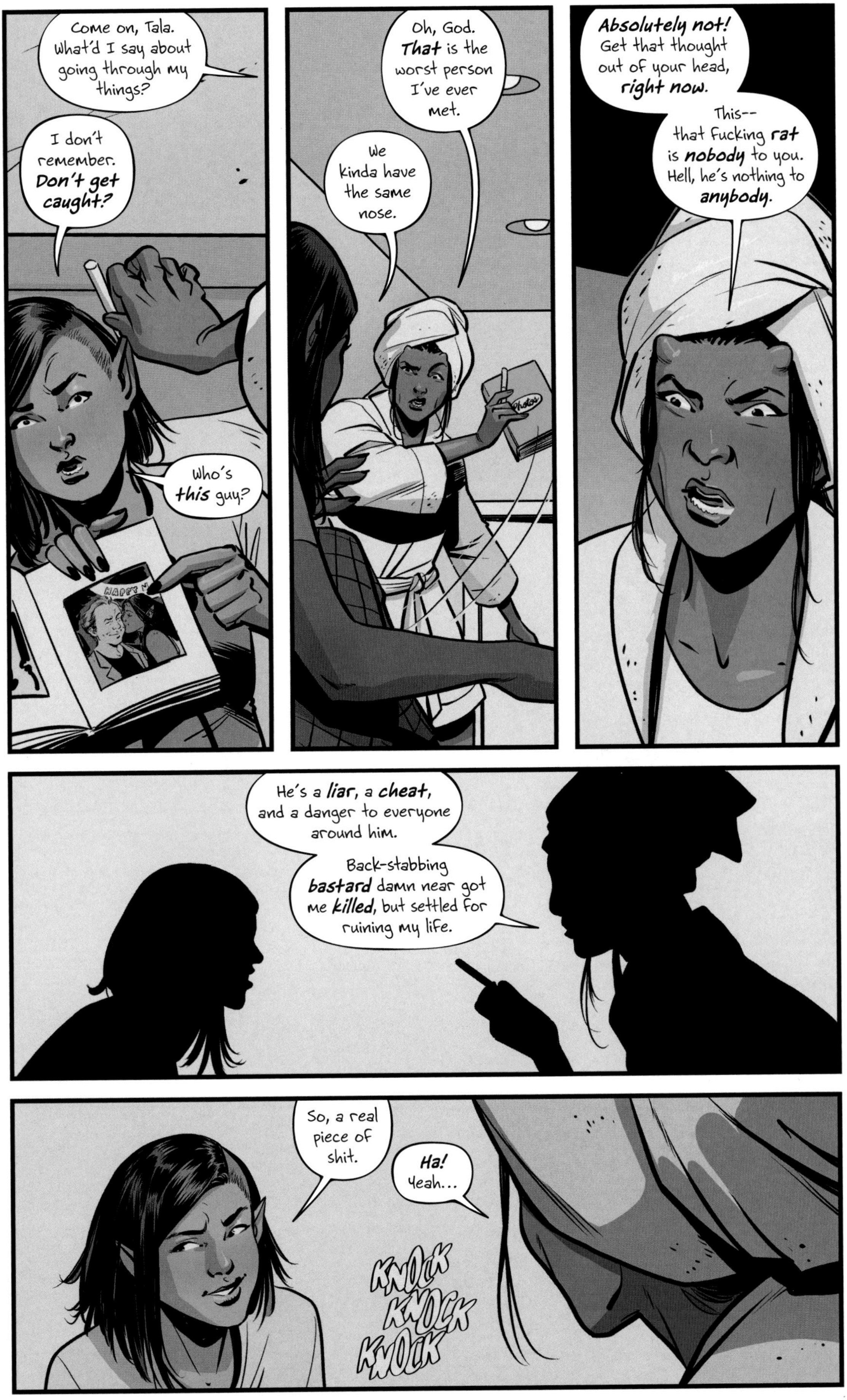
Come on, Tala. What'd I say about going through my things?
I don't remember. Don't get caught?
Who's this guy?
HAPPY N
Oh, God. That is the worst person I've ever met.
We kinda have the same nose.
Photos
Absolutely not! Get that thought out of your head, right now.
This-- that fucking rat is nobody to you. Hell, he's nothing to anybody.
He's a liar, a cheat, and a danger to everyone around him.
Back-stabbing bastard damn near got me killed, but settled for ruining my life.
So, a real piece of shit.
Ha! Yeah...
KNOCK
KNOCK
KNOCK

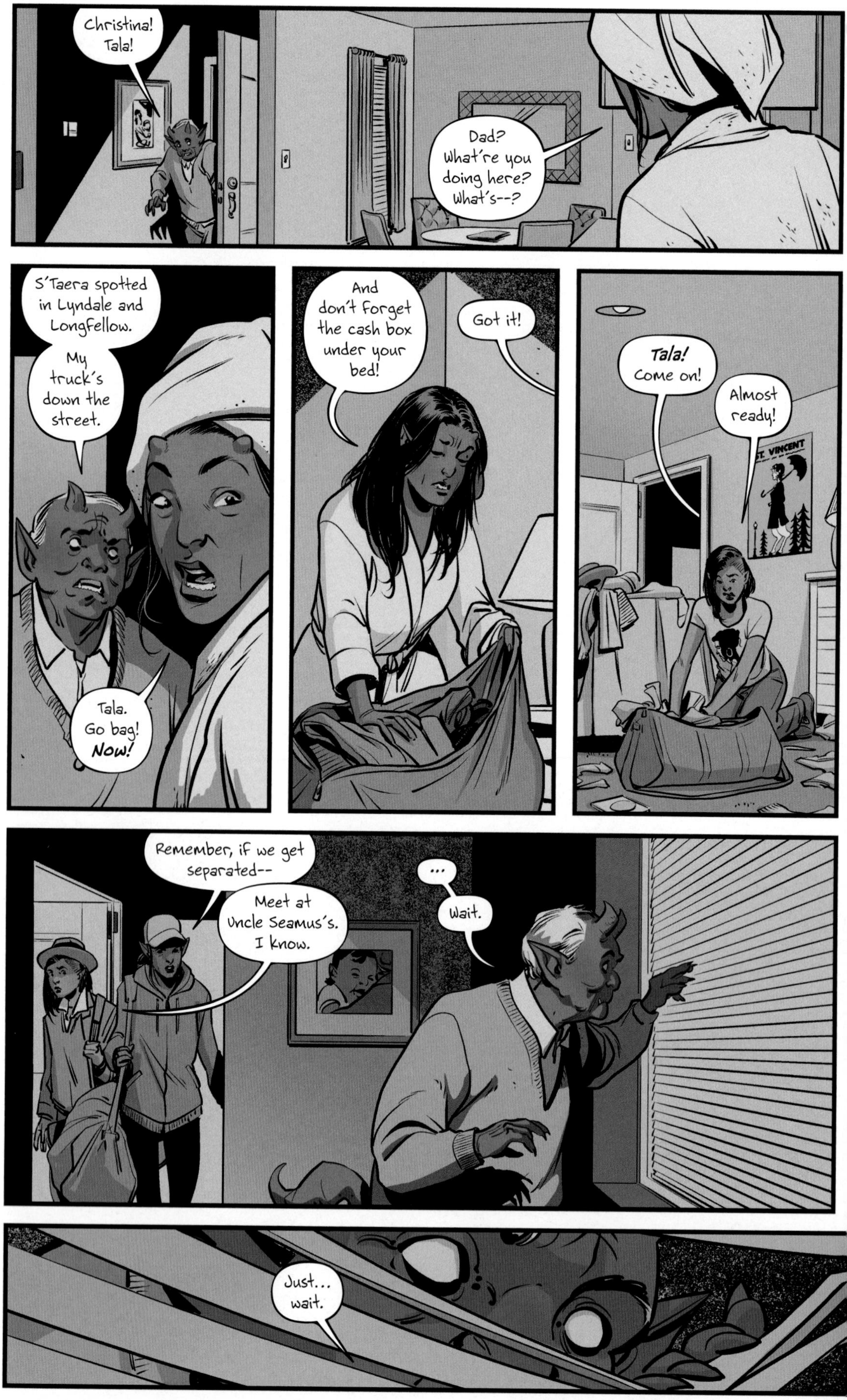
Christina!
Tala!
Dad?
What're you doing here?
What's--?
S'Taera spotted in Lyndale and Longfellow.
My truck's down the street.
Tala.
Go bag!
Now!
And don't forget the cash box under your bed!
Got it!
Tala!
Come on!
Almost ready!
ST. VINCENT
Remember, if we get separated--
Meet at Uncle Seamus's. I know.
...
Wait.
Just... wait.

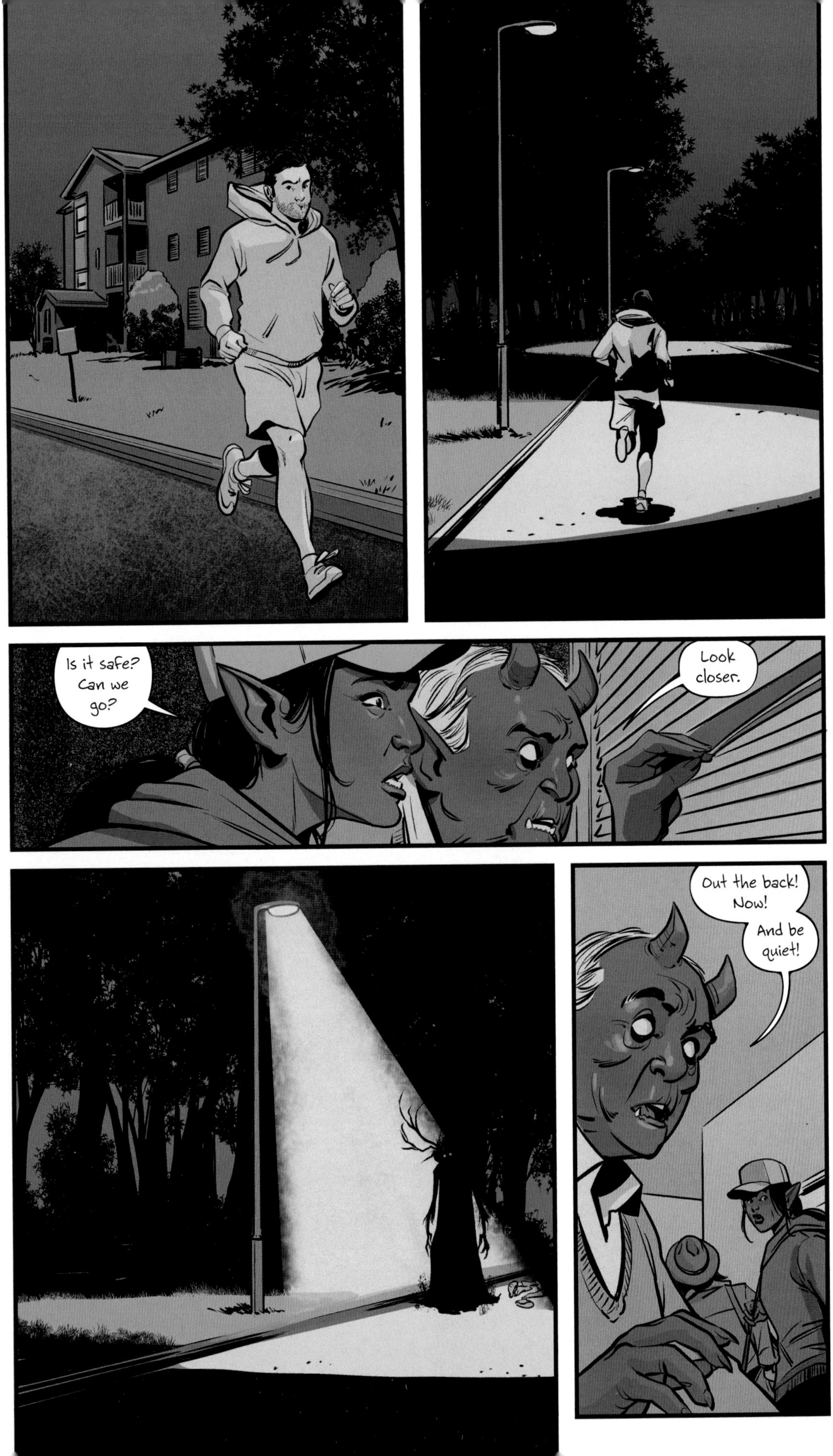
Is it safe? Can we go?
Look closer.
Out the back! Now!
And be quiet!

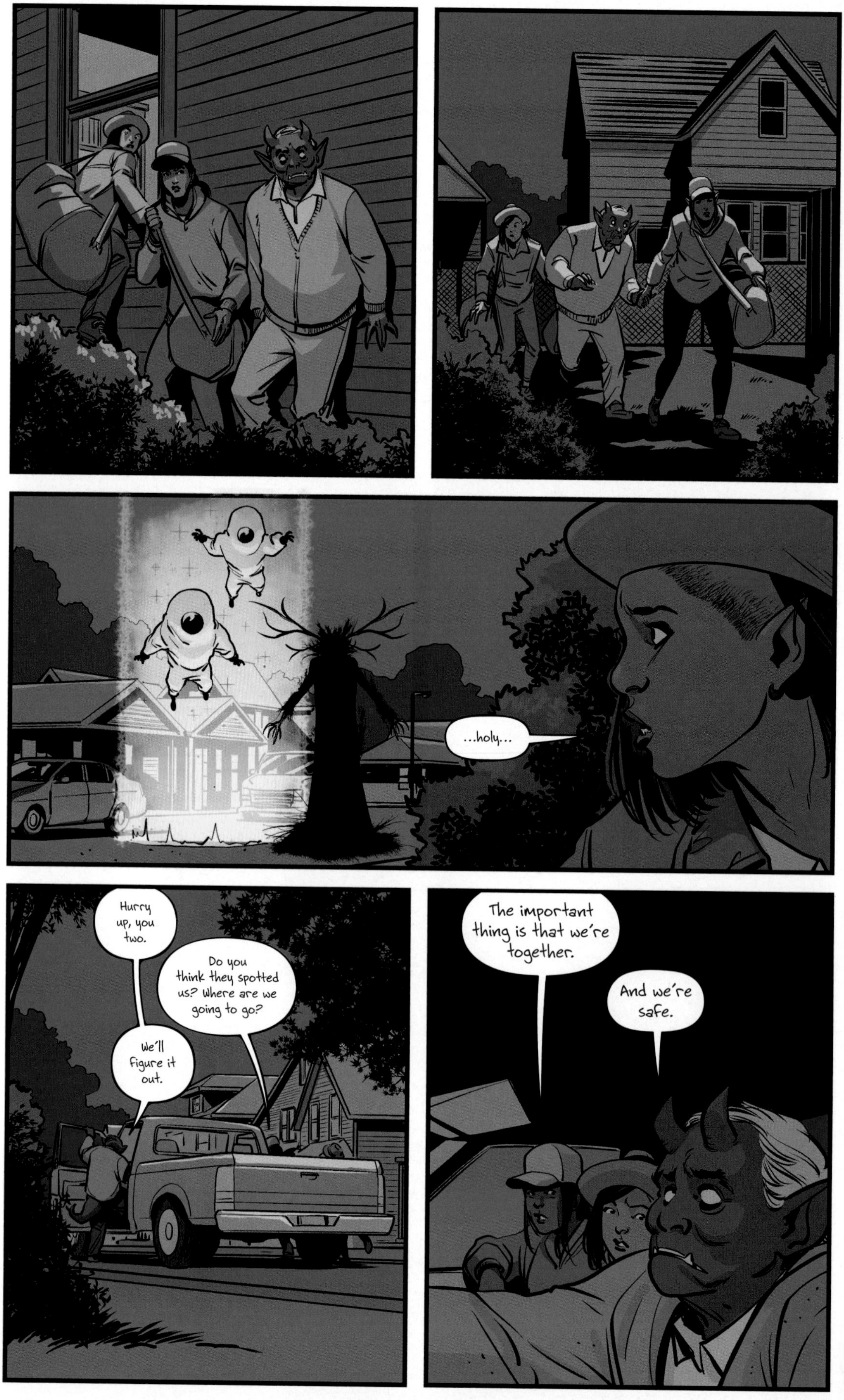
...holy...
Hurry up, you two.
Do you think they spotted us? Where are we going to go?
We'll figure it out.
The important thing is that we're together.
And we're safe.

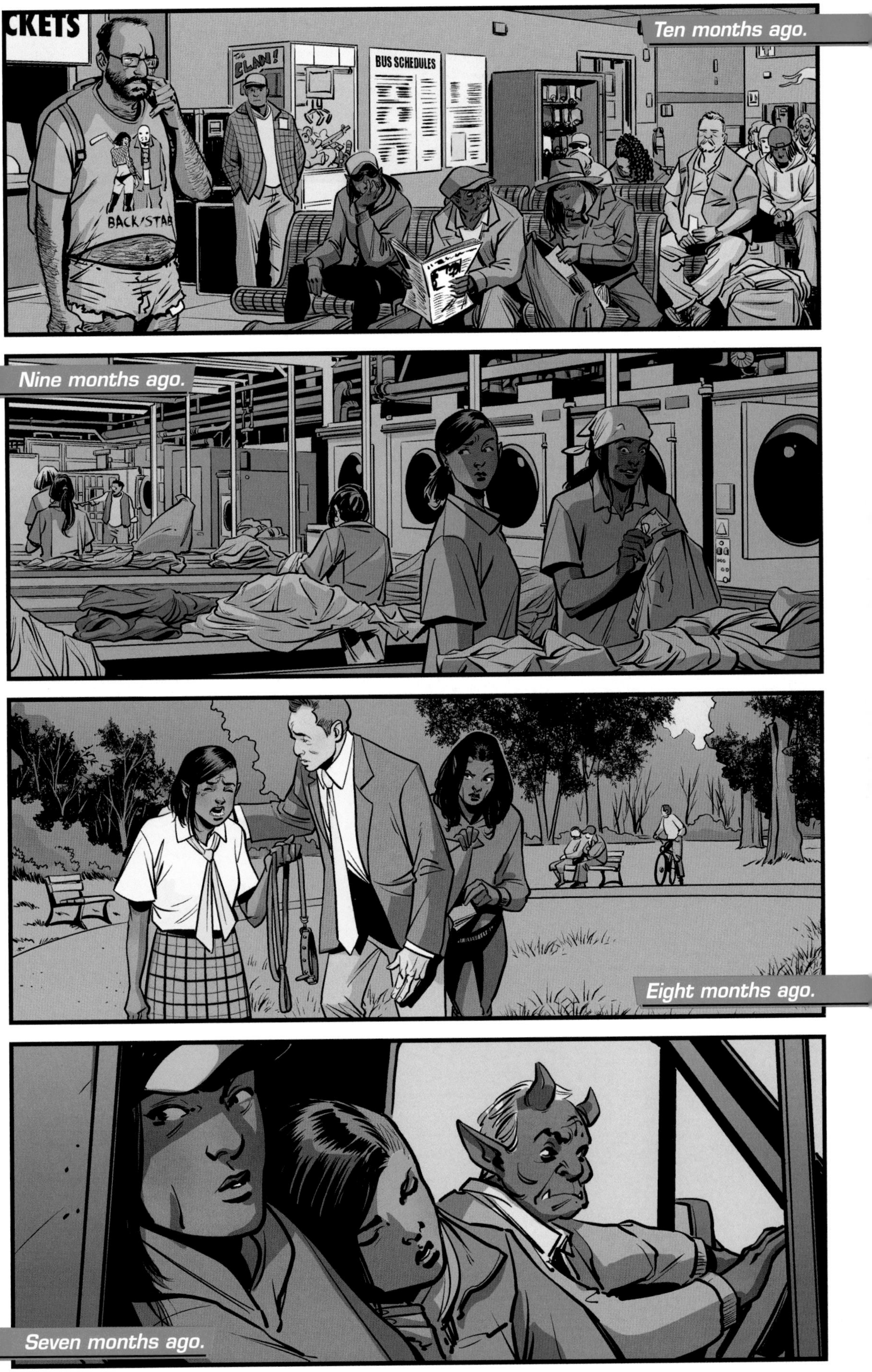
CKETS
THE CLAW!
BUS SCHEDULES
BACK/STAB
Ten months ago.
Nine months ago.
Eight months ago.
Seven months ago.

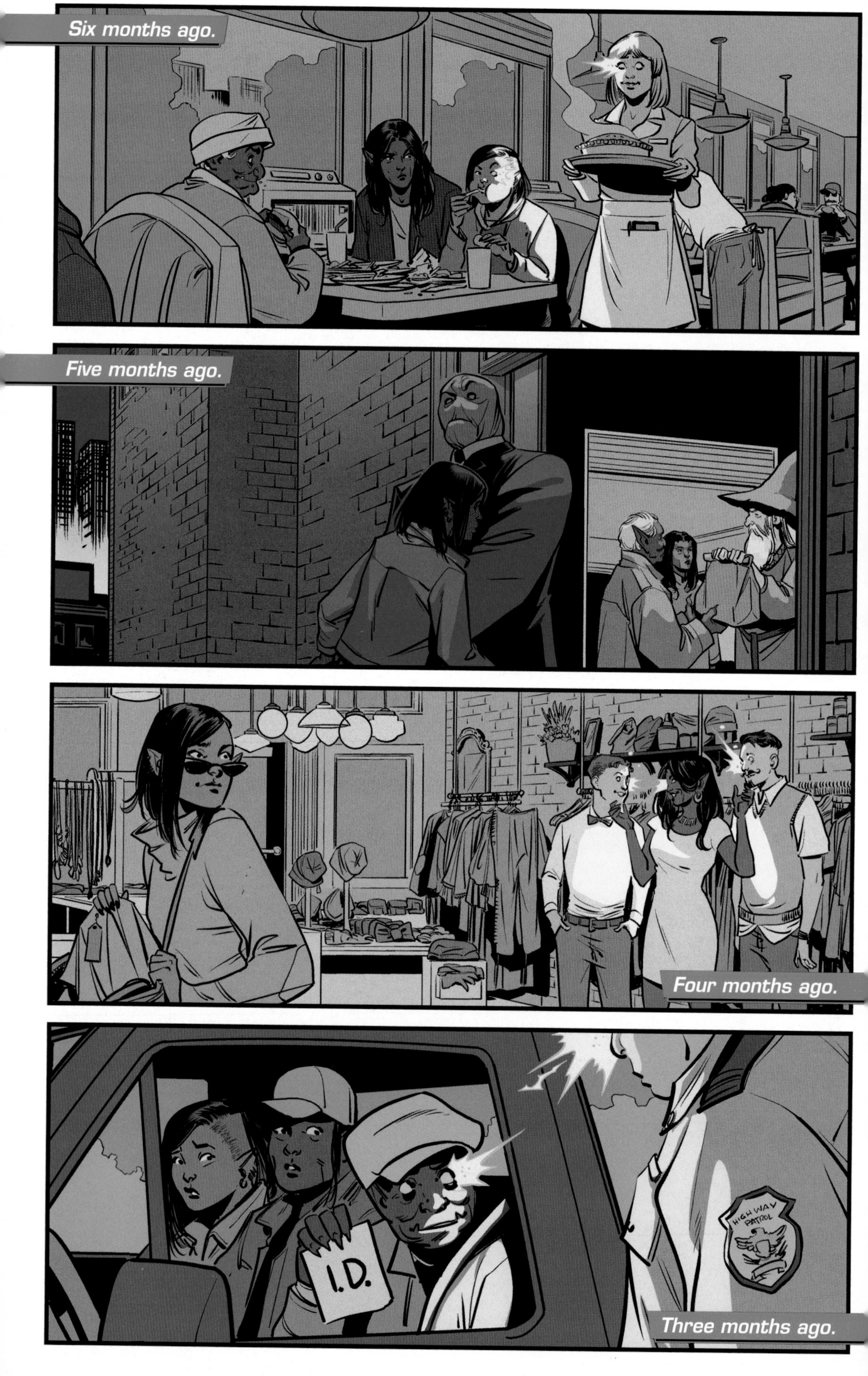
Six months ago.
Five months ago.
Four months ago.
HIGHWAY PATROL
I.D.
Three months ago.

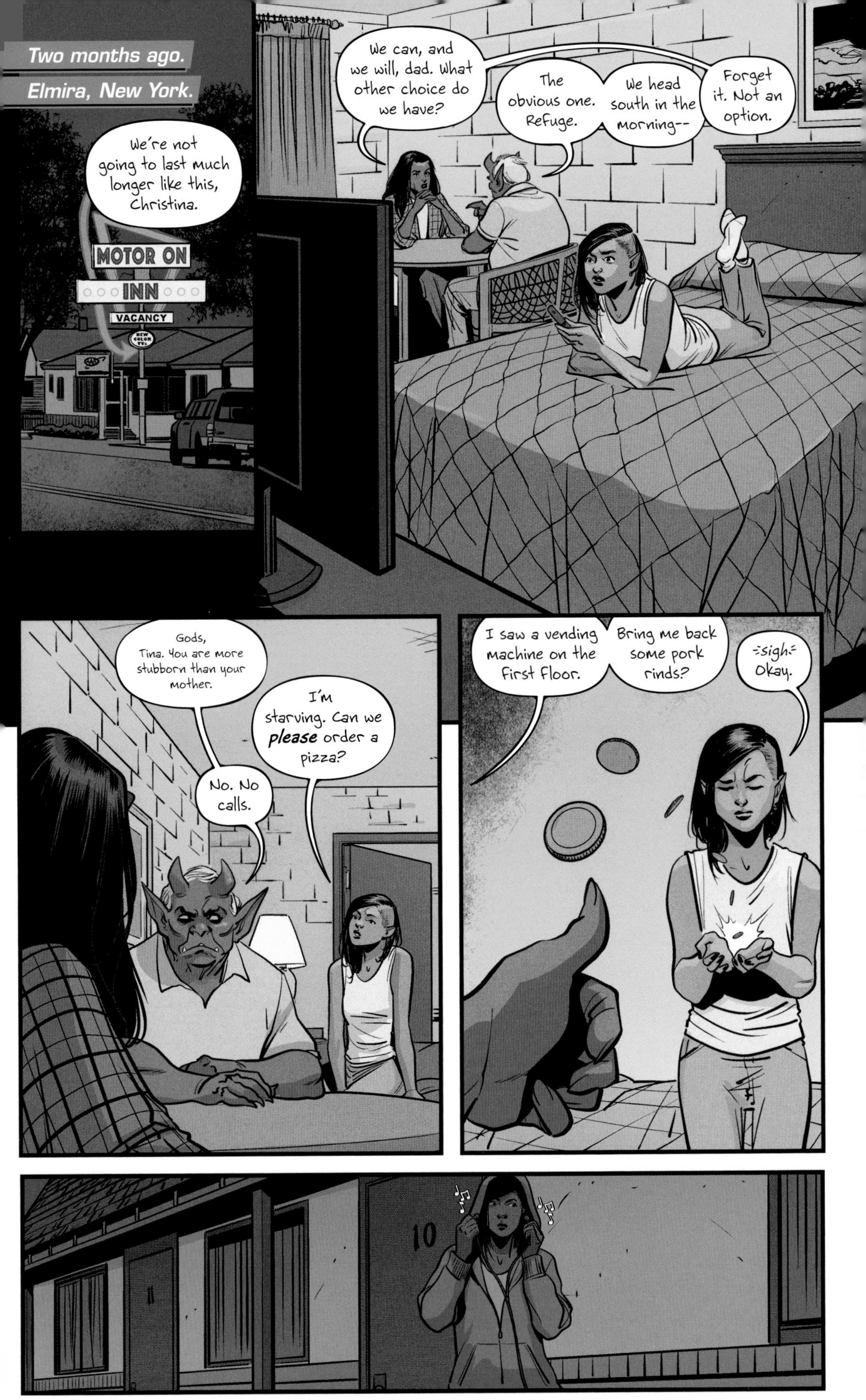
Two months ago.
Elmira, New York.
We're not going to last much longer like this, Christina.
MOTOR ON
INN
VACANCY
We can, and we will, dad. What other choice do we have?
The obvious one. Refuge.
We head south in the morning--
Forget it. Not an option.
Gods, Tina. You are more stubborn than your mother.
No. No calls.
I'm starving. Can we *please* order a pizza?
I saw a vending machine on the first floor.
Bring me back some pork rinds?
=sigh= Okay.
10
11

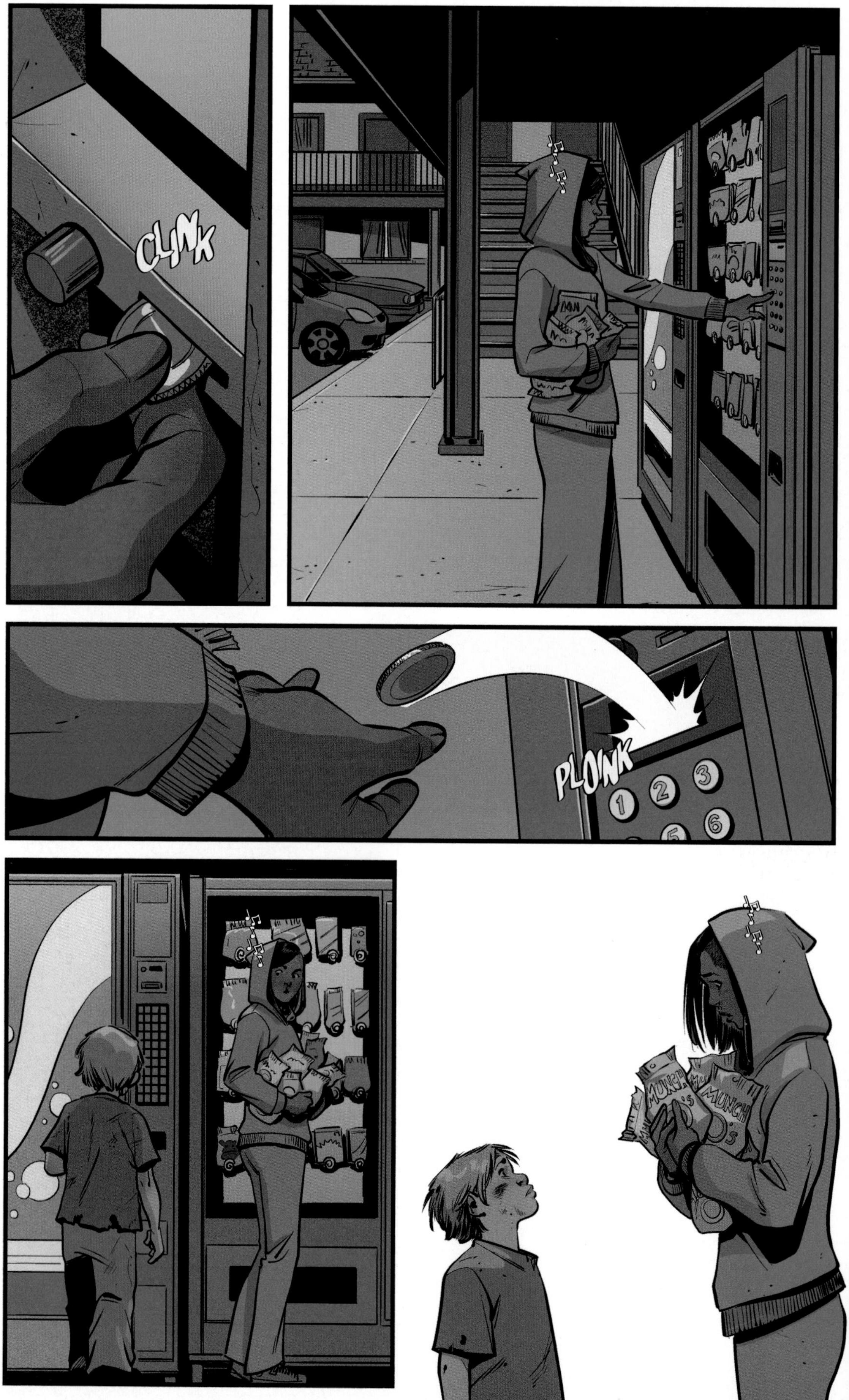
CLINK
PLOINK
1
2
3
5
6
MUNCH O's
MUNCH O's

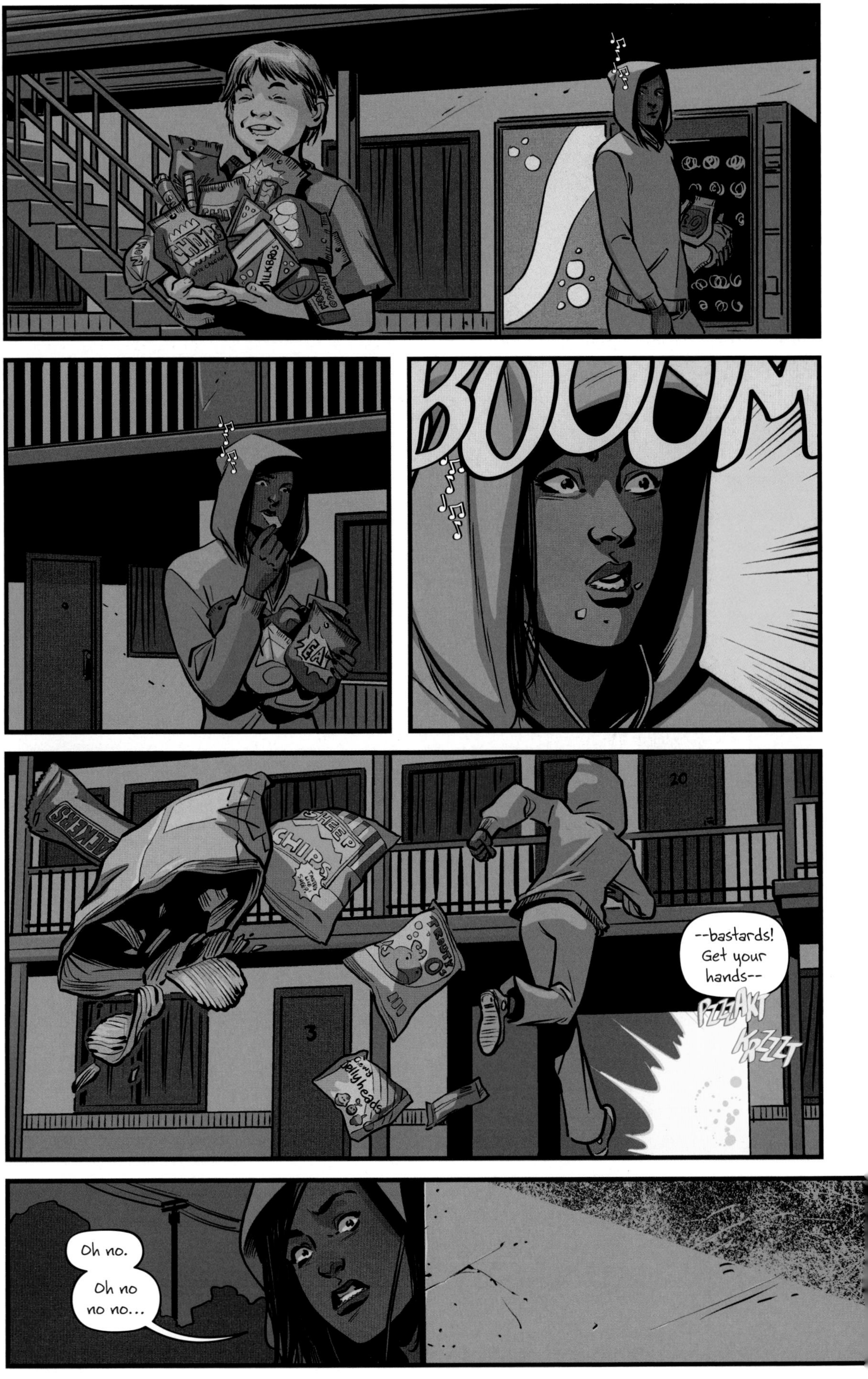
BOOOM
--bastards! Get your hands--
PZZZAKT
KRZZZT
Oh no.
Oh no no no...

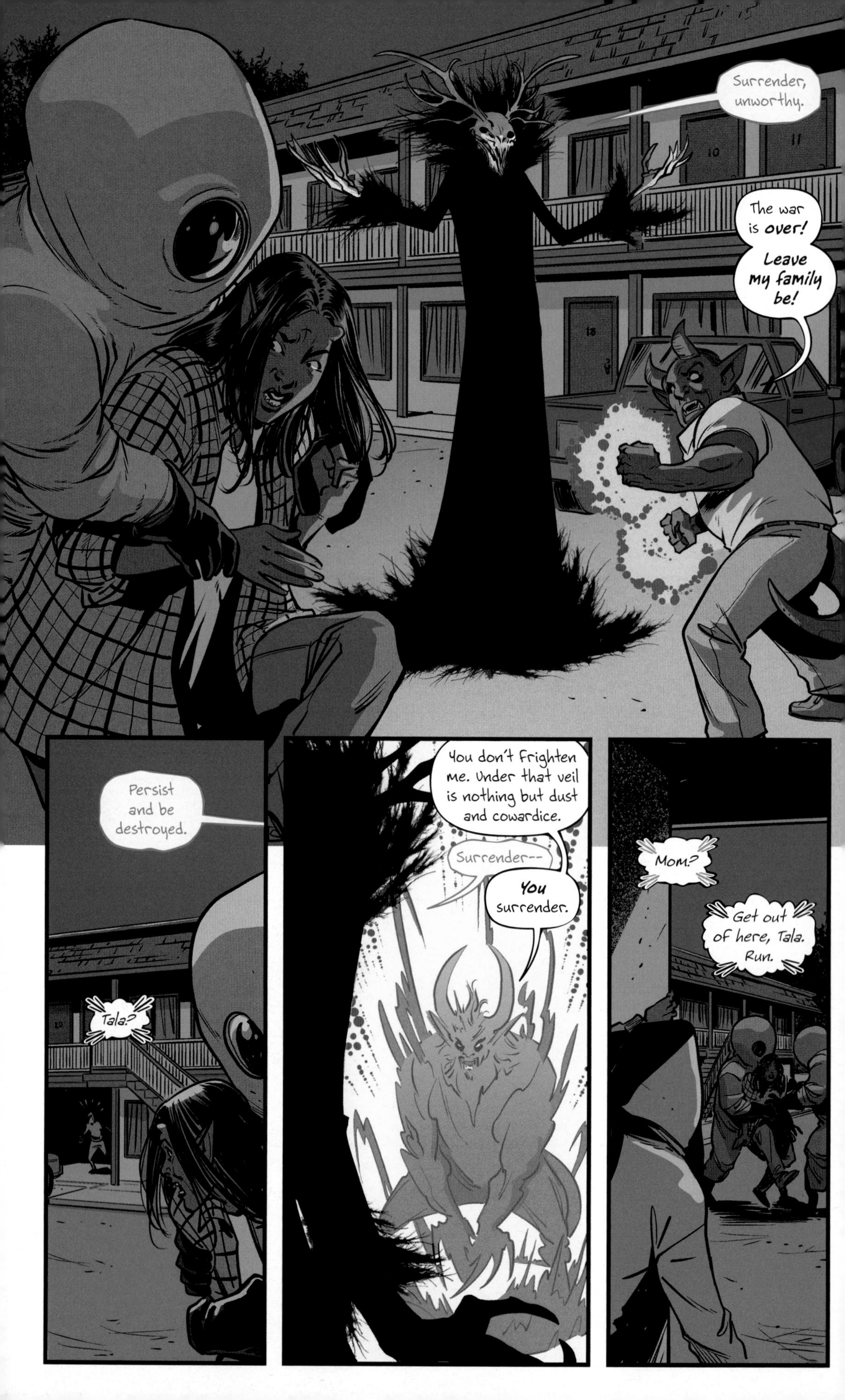

Surrender, unworthy.
The war is over!
Leave my family be!
Persist and be destroyed.
Tala?
You don't frighten me. Under that veil is nothing but dust and cowardice.
Surrender--
You surrender.
Mom?
Get out of here, Tala. Run.

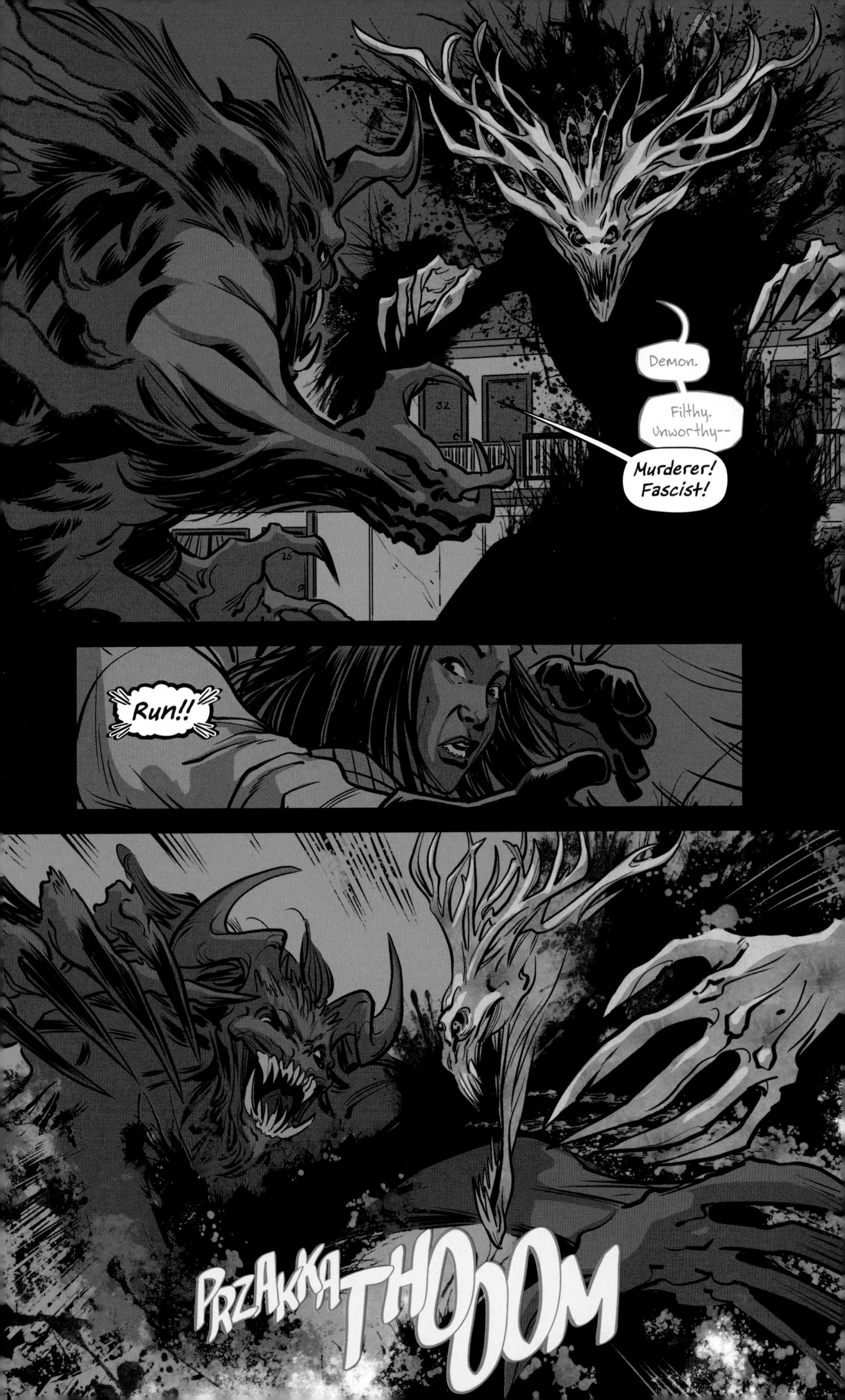
Demon.
Filthy. Unworthy--
Murderer! Fascist!
Run!!
PRZAKKA THOOOM

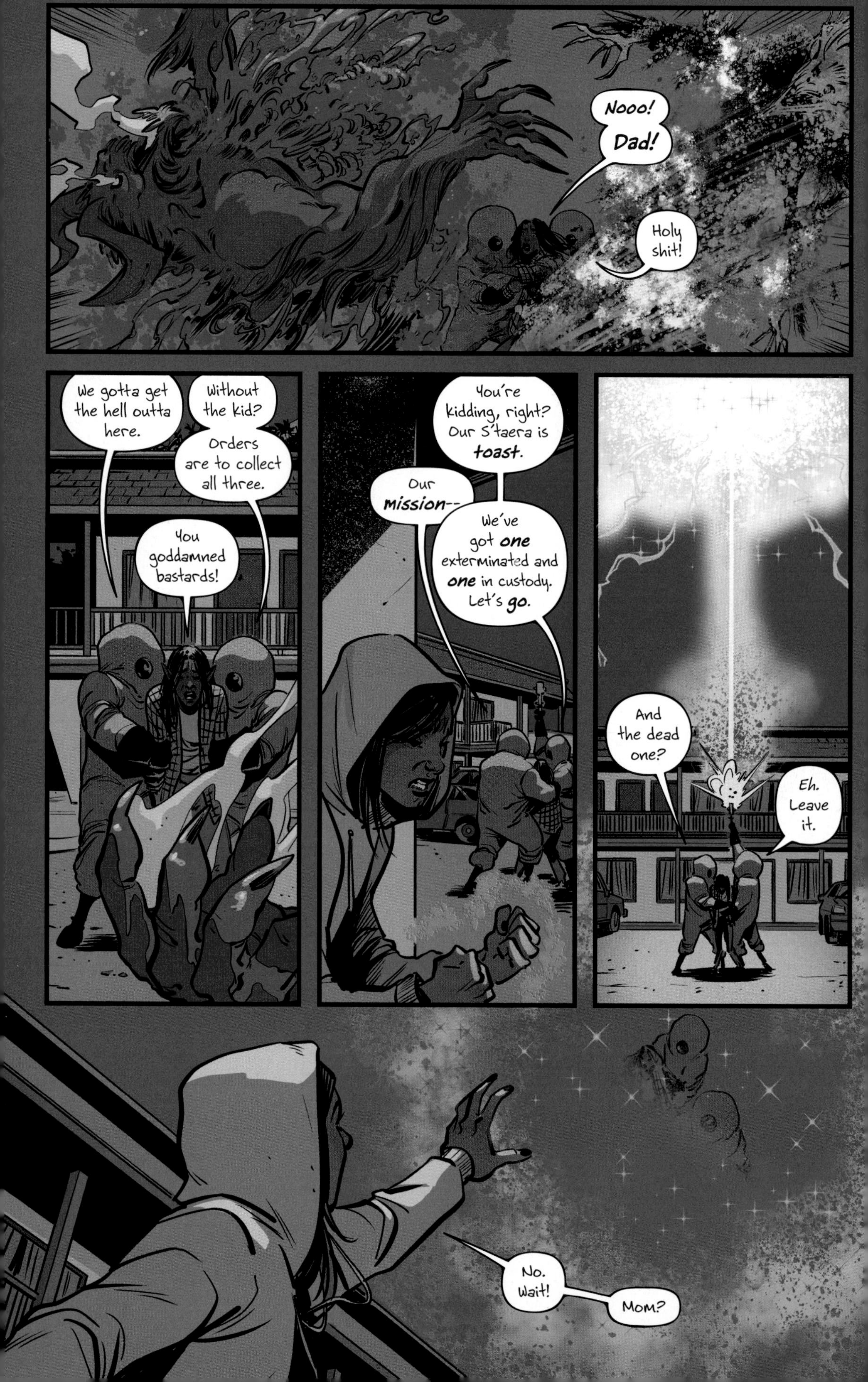
Nooo! Dad!
Holy shit!
We gotta get the hell outta here.
Without the kid?
Orders are to collect all three.
You goddamned bastards!
You're kidding, right? Our S'taera is toast.
Our mission--
We've got one exterminated and one in custody. Let's go.
And the dead one?
Eh. Leave it.
No. Wait!
Mom?

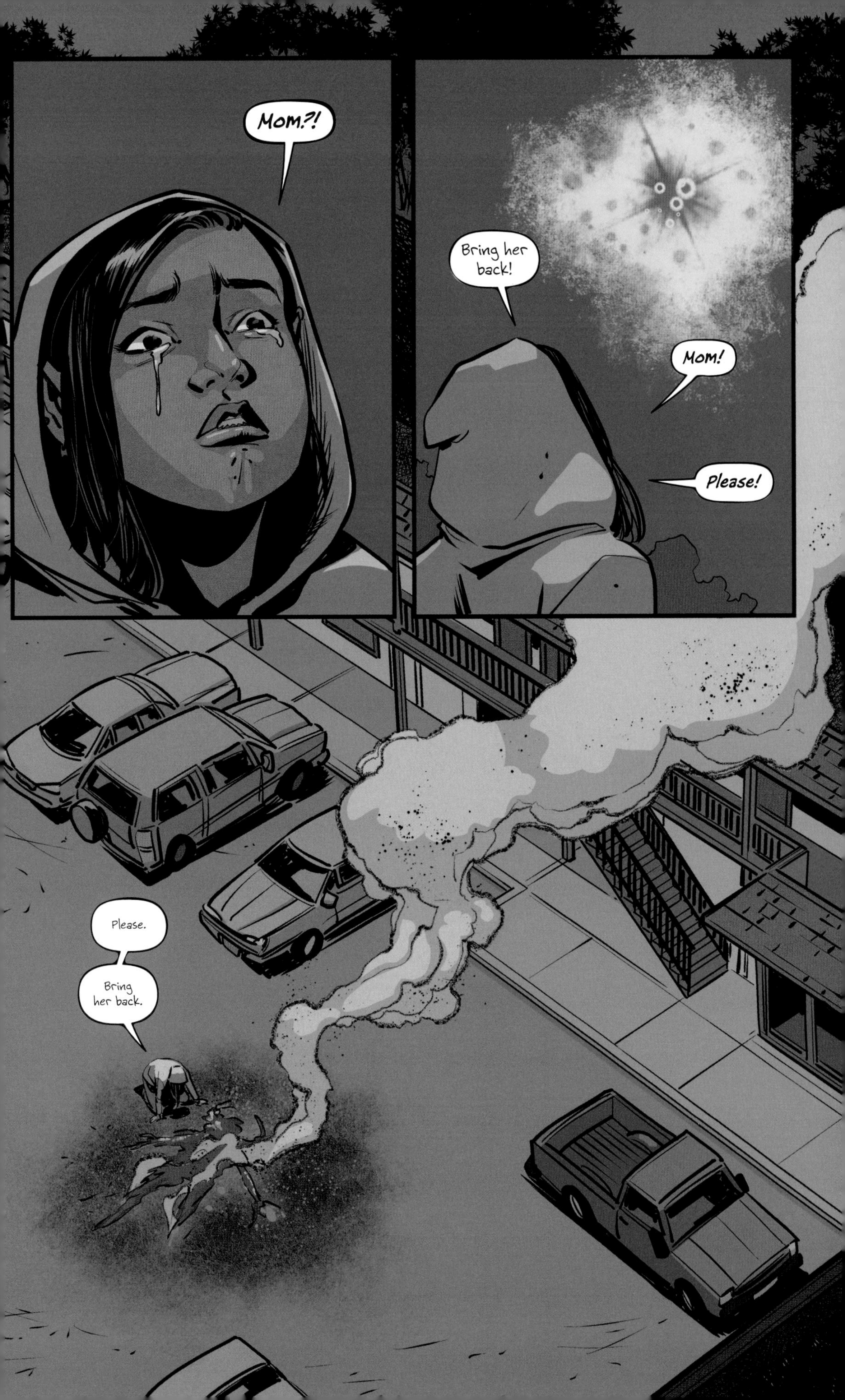
Mom?!
Bring her back!
Mom!
Please!
Please.
Bring her back.

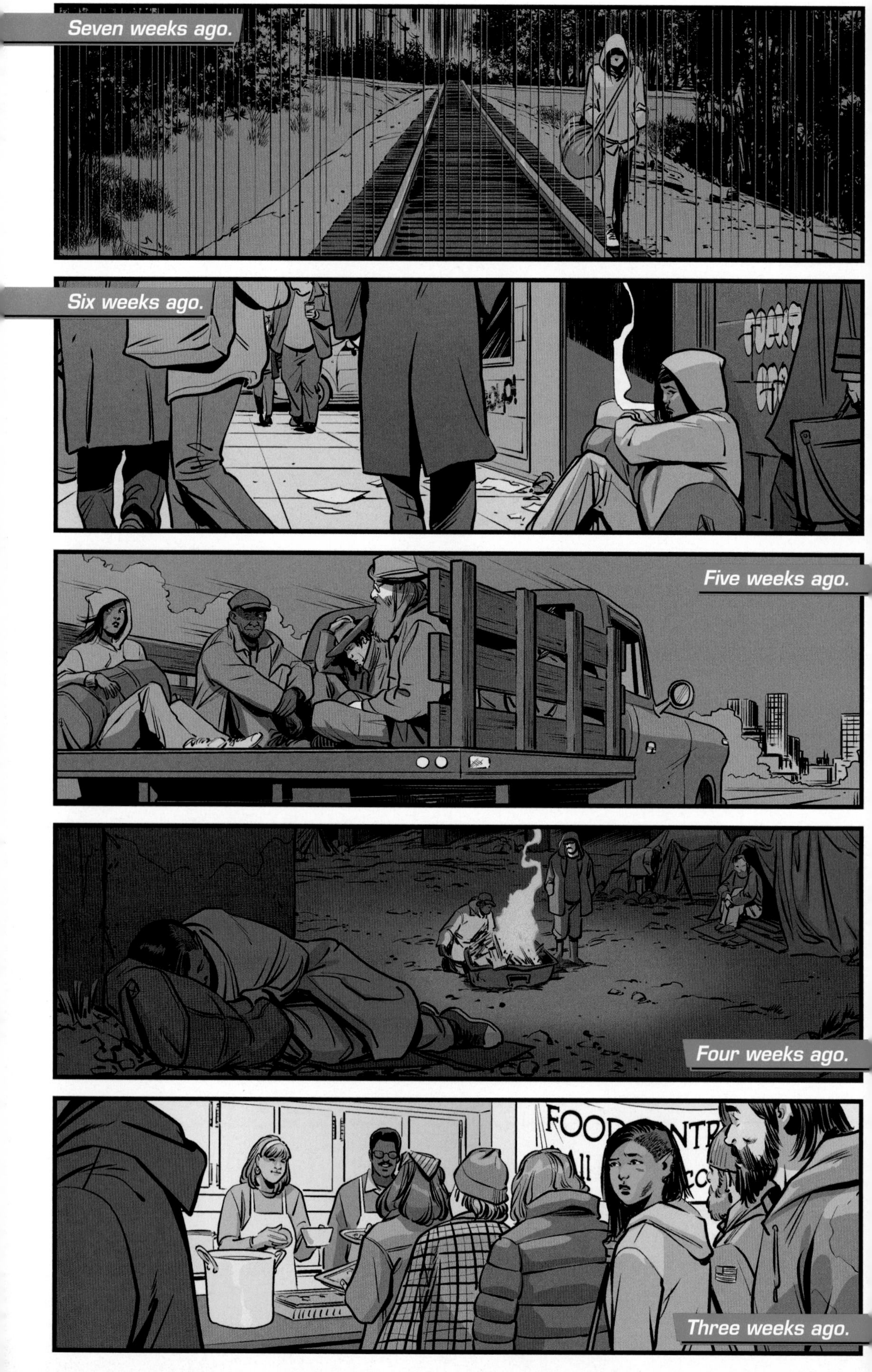
Seven weeks ago.
Six weeks ago.
Five weeks ago.
Four weeks ago.
Three weeks ago.

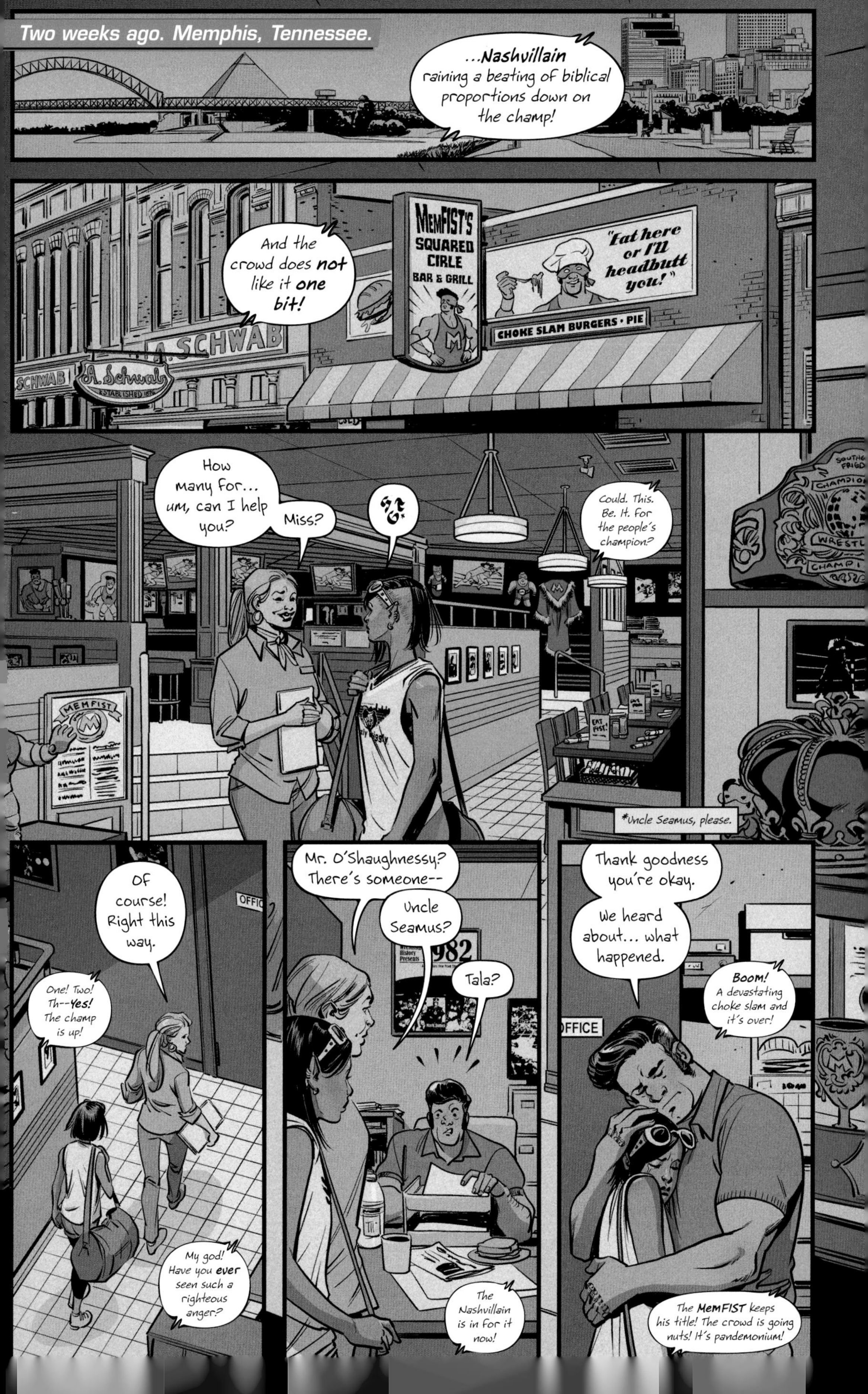

Two weeks ago. Memphis, Tennessee.
...Nashvillain raining a beating of biblical proportions down on the champ!
And the crowd does not like it one bit!
MemFIST'S SQUARED CIRLE BAR & GRILL
"Eat here or I'll headbutt you!"
CHOKE SLAM BURGERS • PIE
A. SCHWAB
How many for... um, can I help you?
Miss?
Could. This. Be. It. For the people's champion?
MEMFIST
*Uncle Seamus, please.
Of course! Right this way.
One! Two! Th--Yes! The champ is up!
My god! Have you ever seen such a righteous anger?
Mr. O'Shaughnessy? There's someone--
Uncle Seamus?
Tala?
The Nashvillain is in for it now!
Thank goodness you're okay.
We heard about... what happened.
Boom! A devastating choke slam and it's over!
The MemFIST keeps his title! The crowd is going nuts! It's pandemonium!

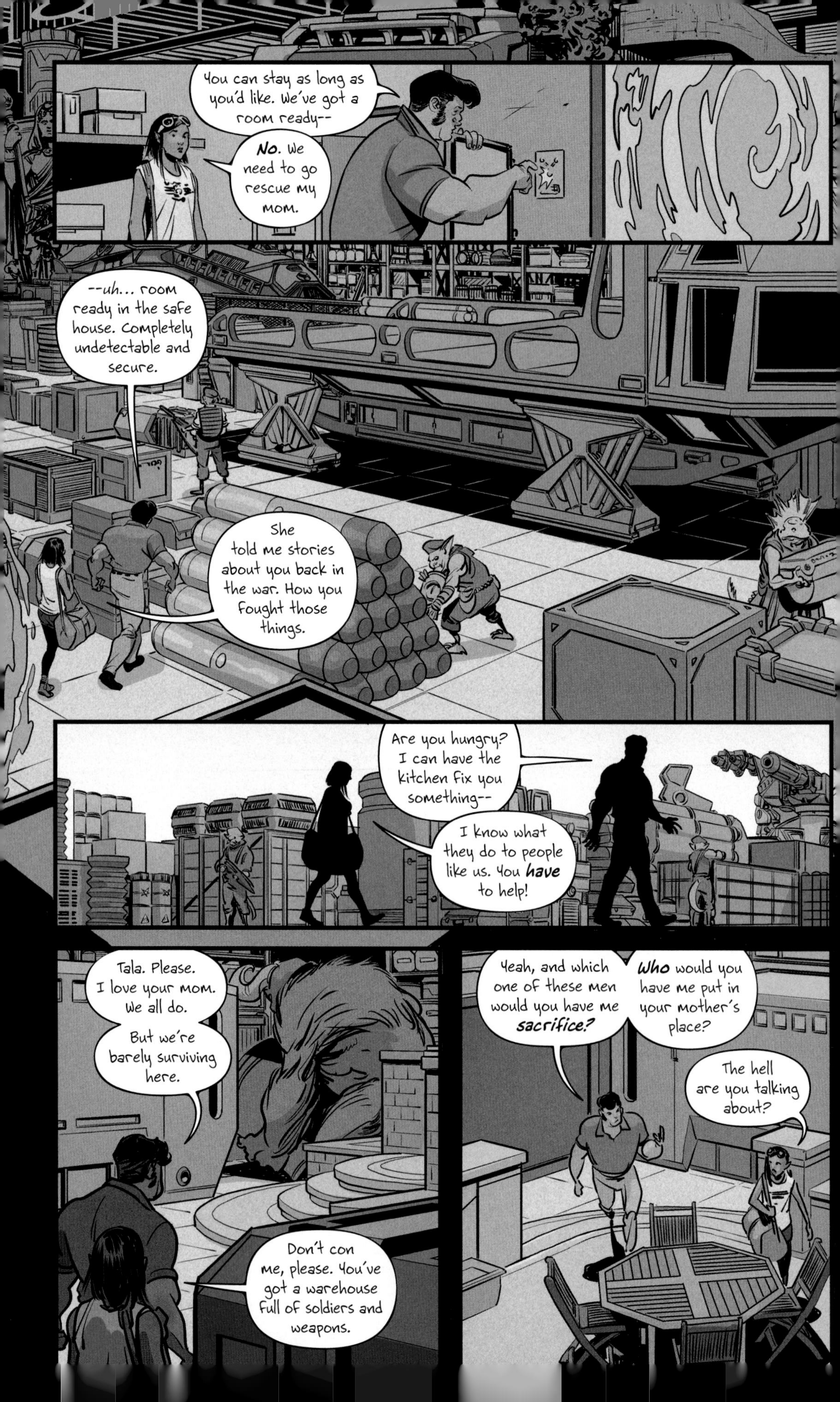
You can stay as long as you'd like. We've got a room ready--
No. We need to go rescue my mom.
--uh... room ready in the safe house. Completely undetectable and secure.
She told me stories about you back in the war. How you fought those things.
Are you hungry? I can have the kitchen fix you something--
I know what they do to people like us. You have to help!
Tala. Please. I love your mom. We all do.
But we're barely surviving here.
Don't con me, please. You've got a warehouse full of soldiers and weapons.
Yeah, and which one of these men would you have me sacrifice?
Who would you have me put in your mother's place?
The hell are you talking about?

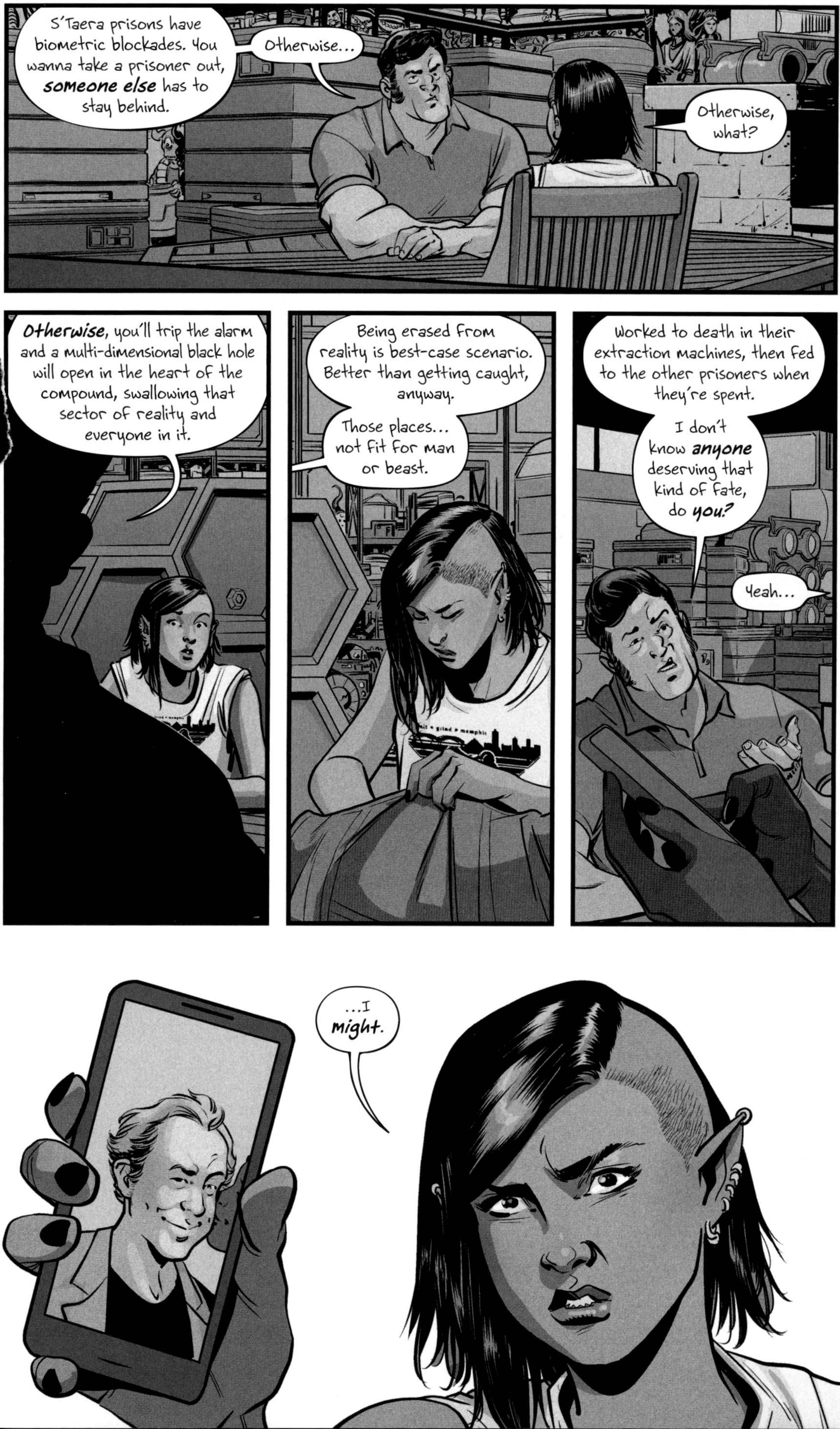
S'Taera prisons have biometric blockades. You wanna take a prisoner out, **someone else** has to stay behind.
Otherwise...
Otherwise, what?
Otherwise, you'll trip the alarm and a multi-dimensional black hole will open in the heart of the compound, swallowing that sector of reality and everyone in it.
Being erased from reality is best-case scenario. Better than getting caught, anyway.
Those places... not fit for man or beast.
Worked to death in their extraction machines, then fed to the other prisoners when they're spent.
I don't know **anyone** deserving that kind of fate, do **you?**
Yeah...
...I **might**.

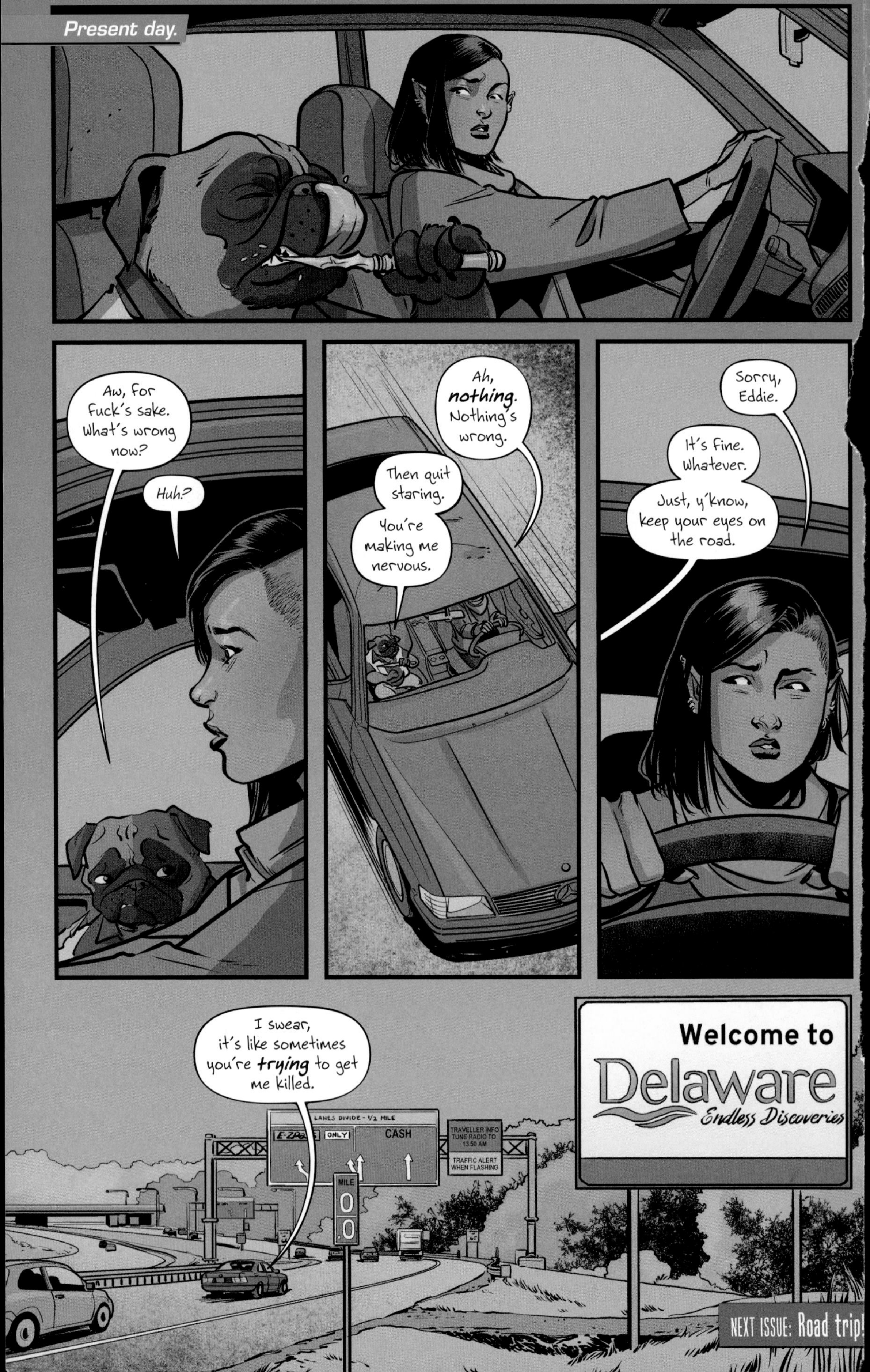
Present day.
Aw, for fuck's sake. What's wrong now?
Huh?
Ah, **nothing**. Nothing's wrong.
Then quit staring.
You're making me nervous.
Sorry, Eddie.
It's fine. Whatever.
Just, y'know, keep your eyes on the road.
I swear, it's like sometimes you're **trying** to get me killed.
LANES DIVIDE - 1/2 MILE
ONLY
CASH
TRAVELLER INFO
TUNE RADIO TO
13.50 AM
TRAFFIC ALERT
WHEN FLASHING
MILE
0
0
Welcome to
Delaware
Endless Discoveries
NEXT ISSUE: Road trip!

SKETCHBOOK

One of the most fun parts about working on GRUMBLE is watching Mike turn my rough (and often incomprehensible) sketches into fully realized characters. I basically try to give a general idea for each creature, without handcuffing Mike into following a rigid design. So far, so good!

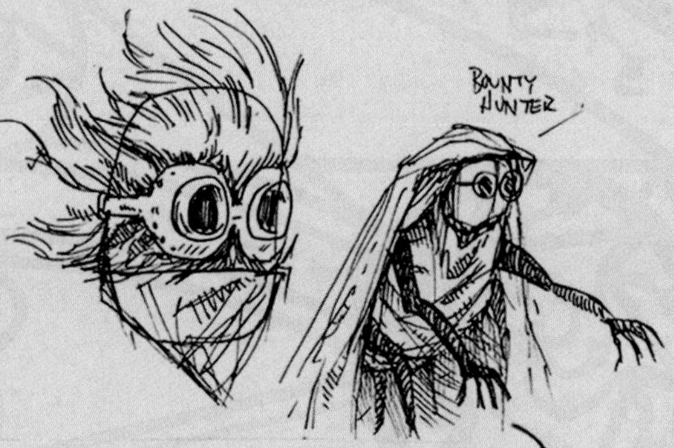
BOUNTY
HUNTER

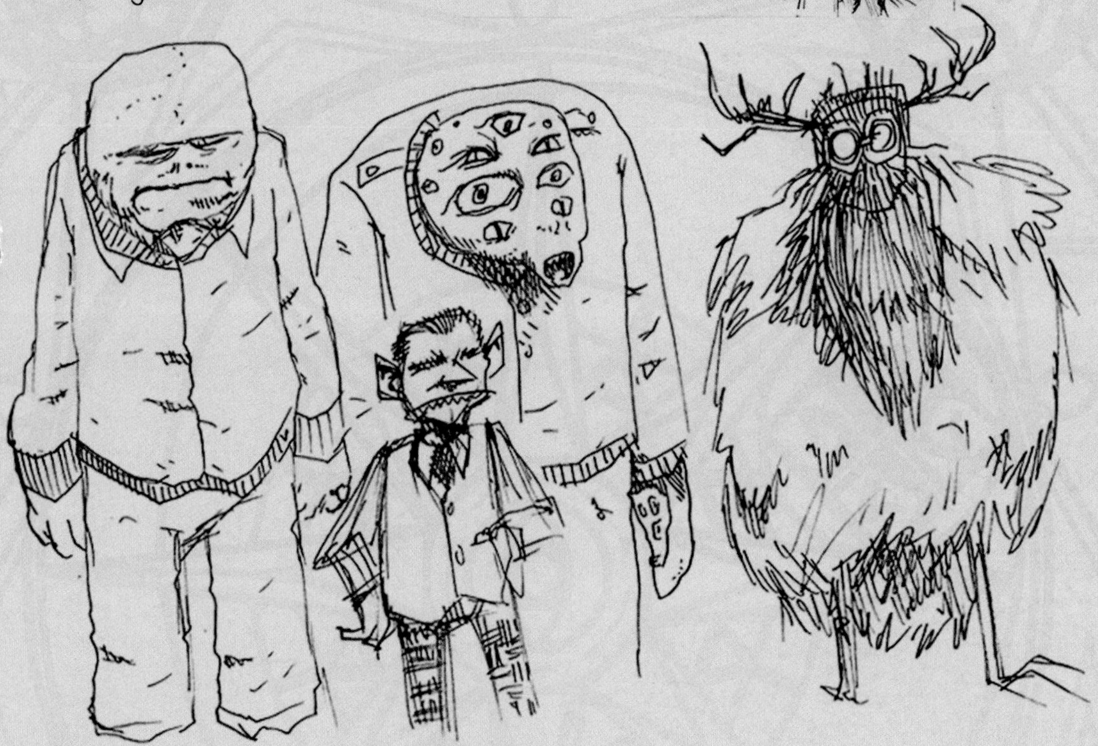

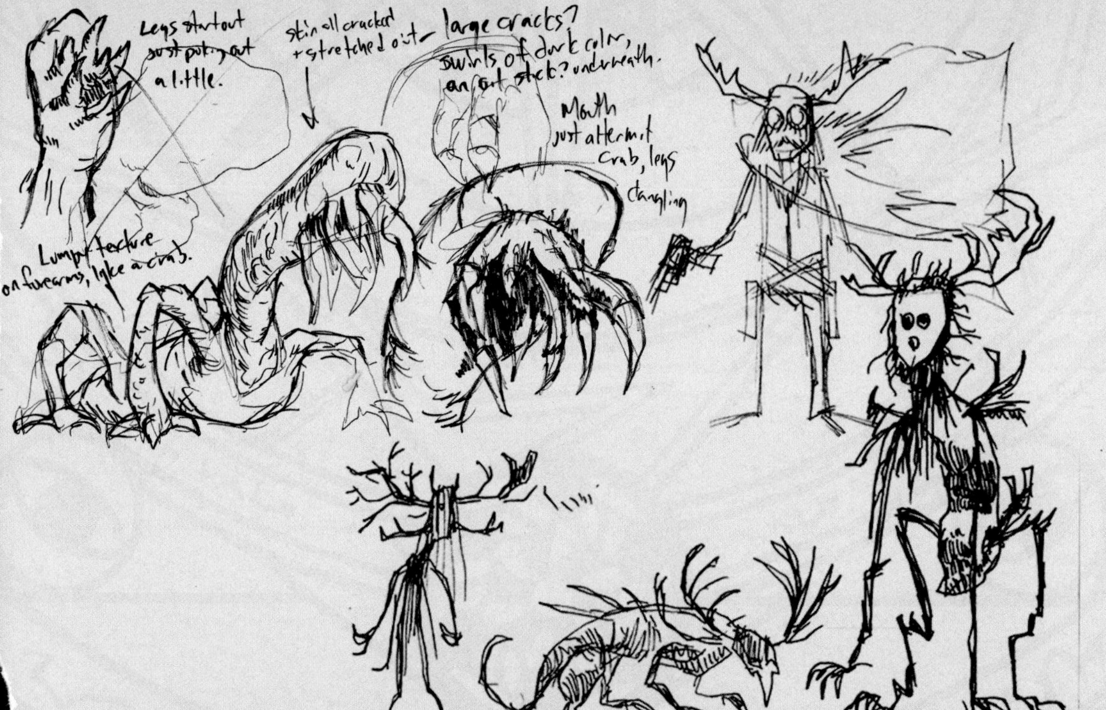
Legs start out
a little.
skin all cracked
+ stretched out
large cracks?
Mouth
crab, legs
dangling
Lumpy texture
on forearms, like a crab.

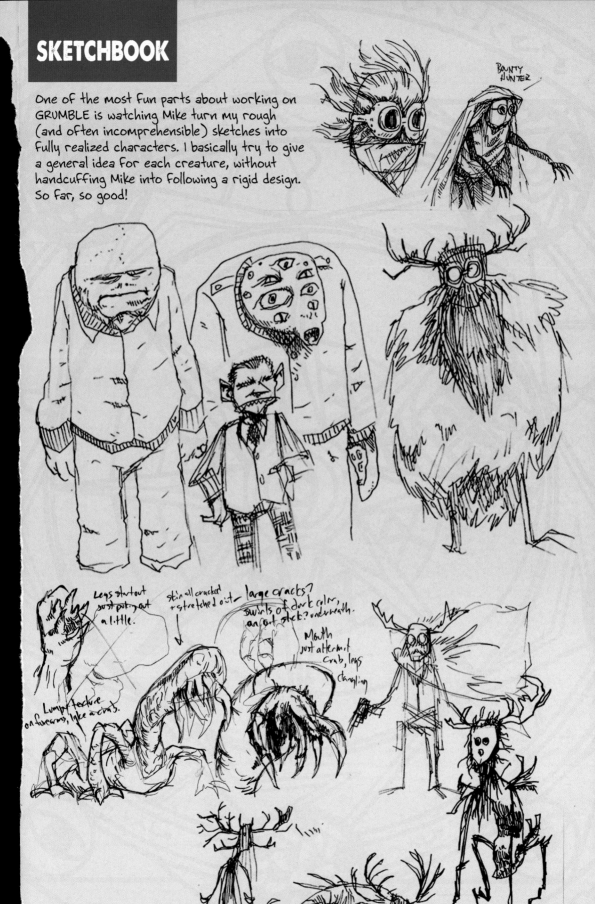

SKETCHBOOK

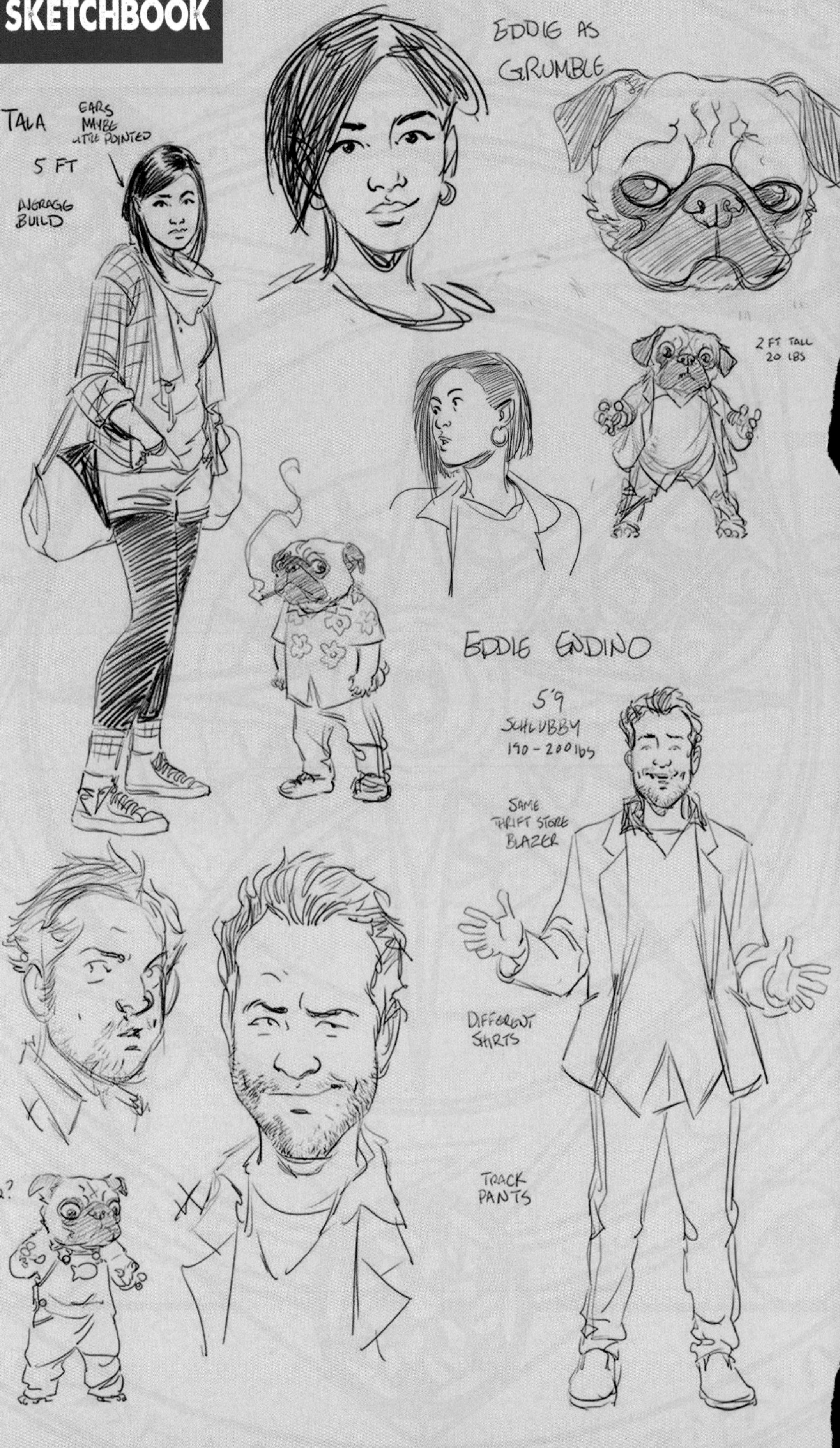
TALA
EARS MAYBE LITTLE POINTED
5 FT
AVERAGE BUILD
EDDIE AS GRUMBLE
2 FT TALL
20 LBS
EDDIE ENDINO
5'9
SCHLUBBY
190 - 200 lbs
SAME THRIFT STORE BLAZER
DIFFERENT SHIRTS
TRACK PANTS
DA FUQ?

THE CREATORS

Rafer Roberts is the writer and co-creator of **Modern Fantasy**, published by Dark Horse Comics, and was the writer on **A&A: The Adventures of Archer & Armstrong** and **Harbinger: Renegades** for Valiant Comics. His self-published work includes the long running **Plastic Farm**, **Nightmare the Rat**, and the Tumblr famous **Thanos and Darkseid: Carpool Buddies of Doom.**

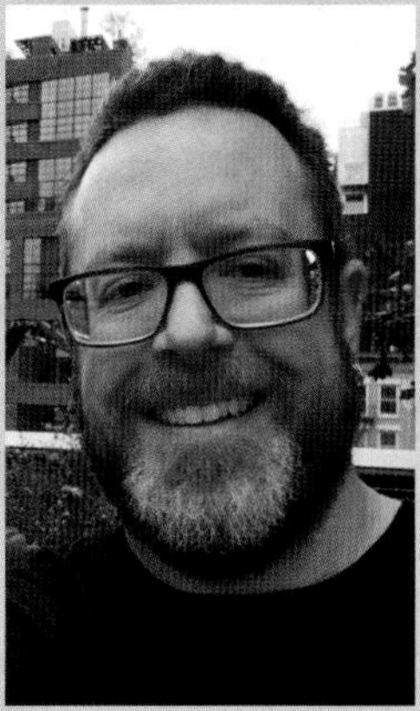

Mike Norton is the creator of the Eisner and Harvey award-winning webcomic **Battlepug** and the co-creator and artist of **Revival.** He has worked for Marvel, DC, Dark Horse and just about everybody else. He has a webcomic called **Lil' Donnie** about the worst president in US history. He lives in Chicago with his wife, two pugs, and a fridge full of beer.

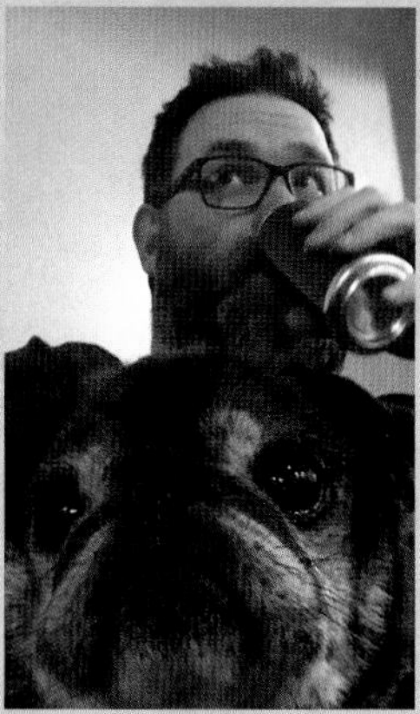

Marissa Louise is a colorist for DC, Dark Horse, Image, and others. She also does a twice monthly Curse of Strahd podcast called Bite Club, wherein she plays multiple loveable scamps.

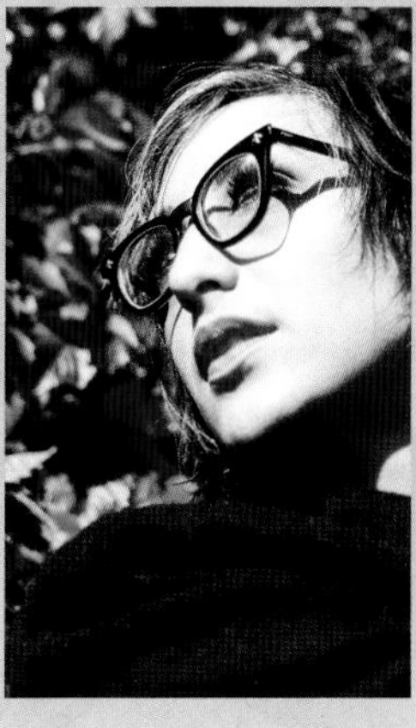

Christopher Crank (crank!) letters a bunch of books put out by Image, Dark Horse, Oni Press, Dynamite, and elsewhere. He also has a podcast with comic artist Mike Norton and members of Four Star Studios in Chicago (crankcast.com) and makes music. (sonomorti.bandcamp.com)

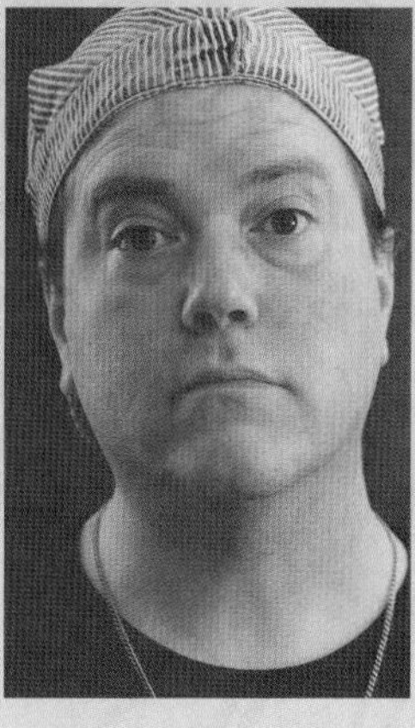

Danny Khazem is a New York City-based editor who worked with Mike and Rafer on Valiant's **A&A: The Adventures of Archer & Armstrong.** He immediately abandoned the team after a call up to the big leagues—what an ass, right?

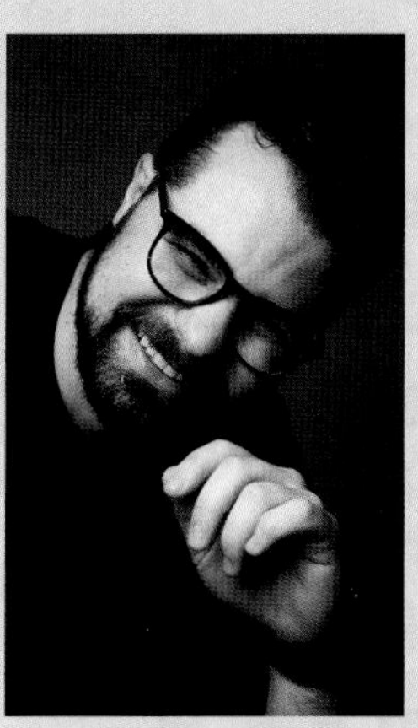

In addition to Grumble, Alejandro Arbona currently edits **Lazarus: Risen, Black Magick,** and **The Old Guard** for Image Comics, and recently edited **Ghost in the Shell: Global Neural Network** for Kodansha/Penguin Random House. He also wrote the non-fiction kids' books **Awesome Minds: Video Game Creators** and **Awesome Minds: Comic Book Creators.** Alejandro lives in New York City with a dog who only speaks Spanish.

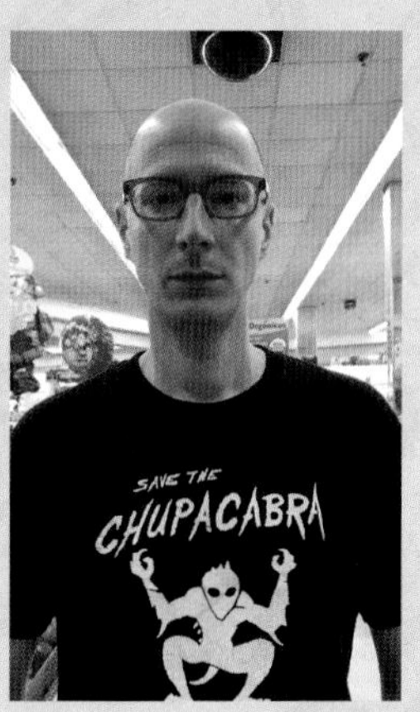
SAVE THE
CHUPACABRA

LOOK FOR THESE OTHER ALBATROSS TITLES!

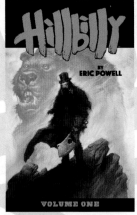

HILLBILLY VOLUME 1
ISBN: 978-0-9983792-0-3
$17.99

HILLBILLY VOLUME 2
ISBN: 978-0-9983792-3-4
$17.99

HILLBILLY VOLUME 3
ISBN: 978-0-9983792-4-1
$17.99

HILLBILLY VOLUME 4 RED EYED WITHCERY FROM BEYOND
ISBN: 978-0-9983792-8-9
$17.99

SPOOK HOUSE VOLUME 1
ISBN: 978-0-9983792-1-0
$17.99

SPOOK HOUSE VOLUME 2
ISBN: 978-0-9983792-7-2
$17.99

'NAMWOLF: HEART OF DARKNESS
ISBN: 978-0-9983792-2-7
$17.99

GALAKTIKON
ISBN: 978-0-9983792-5-8
$17.99

THE GOON: BUNCH OF OLD CRAP AN OMNIBUS VOLUME 1
ISBN: 978-0-9983792-9-6
$29.99

GRUMBLE VOLUME 1
ISBN: 978-1-949889-90-1
$17.99

MEGAGHOST VOLUME 1
ISBN: 978-1-949889-99-4
$17.99

ALBATROSSFUNNYBOOKS.COM